VETERANS: BENEFITS, ISSUES, POLICIES AND PROGRAMS

Additional books in this series can be found on Nova's website under the Series tab.

Additional e-books in this series can be found on Nova's website under the e-book tab.

VETERANS: BENEFITS, ISSUES, POLICIES AND PROGRAMS

VETERANS

BENEFITS, ISSUES, POLICIES, AND PROGRAMS

VOLUME 4

VETERANS

BENEFITS, ISSUES, POLICIES, AND PROGRAMS

VOLUME 4

TIMOTHY C. ROBERTS
EDITOR

nova publishers
New York

For permission to use material from this book please contact us:
Telephone 631-231-7269; Fax 631-231-8175
Web Site: http://www.novapublishers.com

Additional color graphics may be available in the e-book version of this book.

Library of Congress Cataloging-in-Publication Data

ISSN: 2326-7518

ISBN: 978-1-63321-722-5

Published by Nova Science Publishers, Inc. † New York

CONTENTS

PREFACE

This book provides an overview of the benefits, issues, policies and programs relating to our military service members. Topics discussed in this issue include VA housing; VA health care services; additional steps needed to strengthen beneficiary travel program management and oversight; and the Patriotic Express.

Chapter 1 – The Department of Veterans Affairs (VA) has assisted veterans with homeownership since 1944, when Congress enacted the loan guaranty program to help veterans returning from World War II purchase homes. The loan guaranty program assists veterans by insuring mortgages made by private lenders, and is available for the purchase or construction of homes as well as to refinance existing loans. The loan guaranty has expanded over the years so that it is available to (1) all veterans who fulfill specific duration of service requirements or who were released from active duty due to service-connected disabilities, (2) members of the reserves who completed at least six years of service, and (3) spouses of veterans who died in action, of service-connected disabilities, or who died while receiving (or were entitled to receive) benefits for certain service-connected disabilities. Under the loan guaranty, the VA agrees to reimburse lenders for a portion of losses if borrowers default. Unlike insurance provided through the Federal Housing Administration (FHA) insurance program, the VA does not insure 100% of the loan, and instead the percentage of the loan that is guaranteed is based on the principal balance of the loan.

Veterans who enter into VA-guaranteed loans must pay an up-front fee based on a number of factors that include the type of loan entered into (for example, purchase or refinance), whether service was active duty or in the reserves, whether the loan is the first or subsequent VA loan a borrower has entered into, and the amount of down payment. Borrowers are not required to make a down payment for a VA-guaranteed loan, but the up-front fee is reduced if there is a down payment of 5% or more. Most borrowers (88% in FY2011) do not make a down payment.

In addition to guaranteeing loans from private lenders, the VA also makes direct loans to borrowers in certain circumstances. The original VA direct loan, which was targeted to veterans in rural areas, is now available only to veterans or servicemembers with certain service-connected disabilities. Another direct loan program, originally enacted as a demonstration program in 1992, serves Native American veterans, including veterans living in American Samoa, Guam, and the Commonwealth of the Northern Mariana Islands. In addition, the VA may enter into direct loans in cases where a borrower is delinquent or defaults on a VA-guaranteed loan. The VA may either acquire a loan from a lender and continue servicing itself (called “acquired loans”) or, in cases of foreclosure, the VA may purchase the property and resell it. In these cases, the VA may enter into a loan with a purchaser whether he or she is a veteran or not (called “vendee loans”).

A third way in which the VA provides housing assistance to both veterans and active duty servicemembers is through the Specially Adapted Housing (SAH) Program. Through the SAH program, veterans with certain service-connected disabilities may obtain grants from the VA to purchase or remodel homes to fit their needs. The amount of a grant depends on the disability, and in some cases grants can be used to modify the homes of family members with whom veterans or servicemembers are staying.

This report discusses these three types of housing assistance—the loan guaranty program, direct loan programs, and Specially Adapted Housing program—their origins, how they operate, and how they are funded. The report also has a section that discusses the default and foreclosure of VA-guaranteed loans.

Chapter 2 – It’s a simple question—how many veterans use services at the Veterans Health Administration (VHA)? It’s a question being asked a lot these days, and it is important, baseline information to know when changes are being contemplated to the way in which VA delivers health care to veterans.

In the course of an investigation into allegations that veterans seeking health care services from the VHA experienced long delays in treatment, the Department of Veterans Affairs (VA) Office of Inspector General (OIG) released an interim report that substantiated the delays. Final determinations by the OIG of the full scope and impact of the problems, including whether delays in treatment resulted in harm to or the death of any veterans, will not be available until the OIG completes its investigation and issues a final report.

The issue of wait times for VA health care is not new. Approaches to providing timely access to care for veterans enrolled in VA health care have included the use of non-VA care reimbursed by the VA. The need to rely on non-VA care in some cases has raised questions about the VA's capacity to provide services to the veteran population now and in the future. Knowing how many veterans there are is essential to answering those questions.

Chapter 3 – The Department of Veterans Affairs (VA) provides benefits to veterans who meet certain eligibility criteria. Benefits to veterans range from disability compensation and pensions to hospital and medical care. The VA provides these benefits through three major operating units: the Veterans Health Administration (VHA), the Veterans Benefits Administration (VBA), and the National Cemetery Administration (NCA). This report focuses on funding for the VHA. The VHA is primarily a direct service provider of primary care, specialized care, and related medical and social support services to veterans through the nation's largest integrated health care system. Eligibility for VA health care is based primarily on previous military service, disability, and income.

The President's FY2015 budget request was submitted to Congress on March 4, 2014. The President's budget is requesting $158.6 billion in budget authority for the VA as a whole. This includes $93.5 billion in mandatory funding and $65.1 billion in discretionary funding. For FY2015, the Administration is requesting $56.6 billion for VHA. This includes $45.4 billion for the medical services account, $5.9 billion for the medical support and compliance account, $4.7 billion for the medical facilities account, and nearly $589 million for the medical and prosthetic research account. Furthermore, as required by the Veterans Health Care Budget Reform and Transparency Act of 2009 (P.L. 111-81), the President's budget is requesting $58.6 billion in advance appropriations for the three medical care accounts (medical services, medical support and compliance, and medical facilities) for FY2016.

On April 3, 2014, the House Military Construction and Veterans Affairs Subcommittee approved its version of a Military Construction and Veterans Affairs and Related Agencies Appropriations bill for FY2015 (MILCON-VA Appropriations bill). The full House Appropriations Committee approved a draft measure by voice vote on April 9, 2014, and the House passed MILCON-VA Appropriations bill for FY2015 (H.R. 4486; H.Rept. 113-416) on April 30, 2014. The House-passed version of the MILCON-VA Appropriations bill for

FY2015 proposes a total of $158.2 billion for the VA as whole. For FY2015, H.R. 4486 proposes $56.2 billion for VHA. This includes $45 billion for the medical services account, $5.9 billion for the medical support and compliance account, $4.7 billion for the medical facilities account, and nearly $589 million for the medical and prosthetic research account. H.R. 4486 (H.Rept. 113-416) includes $58.6 billion in advance FY2016 funding for the medical services, medical support and compliance, and medical facilities accounts—the same level included in the President's request.

Chapter 4 – VHA's Beneficiary Travel Program is designed to encourage eligible veterans to seek medical care by reducing travel costs to medical appointments. Veterans are eligible to receive reimbursement for some travel expenses, such as mileage, through the program that is administered by VA medical centers. In February 2013, the VA Office of Inspector General identified issues with inadequate management and oversight. VHA has identified the program as susceptible to significant improper payments and has estimated $71 million in improper payments for fiscal year 2012.

GAO was asked to examine VHA's Beneficiary Travel Program. In this report, GAO examined recent efforts VHA has developed or implemented to improve the program. GAO reviewed documents and interviewed VHA officials about these efforts; and determined whether VHA applied the appropriate internal controls. GAO also reviewed documents and interviewed officials from six VA medical centers, which vary on the basis of fiscal year 2012 mileage reimbursement spending, geographic location, and other factors.

Chapter 5 – In June 2007, SBA established the Patriot Express Pilot Loan Program within its 7(a) loan guarantee program to provide small businesses owned and operated by veterans and other eligible members of the military community access to capital. Through Patriot Express, SBA guarantees individual small business loans that lenders originate. GAO was asked to evaluate the program. This report examines (1) trends in the volume and performance of Patriot Express and related SBA loan programs; (2) the effect of the program on eligible members of the military community; and (3) SBA internal controls to ensure that only eligible borrowers participate. GAO analyzed data on performance and costs of Patriot Express and other similar SBA loan programs from 2007 through 2012; interviewed selected borrowers, lenders, and veteran service organizations; and reviewed SBA internal control guidance on borrower eligibility.

In: Veterans
Editor: Timothy C. Roberts
ISBN: 978-1-63321-722-5

Chapter 1

VA HOUSING: GUARANTEED LOANS, DIRECT LOANS, AND SPECIALLY ADAPTED HOUSING GRANTS*

Libby Perl

SUMMARY

The Department of Veterans Affairs (VA) has assisted veterans with homeownership since 1944, when Congress enacted the loan guaranty program to help veterans returning from World War II purchase homes. The loan guaranty program assists veterans by insuring mortgages made by private lenders, and is available for the purchase or construction of homes as well as to refinance existing loans. The loan guaranty has expanded over the years so that it is available to (1) all veterans who fulfill specific duration of service requirements or who were released from active duty due to service-connected disabilities, (2) members of the reserves who completed at least six years of service, and (3) spouses of veterans who died in action, of service-connected disabilities, or who died while receiving (or were entitled to receive) benefits for certain service-connected disabilities (see Table 1). Under the loan guaranty, the VA agrees to reimburse lenders for a portion of losses if borrowers default. Unlike insurance provided through the Federal Housing Administration (FHA) insurance program, the VA does not insure 100% of the loan, and

* This is an edited, reformatted and augmented version of a Congressional Research Service publication, No. R42504, dated February 4, 2013.

instead the percentage of the loan that is guaranteed is based on the principal balance of the loan (see Table 3).

Veterans who enter into VA-guaranteed loans must pay an up-front fee based on a number of factors that include the type of loan entered into (for example, purchase or refinance), whether service was active duty or in the reserves, whether the loan is the first or subsequent VA loan a borrower has entered into, and the amount of down payment (see Table 6). Borrowers are not required to make a down payment for a VA-guaranteed loan, but the up-front fee is reduced if there is a down payment of 5% or more. Most borrowers (88% in FY2011) do not make a down payment.

In addition to guaranteeing loans from private lenders, the VA also makes direct loans to borrowers in certain circumstances. The original VA direct loan, which was targeted to veterans in rural areas, is now available only to veterans or servicemembers with certain service-connected disabilities. Another direct loan program, originally enacted as a demonstration program in 1992, serves Native American veterans, including veterans living in American Samoa, Guam, and the Commonwealth of the Northern Mariana Islands. In addition, the VA may enter into direct loans in cases where a borrower is delinquent or defaults on a VA-guaranteed loan. The VA may either acquire a loan from a lender and continue servicing itself (called "acquired loans") or, in cases of foreclosure, the VA may purchase the property and resell it. In these cases, the VA may enter into a loan with a purchaser whether he or she is a veteran or not (called "vendee loans").

A third way in which the VA provides housing assistance to both veterans and active duty servicemembers is through the Specially Adapted Housing (SAH) Program. Through the SAH program, veterans with certain service-connected disabilities may obtain grants from the VA to purchase or remodel homes to fit their needs. The amount of a grant depends on the disability, and in some cases grants can be used to modify the homes of family members with whom veterans or servicemembers are staying (see Table 7).

This report discusses these three types of housing assistance—the loan guaranty program, direct loan programs, and Specially Adapted Housing program—their origins, how they operate, and how they are funded. The report also has a section that discusses the default and foreclosure of VA-guaranteed loans.

INTRODUCTION

The U.S. Department of Veterans Affairs (VA) administers several programs that assist individual veterans in purchasing and/or rehabilitating homes. The specific ways in which the VA assists veterans include (1) guaranteeing home mortgages from private lenders (through the Loan Guaranty Program, a form of insurance) to help veterans obtain financing for home purchases, improvements, or refinancing; (2) providing direct loans for home purchases to Native American veterans and to purchasers of homes that are in the VA inventory due to default and foreclosure; and (3) extending grants and loans to veterans with service-connected disabilities so that they can adapt housing to fit their needs through the Specially Adapted Housing Program.

This report discusses some of the legislative history behind each of these housing programs, and provides details about how the programs currently operate. There is a separate section on funding for VA loan programs, and the final section of the report discusses VA efforts to assist borrowers who face default and foreclosure. While the VA also provides housing assistance for homeless veterans, this report does not address these programs.

THE VA LOAN GUARANTY PROGRAM

The VA Loan Guaranty Program is a mortgage insurance program through which eligible veterans enter into mortgages with private lenders, and the VA guarantees that it will pay lenders a portion of losses that may be suffered as a result of borrower default. VA-guaranteed loans are available for the purchase, construction, or repair/rehabilitation of a "dwelling"—defined to include homes with up to four units, single condominium units, and manufactured homes classified as real property[1]—or a farm and farm residence. The guaranty is also available to finance the purchase of a manufactured home not classified as real property, and to refinance an existing loan.

The VA loan guaranty came about as an alternative to a cash bonus for veterans returning from World War II, considered less expensive than a bonus, but still a way to provide benefits to veterans.[2] Credit was seen as one of the areas where veterans were at a disadvantage compared to their non-veteran counterparts because they had not had the time to establish a career or credit history that would allow them to obtain a mortgage without a guaranty.[3] The Servicemen's Readjustment Act of 1944 (P.L. 78-346) created the loan guaranty as part of a package of benefits for returning veterans. The act also included educational benefits (the 1944 Act introduced the GI Bill), employment counseling and placement services, and payments for unemployed veterans. The package of benefits was meant to help veterans reintegrate into the civilian economy.[4] The law provided that the VA would guaranty loans for veterans to purchase or construct a home, purchase a farm or farm equipment, or purchase a business. The guaranty was limited to the greater of 50% of the loan or $2,000, and loans could not have an interest rate above 4%. The VA paid the interest on the guaranteed portion of the loan during its first year. Veterans had the greater of two years from the termination of the war, or two years from their date of separation from the military, to apply.

Within a year, Congress amended the loan guaranty to address some of the aspects of the program that did not seem to be working (P.L. 79-268). The maximum guaranty was raised to $4,000 (prices of homes had risen), the maximum maturity was increased from 20 to 25 years (the shorter maturity period had resulted in higher payments), and veterans were given 10 years from the end of the war to apply (two years had been too short a time frame).[5]

Over time, the loan guaranty has been expanded to include all veterans who served on active duty from World War II on, with varying length of service requirements, as well as those who served in the selected reserves; the amount of the guaranty has grown; business purchases are no longer eligible and farm purchases have been limited; and the uses have expanded to include refinancing, energy efficiency improvements, and the purchase of manufactured homes. This section of the report describes eligibility for the loan guaranty ("Borrower Eligibility"), ways in which it can be used ("Uses of the Loan Guaranty"), coverage ("Amount of Coverage Provided by the Loan Guaranty"), and how the VA loan guaranty differs from the Federal Housing Administration (FHA) mortgage insurance program ("How the VA Loan Guaranty Differs from FHA Insurance").

Borrower Eligibility

Service Criteria

Veteran eligibility for the VA loan guaranty started narrowly, targeted to individuals who served during World War II. As additional conflicts arose, veterans of those conflicts, as well as peacetime eras, were made eligible for the program.

Table 1. Service Eligibility for the Loan Guaranty

Eligibility Category	Public Law Initiating Eligibility[a]	Time Requirement (if any)
Active Duty[b] Service during World War II (9/16/40 to 7/25/47)	P.L. 78-346	90 days[c]
Active Duty Service during the Korean Conflict (6/27/50 to 1/31/55)	P.L. 82-550	90 days[c]
Active Duty Service during the Vietnam Era (8/5/64 to 5/7/75)	P.L. 95-476	90 days[c]
Active Duty Service Post-	P.L. 100-322	181 days
• World War II (7/26/47 to 6/26/50)		
• Korea (2/1/55 to 8/4/64)		
• Vietnam (5/8/75 to 8/1/90d)		
Service Begun After[e]	P.L. 97-66	• 24 months or
• 9/7/80 (enlisted personnel) or • 10/16/81 (officers[f])		• full period ordered to active duty, but no less than 181 days during peacetime or 90 days[c] during wartime
Service in the Selected Reserveg	P.L. 102-547	720 days (six years)
Released from Active Duty or Selected Reserve due to Service-Connected Disability (any service after 9/15/40)	P.L. 78-346	—
Spouse of a Veteran who Died in Action or of a Service-Connected Disability Who Has Not Remarried[h]	P.L. 81-475	—
Spouse of Member of Active Duty Military who • is missing in action, • captured, or • forcibly detained	P.L. 91-584	—
Surviving Spouse of Veteran Who Died While Receiving Compensation for a Service-Connected Disability Rated Totally Disabling[i]	P.L. 112-154	—

Source: 38 U.S.C. §§3701-3702, 38 U.S.C. §5303A, and U.S. Department of Veterans Affairs, *Manual M26-1 Guaranteed Loan Processing Manual*, September 16, 1996, pp. 2-1 to 2-28, http://www.benefits M26_1.asp.

Note: The two categories not included in the table are (1) sole surviving child in a family where a parent or sibling was killed while in the Armed Forces, captured or missing in action, or permanently disabled and (2) in some circumstances, commissioned officers of the Public Health Service and the National Oceanic and Atmospheric Administration.

[a] Subsequent laws may have extended the period of service or otherwise modified eligibility requirements.

[b] Active duty service refers to full time service in the Army, Navy, Air Force, Marines, or Coast Guard.

[c] A veteran qualifies if any part of his or her 90 days of service was during wartime.

[d] While the Vietnam era extends to August 1, 1990, benefits for veterans who began service after September 7, 1980, are subject to 38 U.S.C. §5303A(b). See tablenote e.

[e] 38 U.S.C. §5303A(b). The two-year minimum service requirement for many veterans' benefits was added to the law in 1980 as part of P.L. 96-342, the Department of Defense Authorization Act of 1981. A year later, P.L. 97-66, the Veterans' Disability Compensation, Housing, and Memorial Benefits Amendments of 1981, amended the law to include officers as well as enlisted personnel, and to exempt those discharged for reduction-in-force purposes. Congress was concerned that "excessive numbers of servicemembers were, through inappropriate or unproductive conduct, bringing about their early discharges, that many of them had enlisted for the purpose of obtaining eligibility for veterans' benefits based on short periods of service, and that it is wasteful for the Federal government to provide veterans' benefits to those who fail substantially to fulfill their active-duty service commitments." U.S. Congress, Senate Committee on Veterans' Affairs, *Veterans' Disability Compensation, Housing, and Memorial Benefits Amendments of 1981*, report to accompany S. 917, 97t[h] Cong., [1st] sess., July 16, 1981, S.Rept. 97-153, pp. 36-37.

[f] The dates for officers and enlisted personnel differ because the original law implementing the 24-month length-of-service requirement (P.L. 96-342) only applied to enlisted personnel and not officers. See U.S. Congress, House Committee on Veterans' Affairs, *Veterans' Compensation Amendments of 1981*, report to accompany H.R. 3995, 97th Cong., [1st] sess., July 16, 1981, H.Rept. 97-179, pp. 20-21. P.L. 97-66 amended the law to apply to officers.

[g] The Selected Reserve includes the Army, Navy, Air Force, Marine Corps, and Coast Guard Reserves, the Army National Guard, and the Air National Guard. 10 U.S.C. §10101.

[h] The term "surviving spouse" is defined at 38 U.S.C. §101 to mean someone who has not remarried.

[i] The disability must meet one of three duration requirements: (1) it was continuously rated totally disabling for 10 or more years before death; (2) it was continuously rated totally disabling for at least five years from the date of discharge from active duty; or (3) it was continuously rated totally disabling for not less than one year, and the veteran had been a prisoner of war and died after September 30, 1999.

A veteran is defined as "a person who served in the active military, naval, or air service, and who was discharged or released there from under conditions other than dishonorable."[6] To be eligible for VA loan benefits (and most other VA benefits), veterans must fulfill specific time period and duration of service requirements. In addition, reservists with at least six years of service are eligible for the loan guaranty.[7] Reservists need not have served on active duty, unlike what is required for some other veterans benefits, as long as they fulfill the duration of service requirement. The spouses of veterans who died in action, died of a service-connected disability, or who are missing in action, captured, or forcibly detained are eligible for the loan guaranty. In addition, P.L. 112-154, enacted in August 2012, expanded eligibility to include spouses of veterans who die *while receiving* compensation (or who were eligible to receive compensation) for a service-connected disability rated totally disabling for a specified duration.[8] Previously, only surviving spouses of veterans who *died from* their service-connected disabilities were eligible for the loan guaranty. See Table 1 for a complete list of eligibility categories.[9]

Financial Criteria

In addition to length of service requirements, the VA loan guaranty has underwriting criteria designed to ensure that veterans have the financial means to make mortgage payments. The statute gives the VA Secretary the authority to set underwriting standards in regulation, which are further supplemented by the *VA Lenders Handbook*.[10] The underwriting standards consider a veteran's income, expenses, and credit history in determining whether he or she qualifies for a guaranteed loan. In seeking to balance income and expenses, a veteran must meet requirements established via a debt-to-income ratio standard and a residual income analysis.

- **Debt-to-Income Ratio:** In the debt-to-income analysis, a lender is to look at the ratio of a veteran's anticipated housing expenses and other long-term monthly obligations compared to his or her stable and reliable monthly income.[11] To be stable and reliable, income is to be expected to continue "for the foreseeable future." Examples of unreliable income include VA education benefits, unemployment compensation, and irregular overtime pay.[12] A veteran's total debt-to-income ratio should not exceed 41%, although there are provisions to allow for exceptions to this requirement in cases where a lender is able to justify the loan to the VA.
- **Residual Income:** The residual income test is used to determine whether a veteran's income after payments for shelter expenses and other debts is adequate to meet living expenses. Unlike the debt-to-

income ratio, the residual income test looks at additional expenses such as food, clothing, health care, and gasoline that are not captured as part of debt.[13] The loan guaranty regulations contain a guide to sufficient residual income by region.[14]

The Loan Guaranty Program does not require veterans to have a specific credit score to qualify for a loan, but the underwriting guidelines require lenders to analyze a borrower's credit history.[15] Lenders must be able to explain decisions to extend credit to borrowers who have an adverse credit history, and certain situations, such as an unpaid court-ordered judgment or a bankruptcy within the previous one or two years, may disqualify a borrower from obtaining a guaranteed loan. A previous foreclosure is not a bar to obtaining a VA-guaranteed loan, but borrowers who had previous VA-guaranteed loans that were foreclosed upon may have to repay the government for any losses suffered prior to obtaining a new loan.[16]

Uses of the Loan Guaranty

Financing the Purchase, Construction, or Improvement of Dwellings or Farm Residences

Loan guarantees are available for the purchase or construction, or to make improvements (including energy efficiency improvements) to either a "dwelling" or farm residence.[17] A dwelling is defined as a building primarily used and occupied as a home (defined as a "place of residence"),[18] and that consists of no more than four single family units (under most circumstances),[19] one of which will be occupied by an eligible veteran. While a daily physical presence is not necessary to occupy the property as a home, occupancy of the property must be more than intermittent.[20] For example, the property should be near a borrower's place of employment, and if his or her job requires an absence for a "substantial amount of time," there must be a history of continuous presence in the community prior to the absence, and there should be no attempt to establish a principal residence elsewhere.[21] Use of a property as a vacation home would not qualify for the VA loan guaranty. An exception exists for instances where veterans are called away for active duty—their spouses or dependent children may satisfy the requirement by occupying the property as a home.[22]

A range of housing qualifies as a dwelling for VA loan guaranty purposes. A single condominium unit qualifies as a dwelling, and a manufactured home may also be a dwelling if the veteran owns the land to which it is affixed and the state classifies it as real property.[23] Note, however, that a manufactured home that does not meet these requirements may qualify separately under the manufactured housing section of the law (for more information, see the next section of this report entitled "Loan Guaranty for Manufactured Housing"). The loan guaranty can also include the purchase of land for both the construction of a single-family home[24] or for placement of a manufactured home.[25]

In addition to purchasing property, an eligible veteran may enter into a guaranteed loan for the construction of housing or to make improvements to property the veteran already owns. In general, the loan guaranty cannot be used to purchase a property that requires significant work (i.e., a fixer-upper) due to minimum property standards for homes purchased with VA-guaranteed loans.[26] However, if a property meets minimum property standards, and a veteran wants to include funds for improvements in a purchase money loan, the appraiser is to take the value of the improvements into account, increasing the loan amount for which a borrower could potentially qualify.[27] The loan guaranty can also be used for loans to make "energy efficiency improvements" to a property a veteran is purchasing or to a property already owned. Energy efficiency improvements were added as a permissible use of the loan guaranty in 1978 as part of the Veterans' Housing Benefits Act (P.L. 95-476). Energy efficiency improvements are limited to $6,000, and may include such things as solar heating and cooling or conservation measures, such as insulation, weatherizing, and furnace replacement.[28]

Loan Guaranty for Manufactured Housing

The VA loan guaranty has evolved so that there are two ways in which manufactured housing is classified and guaranteed. First, as mentioned in the previous section, manufactured housing can be classified as a dwelling that may be guaranteed under the regular guaranty provisions of the statute (38 U.S.C. §3710). In addition, it can be classified and guaranteed under a separate manufactured housing portion of the law (38 U.S.C. §3712). Congress created the latter program first in 1970 (see the Veterans' Housing Act of 1970, P.L. 91-506), and later specified that manufactured housing could be included as a dwelling for the regular guaranty provisions in Section 3710 (see the Veterans' Compensation and Program Improvements Amendments of 1984, P.L. 98-223). Despite this flexibility, it appears that the VA has not guaranteed new manufactured housing loans under Section 3712 of the law since 1996.[29]

The VA has slightly different definitions for manufactured housing based on the portion of the statute under which it is guaranteed. The definitions share in common that manufactured housing is

> [a] movable dwelling unit designed and constructed for year-round occupancy on land by a single family, which dwelling unit contains permanent eating, cooking, sleeping, and sanitary facilities. A double-wide manufactured home is a movable dwelling designed for occupancy by one family consisting of (1) two or more units intended to be joined together horizontally when located on a site, but capable of independent movement or (2) a unit having a section or sections which unfold along the entire length of the unit.[30]

The definitions differ in that the regulations governing the Section 3710 guaranty require that the manufactured home be permanently affixed to a lot and classified as real property under state law. To be permanently affixed, the home must be placed on a foundation in a way that satisfies local building codes.[31] This generally means being placed on a permanent foundation, and in some, but not all cases, connection to utilities and ownership of the land, although long-term rental agreements may suffice.[32] Once a home is permanently affixed, it may be titled as real property rather than personal property (as a vehicle is titled). According to the Census Bureau, in 2010, approximately 73% of new manufactured homes were titled as personal property and 22% as real property.[33]

Separate Loan Guaranty for Manufactured Housing, 38 U.S.C. Section 3712

When Congress created the separate loan guaranty for manufactured housing in 1970, it was concerned that returning Vietnam veterans, some without significant financial resources, were unable to afford conventional homes and the costs of financing.[34] The recommendation to include mobile homes as eligible properties for the loan guaranty originated from the President's Committee on the Vietnam Veteran, whose members saw growing construction costs of conventional homes as a barrier to home ownership for veterans.[35] According to the committee, the lower costs of mobile homes represented "an enormous potential in meeting the housing needs of many veterans with low to moderate incomes."[36] It was necessary to add a new manufactured housing portion to the law because, unlike loans for site-built homes, manufactured housing is often financed with "chattel mortgages," which are designed for moveable property and governed by different laws than mortgages for real property.

Manufactured housing loans that are guaranteed through Section 3712 differ from the Section 3710 loan guaranty in that the term of the mortgage is generally shorter depending on the type of manufactured housing,[37] the maximum loan guaranty amount is set differently (see Table 3), and fees charged by the VA are less than for conventional housing (see Table 6), among other differences. However, as mentioned previously, the VA has not guaranteed loans pursuant to Section 3712 for a number of years. The VA cites several reasons that the Section 3712 loan has not been popular: interest rates are often higher for manufactured homes not permanently affixed to a foundation, the maximum loan amount cannot exceed 95% of the purchase price plus the VA fee[38] (meaning that a veteran must make a down payment), and changed appraisal standards instituted in the 1980s that resulted in sales prices that exceeded appraised values.[39]

Refinancing Loans

Veterans may use the loan guaranty to refinance an existing loan in two different ways: to reduce the interest rate of an existing VA-guaranteed loan (sometimes referred to as an interest rate reduction refinancing loan or IRRRL),[40] or to refinance generally with fewer restrictions. Loans in the latter category are sometimes referred to as "cash out" refinancings because veterans may choose to take out equity as part of the transaction. The ability to refinance a loan on a property owned and occupied by an eligible veteran became part of the loan guaranty law as part of the Veterans' Housing Act of 1970 (P.L. 91-506).[41] Manufactured housing loans became eligible for refinancing as part of the Veterans' Compensation and Program Improvements Amendments of 1984 (P.L. 98-223).

IRRRL

When a veteran refinances a loan that is already guaranteed by the VA as an IRRRL, generally the interest rate on the new loan should be lower than the loan being refinanced.[42] However, a veteran may refinance from an adjustable-rate loan to a fixed-rate loan without the requirement for a lower rate. The amount of the new loan may not exceed the principal balance of the original loan, plus any closing costs, and the term of the new loan cannot exceed the original loan term by more than 10 years.[43] A veteran may also take advantage of energy efficiency improvements as part of an IRRRL, in which case the principal balance of the new loan may be increased by the amount of the improvements.[44] Another aspect of an IRRRL refinancing is that a veteran need not occupy the residence as a home after refinancing as long as it had been occupied as a home prior to refinancing. The limitation on occupancy was removed in 1987 (P.L. 100-198) due to concern that servicemembers who were transferred or stationed elsewhere were unable to take advantage of refinancing.[45] In general, no appraisal and no new underwriting are required for an IRRRL,[46] and, unlike purchase-money VA loans, closing costs may be financed as part of the loan.[47]

"Cash-Out" Refinancing

A veteran may also refinance without the restrictions involved in an IRRRL. The loan or lien being refinanced need not be VA-guaranteed, the new loan does not have to have a lower interest rate, the loan balance on the refinanced loan may be higher than on the original loan, and the veteran may receive cash from the refinancing for any purpose approved by the lender. Property improvements are often undertaken as part of a refinancing.[48] However, there are requirements for cash-out refinancings that are not required for IRRRLs. A veteran must occupy the property as his or her home after the refinancing, and, unlike the IRRRL, an appraisal, credit check, and underwriting are required.[49]

Number and Amount of Loans Guaranteed

VA-guaranteed loans make up a relatively small share of mortgage loans in the United States. According to the 2009 American Housing Survey, approximately 7.6% of primary mortgages outstanding were VA-guaranteed loans.[50] Table 2 shows the number of loans that have been guaranteed by the VA from FY2000 through FY2011 broken down by purchase and refinance loans, the dollar amount of the loans, and the dollar amount of the portion guaranteed.

During periods where interest rates have fallen, refinance loans make up a greater share of the total VA loans extended. And during the mid-2000s, when housing prices were at their height, the numbers of VA-guaranteed purchase loans were lower than the number entered into at both the beginning and end of the last decade. Among the reasons for this are the fact that looser lending standards on private mortgage loans, particularly subprime loans, might have made them more appealing for veteran borrowers. This may have been particularly true in a climate where the ability to close loans quickly was considered appealing to sellers, and bypassing the VA loan fee was appealing to veteran borrowers.[51] In addition, higher home prices during the mid-2000s could have made it difficult for veterans living in high-cost areas to take advantage of the loan guaranty. Until enactment of legislation in 2008, the VA loan guaranty did not cover properties in high cost areas where the cost exceeded $417,000. (For more information about maximum mortgage limits, see the next section of this report entitled "Amount of Coverage Provided by the Loan Guaranty.")

Table 2. VA Loans Guaranteed by Fiscal Year, FY2000-FY2011

Fiscal Year	Number of Loans in Year			Volume of Loans Made in Year ($ in billions)		Cumulative Volume of Loans Outstandinga ($ in billions)	
	Purchase Loans	Refinance Loansb	Total Loans	Amount of Loans	Amount Guaranteed	Amount of Loans	Amount Guaranteed
2000	185,553	13,607	199,160	23.372	7.071	—c	—c
2001	177,158	72,851	250,009	31.255	9.152	218.455	71.431
2002	176,898	140,353	317,251	40.129	11.667	216.042	69.547
2003	148,810	340,608	489,418	63.255	18.245	213.248	67.654
2004	152,395	183,393	335,788	44.131	12.643	207.374	64.683
2005	119,130	46,724	165,854	24.901	6.808	202.073	62.114
2006	122,604	20,104	142,708	24.635	6.486	203.186	61.277
2007	117,941	15,372	133,313	24.890	6.438	207.644	61.456
2008	142,340	37,330	179,670	36.089	9.236	220.839	63.921
2009	180,896	144,794	325,690	68.201	17.492	183.365	50.368
2010	192,625	121,386	314,011	65.051	16.745	214.726	58.080
2011	186,588	171,006	357,594	74.929	19.318	247.648	66.222

Source: The data on the number and dollar amount of guaranteed loans in a fiscal year are from the Department of Veterans Affairs, *Annual Benefits Reports*. The data on the cumulative volume of loans come from the VA *Performance and Accountability Reports*.

[a] The cumulative volume of loans is the total dollar amount of all guaranteed loans that was outstanding at the end of the fiscal year.

[b] Refinance loans include interest rate reduction refinancing loans and cash-out or other refinancing transactions.

[c] *The FY2000 Performance and Accountability Report* did not provide information about the total loan volume.

Amount of Coverage Provided by the Loan Guaranty

While there is technically no limit to the amount that a veteran can borrow and still receive a loan guaranty through the VA, the VA limits the guaranty that it will provide based on the amount of the loan as well as the type of loan (purchase money, refinance, or energy efficiency mortgage). In most cases, the VA guaranty covers at least 25% of the principal balance of a loan. While the VA guaranty does not insure 100% of the loan (as Federal Housing Administration loan insurance does, for example), the guaranty covers what would typically be required as a down payment in a conventional mortgage transaction to avoid the requirement for private mortgage insurance. In cases where the loan guaranty does not cover 25% of the loan amount, a veteran may have to make a down payment.

Freddie Mac Conforming Loan Limit

The conforming loan limit is a ceiling on the value of loans that Freddie Mac, one of the Government Sponsored Enterprises, can purchase from lenders.[52] The single-family home loan limit in statute was initially pegged to the FHA insurance limit—$33,750 in 1970[53]— then revised to follow the loan limits for savings and loans.[54]

However, beginning in 1980 as part of the Housing and Community Development Act (P.L. 96-399), Congress inserted the maximum loan limit directly in the Freddie Mac statute. P.L. 96-399 set the single-family limit at $93,750, and it was to be adjusted administratively each year based on the national average single-family home price.[55] While Congress did not amend the statute to increase the loan limit until 2008, the limit was changed administratively 27 times.[56]

As part of the Housing and Economic Recovery Act of 2008 (P.L. 110-289), Congress amended the Freddie Mac statute to raise the *statutory* conforming loan limit from $93,750 to $417,000, which was the level that had been established administratively for 2006 and 2007. P.L. 110- 289 also added a sentence to the statute allowing the limit to increase in high-cost areas where 115% of the median home price exceeds the conforming loan limit. In these high-cost areas, the loan limit may go up to 115% of the area median home price, not to exceed 150% of the loan limit (or as high as $625,500).

Since the enactment of P.L. 110-289, the Freddie Mac statute itself has not been amended, although Congress temporarily raised the loan limits for high-cost areas through September 30, 2011, via several laws. This limit was the lower of 125% of the area median home price or 175% of the Freddie Mac limit (or $729,750).[57] These temporary limits expired at the end of FY2011.

The statute governing the loan guaranty for home purchase sets out four categories of coverage depending on the principal balance of the loan.[58] (For all guaranty amounts, including manufactured housing, refinance loans, and energy efficiency mortgages, see Table 3.) In general, the amount of the loan guaranty is based on the amount borrowed by a veteran.

- At loan levels at or below $45,000, the VA guaranties 50% of the loan.
- For loans above $45,000 and up to and including $56,250, the guaranty is $22,500.
- At loan levels above $56,250 and up to and including $144,000, the VA guaranty is the lesser of $36,000 or 40% of the loan.
- For loan levels above $144,000, the maximum loan guaranty is the lesser of the "maximum guaranty amount" (described below) or 25% of the loan.

The Maximum Guaranty Amount

The VA loan "maximum guaranty amount" is defined in 38 U.S.C. Section 3703 as 25% of "the Freddie Mac conforming loan limit limitation determined under section 305(a)(2) of the Federal Home Loan Mortgage Corporation Act."[59] The Freddie Mac statute has most recently set the conforming loan limit at $417,000 for single-family homes (for more information about the Freddie Mac conforming loan limit, see the text box).[60] However, for certain high-cost areas, the loan limit may be as high as 115% of the area median home price, though it may not exceed 150% of the conforming loan limit (or $625,500).[61]

However, for two periods—from October 10, 2008, through December 31, 2011, and from August 6, 2012, through December 31, 2014—limits to the VA loan guaranty for loan levels above $144,000 have been higher than the limit in 38 U.S.C. Section 3703. The Veterans' Benefits Improvement Act of 2008 (P.L. 110-389) temporarily increased the "maximum guaranty amount" through 2011 (it did not make the change in statute), and then P.L. 112-154 again increased the limit through 2014. The two laws set the maximum guaranty amount at 25% of the higher of

- the Freddie Mac conforming loan limit, or
- 125% of the area median home price, but no higher than 175% of the limit determined under the Freddie Mac statute.

According to guidance issued by the VA,[62] this means that in certain high-cost areas, the VA can guarantee loans up to a maximum of 175% of

$625,500, or $1,094,625. Loan limits in a number of counties have exceeded the statutory maximum level of $625,500 during these time periods, with three counties reaching $1,094,625 in 2013.[63] Therefore, depending on where a property is located, the maximum VA loan guaranty may be as high as 25% of $1,094,625, or $273,656.

If the amount of a mortgage exceeds the maximum amount at which the VA will guarantee 25% of the loan (for example, the amount of a mortgage is $500,000 in a county where the loan limit is $417,000), then a veteran may have to make a down payment equal to 25% of the amount over the loan limit to qualify for the loan due to secondary market considerations (see the next section of this report entitled "Maximum Loan Amount" for more information about the secondary market). However, the majority of VA-guaranteed loans are made with no down payment (88% of purchase loans in FY2011 had no down payment),[64] so the limits described here will apply to most veteran borrowers.

Maximum Guaranty for Alaska, Hawaii, U.S. Virgin Islands, and Guam

The maximum single-family guaranty limit for Alaska, Hawaii, the U.S. Virgin Islands, and Guam is higher than in the other states and the District of Columbia due to costs of construction.[65] As with the maximum guaranty for the 50 states and Washington, DC, P.L. 110-389 and P.L. 112- 154 have increased the maximum guaranty through the end of 2014.

The statutory Freddie Mac conforming loan limit for Alaska, Hawaii, the U.S. Virgin Islands, and Guam is 50% higher than the $417,000 limit for the rest of the country, resulting in a statutory conforming loan limit of $625,500.[66] Further, with the Freddie Mac statutory provision allowing the area limit to be increased up to 150% of the conforming loan limit for high-cost areas, it is possible for the loan limit in Alaska, Hawaii, the U.S. Virgin Islands, and Guam to be as high as $938,250 (150% of $625,500). In addition, because P.L. 110-389 and P.L. 112-154 increased the maximum limit to as much as 175% of the limit determined under the Freddie Mac statute, the maximum loan limit could be set as high as $1,641,937.50 (175% of $938,250). However, through 2013, only two communities, Honolulu County and St. John, Virgin Islands, saw their limits exceed $625,500.[67]

Maximum Loan Amount

Although there is no limit to the amount a veteran may borrow and still participate in the VA loan guaranty program, lenders may be unwilling to extend a loan that exceeds the limit where the VA will guaranty 25% of the loan. VA loans are securitized through the Government National Mortgage Association (Ginnie Mae). Ginnie Mae may secure certain "high balance loans" originated after October 1, 2008—loans where the balance exceeds the conforming loan limit of $417,000 for single-family properties.[68] However, according to the VA, the "rule of thumb" for Ginnie Mae to purchase a VA loan is that at least 25% of the principal balance either be guaranteed and/or covered by a down payment.[69] As a result, the effective maximum loan limit with no down payment corresponds to the "maximum guaranty amount" described in the previous section.

Table 3. Limits on the Level of Loan Guaranty

Amount of Loan	Limits on Guaranty
Home Loan Guaranty	
• $45,000 or less	• 50% of the loan amount
• from $45,000 up to and including $56,250	• $22,500
• from $56,250 up to and including $144,000	• Lesser of $36,000 or 40% of the loan amounta
• more than $144,000	• Lesser of (1) 25% of the loan amount or (2) 25% of the higher of (a) the Freddie Mac conforming loan limit ($417,000) or (b) 125% of the area median home price, not to exceed 175% of the limit determined under the Freddie Mac Statute (a maximum of 175% of $625,500).
Refinance: Same as for purchase, but in the case of an interest rate reduction refinancing loan (IRRRL), the guaranty may not exceed the greater of the original loan's guaranty or 25% of the loan.	
Energy Efficiency Improvements: The sum of (1) the guaranty amount without the energy efficiency improvements and (2) the guaranty percentage (from step (1)) multiplied by the portion borrowed for energy efficiency improvements.b	
Manufactured Housing Purchase: The lesser of $20,000 or 40% of the loan.	
Manufactured Housing Refinance: If refinancing a VA loan, the guaranty may not exceed the greater of the original loan guaranty or 25% of the refinancing amount.	

Source: 38 U.S.C. §3703(a), P.L. 112-154, §3710(d)-(e), §3712(a),(c).

[a] This effectively means that for loans between $90,000 and $144,000, the maximum guaranty is $36,000.

[b] While the Energy Efficiency Improvement guaranty is effectively the same as the guaranty for home purchase, the separate calculations are meant to ensure that the portion of the guaranty related to the improvements are not counted against the veteran's entitlement. 38 U.S.C. §3710(d)(4). See also, *VA Lenders Handbook*, p. 7-20, http://www.benefits.va.gov/WARMS/docs/admin26 /pamphlet/pam26_7/ ch07.doc.

Subsequent Loans: The Veteran's Entitlement

The term "entitlement" is used to refer to the amount of guaranty to which a veteran is entitled under the loan guaranty statute. It is different from the guaranty amount described in the previous section in that it is technically a lifetime limit on the amount of loan insurance coverage for which a veteran may qualify. However, given the broad circumstances under which entitlement may be restored (described below), veterans may use the guaranty for the purchase of more than one home during a lifetime, though not necessarily more than one home at a time.

The statute governing the VA loan guaranty limits a veteran's entitlement to $36,000 or, for loans that exceed $144,000, the "maximum guaranty amount" described in the previous section (under current law, this amount may be no more than $273,656 in high-cost areas).[70] The term "basic entitlement" is sometimes used to refer to entitlement up to $36,000, and the term "bonus entitlement" is used to refer to entitlement that exceeds $36,000. In general, due to the requirement that VA-guaranteed loans be used to purchase properties that a veteran will occupy as his or her home,[71] unused entitlement cannot be used to purchase more than one home at a time.

In addition to being able to put unused entitlement toward a future guaranteed loan, there are instances in which already-used entitlement may be restored so that a veteran may use the maximum available loan guaranty to purchase another home.[72] These circumstances cover most situations where a veteran has ended the previous loan transaction in some way.

- Entitlement is restored where a veteran has disposed of the property (e.g., through sale) or the property has been destroyed through natural disaster, and either (1) the loan is paid off in full; (2) if the VA suffered a loss on the loan, the loss is repaid; or (3) the VA has been released from liability on the loan.
- When one veteran assumes a guaranteed loan from another, entitlement is restored to the original mortgagor.
- In cases of refinancing, entitlement is restored either when a veteran has paid off the original loan prior to entering into a new loan or where proceeds from the refinancing will be used to pay off the original loan.[73]
- Where a veteran has paid off a VA-guaranteed loan, but has not yet sold the property that secured it, the VA may do a one-time restoration of entitlement to be used toward the purchase of another property.[74]

If available entitlement is less than 25% of the loan, then a lender may require a veteran to make a down payment to make up the difference between the loan guaranty and 25% of the loan to meet secondary market requirements.[75]

How the VA Loan Guaranty Differs from FHA Insurance

Both the Federal Housing Administration (FHA) loan insurance program and the VA loan guaranty program provide borrowers with the federal government's promise to reimburse lenders in the event of borrower default on private mortgages. Due to the insurance features of each program, borrowers who might not otherwise have the resources for a conventional mortgage may still be able to purchase a home. Despite similar purposes, however, the programs differ in their specifics. Aside from the requirement that a borrower through the VA meet service requirements, other features such as the amount of coverage, borrower fees, loan processing and underwriting, terms of the loan, etc., vary between the two.

- **Amount of Coverage:** As discussed earlier in the "Amount of Coverage Provided by the Loan Guaranty" section, the VA loan guaranty covers only a portion of the mortgage loan in the event of a borrower's default. Insurance through FHA covers 100% of the loan amount (up to a certain limit).
- **Maximum Loan Amount:** As a practical matter, the maximum loan amount for the VA loan guaranty in certain high-cost areas is may be as high as $1,094,625 (see the "Maximum Loan Amount" section of this report). In the case of FHA, the insurance will currently cover loans up to $729,750 in certain high-cost areas.[76]
- **Borrower Fees:** Fees paid by veterans participating in the VA loan guaranty program are paid up front as a percentage of the loan (see Table 6), and borrowers do not pay additional annual premiums. Borrowers who go through the FHA program currently pay an up-front fee of 1.75% of the loan amount, and then pay annual premiums that range between 1.20% and 1.50% of the mortgage balance, depending on the loan-to-value ratio and size of the mortgage.[77]
- **Down Payment:** Veteran borrowers who participate in the VA loan guaranty program are not required to make a down payment. However, if the loan balance exceeds loan limits, the borrower

generally must make up the difference between the guaranty and 25% of the loan amount. In general, borrowers through FHA must make a 3.5% down payment (10% for credit scores ranging from 500 to 579).[78]

- **Fees Charged at Closing:** While both the VA loan guaranty and the FHA insurance program have rules about what lenders may charge borrowers at closing, the VA loan guaranty is more restrictive. VA loan guaranty regulations list services where lenders are allowed to charge itemized fees to borrowers (such as appraisal, recording, and credit report fees),[79] and any other fees must be recouped through a flat fee not to exceed 1% of the loan, limiting such charges as application fees, document preparation, interest rate lock-in fees, and charges from mortgage brokers.[80] FHA rules are more general, specifying that lenders "may only collect fair, reasonable, and customary fees and charges" from borrowers.[81]
- **Minimum Credit Score:** The VA loan guaranty does not require a specific credit score from a borrower, while FHA requires a credit score of at least 500.[82]
- **Appraisal:** Appraisers for properties that are to be guaranteed through the VA loan guaranty program must go through a separate VA certification procedure, and they are chosen by the VA rather than lenders.[83] The statute requires the VA to review appraisals prior to loan closings, although the VA has a program in place to allow lenders to process appraisals after application and training.[84] FHA does not have similar policies regarding appraisers, and they may be selected by lenders.

In addition, for a number of years, veterans were given special terms when entering into FHA loans. The Housing and Urban Development Act of 1965 (P.L. 89-117) first allowed veterans to enter into FHA loans with slightly higher maximum mortgages compared to nonveteran borrowers, and it also exempted them from what was then a 3% cash down payment requirement on the first $15,000 of the loan. Over time, some of the specifics of the maximum mortgage and down payment requirements changed, but veterans still retained favorable levels compared to nonveterans. In 2002, the FHA Downpayment Simplification Act (P.L. 107-326) removed statutory language that allowed for higher maximum mortgages for veteran borrowers.[85] And when the Housing and Economic Recovery Act of 2008 (P.L. 110-289) was enacted, it eliminated the provision exempting veterans from the requirement of what had previously been a 3% down payment in cash or its equivalent.[86]

DIRECT VA LOANS

In addition to the VA loan guaranty program, through which the VA insures loans made to veterans by private lenders, there are several circumstances under which the VA makes loans directly to veterans, as well as occasionally to nonveterans. The direct loans through the VA can be put into two broad categories. The first category involves loans that are targeted to specific veteran populations: one program was created to address the needs of rural veterans, but has evolved to serve veterans with certain disabilities, and the other program is designed for Native American veterans. The second category involves loans made as the result of borrower default on guaranteed loans—these are referred to as "acquired loans" and "vendee loans."

The Original Direct Loan for Veterans in Rural Areas, Now Limited to Veterans with Disabilities

The VA first made direct housing loans available to veterans who were unable to obtain mortgages through private lenders and were therefore unable to participate in the loan guaranty program. The direct loan portion of the program was enacted as part of the Housing Act of 1950 (P.L. 81-475), and was meant to be a "last resort" where private financing was not available to veterans.[87] The enacting legislation did not specify that the program was directed to veterans in rural areas, but about eight years later, in 1958, Congress changed the law to apply specifically to veterans living in rural areas and small towns as part of P.L. 85-857.[88] The law provided that the VA Secretary would designate an area without private loan options for veterans as a "housing credit shortage area" and make loans to veterans at a rate not exceeding the rate set for guaranteed loans at a maximum principal balance (at the time the law was enacted) of $13,500. In the Veterans' Housing Act of 1970 (P.L. 91-506), Congress made direct loans available to veterans who qualified for Specially Adapted Housing grants for veterans with certain disabilities, who it recognized might also have difficulty obtaining credit for home purchases.[89]

The VA direct loan program continues to exist today, but in limited form.[90] A 1980 review of the direct loan program found that 98% of veterans in rural areas received loans from private lenders, and only 2% received VA direct loans.[91] As a result of the increased availability of private loan funds in rural areas, beginning in the FY1981 Department of Housing and Urban Development-Independent Agencies Appropriation Act (P.L. 96-526), Congress specified that VA direct loans be made only for veterans with disabilities through the Specially Adapted Housing Program (described in a later section of this report entitled "The Specially Adapted Housing Program"). Congress has continued to include similar language in subsequent appropriations acts.[92] Currently, direct loans are limited to $500,000 in obligations for Specially Adapted Housing loans of not more than $33,000 apiece.[93] Interest rates on the loans are to be determined by the VA Secretary, and veterans are eligible as long as they qualify for the loan guaranty program.

Direct Loans for Native American Veterans (Including Guam, American Samoa, and CNMI)

While the VA loan guaranty program is available to Native American veterans,[94] due in part to certain tribal land ownership issues, Congress enacted a direct loan program specifically to provide mortgage assistance for Native American veterans. The direct loan program may also be used by veteran borrowers who are Native Hawaiians, Alaska Natives, and those who are native to American Samoa, Guam, and the Commonwealth of the Northern Mariana Islands (CNMI).[95]

Prior to enactment of the direct loan program for Native American veterans, VA housing assistance to Native American veterans was minimal. In fact, the Advisory Committee on Native American Veterans had been unable to find a single instance of a Native American veteran benefitting from the loan guaranty program.[96] While factors such as poverty and unemployment among Native American veterans may have contributed to their lack of participation, the unique nature of tribal land also presented obstacles to private lenders entering into mortgages. Much of tribal land is held in trust by the federal government, either for a tribe or for individual Native Americans (the latter situation is sometimes referred to as an allotment). Of the approximately 56 million acres of trust land, 45 million are held in trust for tribes and 11 million for individuals.[97] In the case of tribal trust land, the land may be assigned or leased to individual tribal members. However, in neither case (tribal or individual trust) may the land be encumbered or transferred without federal government approval.[98] Lenders could be reluctant to enter into mortgage arrangements where they would be unable to have the land transferred to them in the event of a veteran's default.[99]

Similar issues apply to residents of American Samoa and CNMI, where land ownership is restricted. In American Samoa, approximately 90% of land is communally held,[100] it may not be transferred without government approval, and it may not be transferred to anyone who is "less than one half Samoan."[101] The CNMI Constitution restricts land ownership and long-term interests (such as leases) to those of Northern Marianan descent.[102] As with tribal land, a private lender may not be willing to extend a loan where transfer of the land in the event of default would violate territorial law. Guam does not have these restricted land ownership issues.

After finding that only 15 of 24,000 veterans living on trust land had participated in any sort of housing benefit—all of whom received the Specially Adapted Housing benefit and none the loan guaranty—Congress initially enacted a demonstration program to make loans to Native American veterans that was included in the Veterans Home Loan Program Amendments of 1992 (P.L. 102- 547).[103] The program was made permanent as part of the Veterans' Housing Opportunity and Benefits Improvement Act of 2006 (P.L. 109-233). In order to participate in the VA direct loan program, and circumvent the issues of land ownership, a tribe must enter into a memorandum of understanding (MOU) with the VA to provide avenues for addressing default and foreclosure.

Typically individuals enter into long-term leases for use of trust land. The MOU requires that a participating tribe set up a process through which a veteran borrower's leasehold interest in a property can be transferred to a lender, whether private or government, or their assignee in the event of default.[104] The tribe must also establish a procedure for evicting and foreclosing on the veteran's interest in the land and property.

As of FY2011, the VA had entered into MOUs with 83 tribes or Pacific Island territories.[105] Through FY2011, the VA had entered into 869 loans through the direct loan program, 41 of which were made in that year.[106] The Direct Loan program for Native American veterans has had much of its participation in Hawaii and the territories. Prior to the program being made permanent in 2006, the VA noted in hearing testimony that the program was most successful in American Samoa, Guam, CNMI, and Hawaii, with 90% of loans at the time made in American Samoa and Hawaii.[107] Reasons behind the lack of lending to Native American veterans were thought to include low income, lack of infrastructure, and poor credit.[108] As of calendar year 2011, 90% of loans were still made in American Samoa and Hawaii.[109]

Table 4. Direct Loans for Native American Veterans, FY2000-FY2011

Fiscal Year	Number of Loans	Amount of Loans Made During the Year ($ in millions)
2000	21	1.871
2001	20	1.544
2002	62	5.620
2003	120	10.637
2004	56	4.924
2005	38	3.266
2006	30	4.957
2007	53	7.378
2008	42	8.288
2009	99	15.725
2010	103	15.835
2011	41	7.492

Source: U.S. Department of Veterans Affairs, *Annual Benefits Reports*, FY2000 to FY2011.

Direct Loans Resulting from Borrower Delinquency or Default (Acquired and Vendee Loans)

The VA may also enter into a direct loan arrangement in two situations involving a veteran's delinquency and/or default on a guaranteed loan.

- **Acquired Loans:** In situations where a veteran borrower with a guaranteed loan has difficulty making payments, the VA may purchase the loan from the lender (or current servicer) and continue to hold and service the loan.[110]
- **Vendee Loans:** In cases where a veteran defaults on a guaranteed loan and the lender forecloses, the VA often acquires the property from the servicer and then resells it. As part of the resale, the VA may enter into a direct loan with a purchaser of the home, whether or not the purchaser is a veteran. The VA briefly suspended the vendee loan program in 2003, but Congress reinstated it as part of the Veterans

Benefits Act (P.L. 108-183). The law also amended the statute to require that, of the properties acquired and sold by the VA as the result of veteran default, between 50% and 85% are to be financed by the VA as part of their purchase.[111]

Generally, the VA has had the authority to bundle and sell pools of vendee loans.[112] The loans are sold to a trust, which in turn issues certificates that are backed by the mortgages and sold to investors. The VA guarantees that investors in the certificates will receive "full and timely" payments of principal and interest from the loans as well as against losses at foreclosure.[113] The bundled loans appear in the VA budget as "Guaranteed Loan Sales Securities." The authority to bundle and sell the loans had expired on December 31, 2011, but was reinstated through December 31, 2016, as part of P.L. 112-154, enacted August 6, 2012.

Table 5. Guaranteed Loans Acquired by VA, Vendee Loans Extended, and Direct Loans Sold

Fiscal Year	Loans Acquired and Serviced by VA	Vendee Loans Entered Into by VA as Part of Property Sale	Vendee Loans Sold by VA
1998	2,001	15,856	—a
1999	1,573	16,871	11,952
2000	4,256	13,698	18,434
2001	2,775	11,186	9,282
2002	2,693	8,786	11,714
2003	1,740	4,621	3,333
2004	1,171	3	3,397
2005	1,161	1,419	0
2006	1,150	788	0
2007	642	501	0
2008	386	626	2,532
2009	81	435	0
2010	36	1,081	2,190
2011	92	4,660	1,725

Source: VA Budget Justifications for Veterans Benefits Programs, FY2000-FY2013. a. The number of vendee loans for FY1998 was not available.

The number of loans acquired by the VA, vendee loans entered into, and sales of vendee loans in a given year depend on borrower defaults, purchaser interest in foreclosed VA homes, and investor interest in VA securities. Table 5 shows the number of acquired loans, vendee loans entered into, and vendee loans sold from FY1998 through FY2011. As a result of the vendee loan program suspension in 2003, the number of vendee loans sold decreased during the following years and has only recently begun to pick up again. This has also resulted in the sale of fewer vendee loans. In addition, the number of VA acquired loans has fallen in recent years. According to the VA, there have been fewer acquired loans since the 1990s and early 2000s because both the VA and loan servicers focused efforts on loan modification and other options to help borrowers keep their homes, reducing the need for the VA to acquire loans.[114] Efforts particularly increased in 2008 and thereafter, when the VA offered new incentives for servicers to work with borrowers (see the section of this report "Options to Prevent Foreclosure").

Federal Credit Reform Act of 1990

The FCRA (P.L. 101-508)[115] changed the way in which the federal government budgets for loan and loan guaranty programs like those administered by the VA. Prior to the FCRA, if a federal agency extended direct loans to borrowers in a given fiscal year, the disbursement of the principal balance of the loans was recorded as an outlay in that year, and the budget did not account for the fact that the government would recoup principal and interest payments in future years. Loan guarantees, by contrast, could appear costless in the early years, or even income-generating if fees were collected, but did not reflect potential costs due to defaulted loans in the future.

Beginning in 1992, the FCRA required agency budgets to reflect the *net present value* of outflows and inflows of a loan over its lifetime. The estimated cash inflows and outflows of a program are discounted to the present fiscal year using a discount rate. A credit subsidy in the form of an appropriation from the federal government may be required to support loan programs when the net present value is positive. Due to the uncertainty involved in making the net present value estimates, OMB and federal agencies re-estimate the credit subsidy each year to determine the actual subsidy required. Additional funding in subsequent years that may be required due to underestimates of the subsidy comes from "permanent indefinite authority" provided through the FCRA rather than annual discretionary appropriations.

Within their budgets, federal agencies account for loans entered into prior to 1992 separately, in a liquidating account.

Funding for the VA Direct and Guaranteed Loan Programs

Both the VA direct loan and loan guaranty programs are funded through several sources. These sources include congressional appropriations, fees paid by borrowers, proceeds from the rental or sale of foreclosed properties, collection of principal and interest payments made by borrowers, and any penalties paid by lenders.[116] An important aspect of understanding how VA loans are funded, apart from the sources of funding, is how loans are accounted for in the federal budget.

In most federally funded *grant* programs, the cost to the federal budget is the amount appropriated, and federal involvement in funding generally ends after the outlay of funds. By contrast, the cost of *loan* programs may involve both an up-front outlay of funds as well as the recoupment of costs through payments of principal and interest, and/or collection of fees and penalties, over the lifetime of the loans. Loan programs may also suffer losses in subsequent years through defaults or lower-than-expected collection of fees. As a result, it is not always possible to capture the budgetary effects of loans in one particular year. Current government practice, instituted in 1992, is to determine the *net present value* of loans over their lifetime and to record this amount in the budget in the year the loans are extended. (See the text box for an explanation of the law implementing this budget process.)

The concept of net present value is helpful both in understanding how funds are appropriated for VA loans and in reading VA budget documents. The federal funding process is described briefly in the following subsection of this report, "The VA Budget and Congressional Appropriations for VA Loan Programs." The two subsequent subsections describe loan fees paid by borrowers, and funds obtained through loan payments and property sales.

Sources of Funding for Loan Programs

The VA Budget and Congressional Appropriations for VA Loan Programs

The VA direct and guaranteed loan programs receive both discretionary and mandatory appropriations from Congress. The discretionary funds pay for the administrative expenses of the VA loan programs. The mandatory funding supports the loans themselves, and typically appears in appropriations laws as "such sums as necessary."

Mandatory funding for the loan guaranty and direct loan programs is expressed as a percentage of the total loan volume. This is sometimes referred to as the "subsidy rate"; each year the estimated subsidy rate appears in the President's Budget Appendix for the Department of Veterans Affairs. The estimated subsidy rate of loans guaranteed or made in a given fiscal year is based on the net present value of expected expenses in the event of borrower defaults as well as expected income through fees and other sources. If the estimated present value of payments by the VA for a cohort of loans guaranteed or extended in a given fiscal year exceeds the estimated present value of fees paid by borrowers, recoveries, and other collections, then the subsidy rate is positive (i.e., the government subsidizes the loan program), and the program receives mandatory funding. If the net present value of cash flows for a cohort of loans is expected to result in a surplus of funds (more taken in than paid out), then the subsidy rate is negative (i.e., the program has excess revenue that is returned to Treasury).

As part of the annual budget process, the VA estimates individual subsidy rates for each of the four types of loans either made directly by the VA or guaranteed by the VA. The four programs for which the VA estimates subsidy rates are guaranteed loans, guaranteed loan sale securities, acquired loans, and vendee loans. The initial estimated subsidy rate for each of these programs for a given fiscal year represents the net present value for that year's cohort of loans. However, the initial estimated subsidy rate may differ from the actual subsidy rate for the cohort of loans over their lifetime. Projecting the net present value of cash flows is uncertain, so subsidy reestimates are made by the VA each year, and additional mandatory funding is permanently available by the FCRA to cover any shortfalls.[117] Factors that can affect the subsidy rate (and resulting mandatory appropriation) include changes in the interest rate used to determine the present value of future funding streams, revisions in estimates of borrower default or prepayment rates, the outcomes of property management decisions, and changes in the amount of fees actually paid by borrowers (compared to what was expected). Due to reestimates, a negative subsidy rate calculated in one year may be recalculated as positive in a subsequent year, resulting in an increased amount of mandatory funding needed for a loan program. Or, if the subsidy rate is recalculated as negative, funds are returned to Treasury.

Appropriations for VA direct and guaranteed loans are captured in one "on-budget" account, called the Veterans Housing Benefit Program Fund, sometimes referred to as the program account.[118] (Note that direct loans for Native American veterans are funded separately.) In addition, several separate, off-budget accounts reflect inflows and outflows for direct and guaranteed loan cohorts, depending on when the loans were extended. Funds for direct and guaranteed loans made prior to 1992 are shown in a housing liquidating account, and funds for loans extended after 1992 are shown in direct and guaranteed loan financing accounts. The multiple accounts may be cause for confusion, so it is useful to keep in mind that appropriations appear in the Veterans Housing Benefit Program Fund, while the financing and liquidating accounts reflect the specific income and expenses associated with particular loan cohorts.

Fees from Borrowers

The costs of the VA direct and loan guaranty programs are supported, in part, by fees paid by the borrowers. The amount of a borrower's fee is based on the amount of down payment, if any; whether the loan is extended through the loan guaranty or direct loan program; whether the borrower had active duty service or was a reservist; when the loan closed; whether the loan is purchase money or a refinance; whether the borrower is accessing the guaranty for the first time or entering into a subsequent loan; and whether the property is purchased under the manufactured housing portion of the loan guaranty statute.[119] (See Table 6.) Fees may be waived for veterans receiving compensation for a service-connected disability, for the surviving spouse of a servicemember who died of a service-connected disability, or for the surviving spouse of a veteran who died while receiving (or was entitled to receive) compensation for certain service-connected disabilities.[120] Veterans may finance the fees as part of the loan, and the guaranty is based on the loan amount, including the fees.[121]

Veterans were not always charged fees as part of the loan guaranty transaction and, in general, fees were not required prior to 1982.[122] When the loan guaranty program was created, it was considered a benefit or entitlement for veterans. However, in 1982, the VA administrator wrote a letter to the Speaker of the House, together with draft legislation, suggesting that the VA require veterans to pay a 0.5% fee on the principal balance of each loan.[123] The letter expressed concern regarding the "costs to the taxpayers of operating the program," and noted that "paying claims on the approximately 3.7 percent of the loans resulting in foreclosure are significant."[124] Despite objections from veterans groups,[125] Congress instituted the fee as part of the Omnibus Budget Reconciliation Act of 1982 (P.L. 97-253). The fee was to be in effect for transactions entered into from FY1983 through FY1985, with an exemption for veterans with service-connected disabilities. Congress continued the fee beyond FY1985, and after the fee was raised to 1% as part of the Deficit Reduction Act of 1984 (P.L. 98-369), Congress began to institute the more complicated fee schedule that exists today, with fees varying based on amount of down payment and whether the veteran received a loan guaranty or direct loan (Veterans' Benefits Amendments of 1989, P.L. 101-237).

Table 6. Current Loan Guaranty Fees Effective Until October 1, 2017

Loan Type	Down Payment	First Loan or Subsequent	Fee as % of Loan Amount	
			Active Duty	Reservist
Loan to Purchase or Construct Dwelling (38 U.S.C. §3710(a))	Less than 5% Less than 5% 5%-10% 10% or more	First Subsequent First or Subsequent First	2.15% 3.30% 1.50% 1.25%	2.40% 3.30% 1.75% 1.50%
Cash-Out Refinancing Loan (38 U.S.C. §3710)	NA NA	First Subsequent	2.15% 3.30%	2.40% 3.30%
Manufactured Housing Loan to Purchase or Construct or for Cash-Out Refinancing (38 U.S.C. §3712)	Any	Either	1.00%	1.00%
Interest Rate Reduction Refinancing Loan (38 U.S.C. §3710, §3712, and §3762)	NA	Either	0.50%	0.50%
Direct Loan for Specially Adapted Housing (38 U.S.C. §3711)	Any	Either	1.00%	1.00%
Direct Loans for Native American Veterans to Purchase or Construct (38 U.S.C. §3762)	Any	Either	1.25%	1.25%
Assumption of Guaranteed Loan (38 U.S.C. §3714)	Any	Either	0.50%	0.50%
Vendee Loan (38 U.S.C. §3733(a))	Any	Either	2.25%	2.25%

Source: 38 U.S.C. §3729 as amended by P.L. 112-26, P.L. 112-56, and P.L. 112-154 and the *VA Lenders Handbook*, p. 8-21.

The most recent changes to borrowers' fees occurred as part of P.L. 112-56, which was enacted on November 21, 2011. Prior to the enactment of P.L.

112-56, fees for both active duty and reserve veterans entering into purchase money guaranteed loans were scheduled to be reduced starting on October 1, 2011, pursuant to the Veterans Benefits Act of 2003 (P.L. 108-183). However, the Veterans Health Care Facilities Capital Improvement Act of 2011 (P.L. 112-37), enacted on October 5, 2011, initially extended the existing, higher fees implemented in P.L. 108-183 through November 18, 2011. Then, P.L. 112-56 further extended existing fees through October 1, 2016.[126]

The fees in P.L. 112-56 took effect on the date of enactment. For loans that closed from October 1 through October 5, and from November 18 through November 21, the VA issued guidance stating that the lower fees in P.L. 108-183 applied.[127] In August of 2012, the existing fees were further extended through October 1, 2017, as part of P.L. 112-154.

Collection of Loan Payments and Property Sales

In its direct loan portfolio, the VA owns some loans on which it collects principal and interest payments (acquired loans), and it also sells properties that it has acquired through foreclosure and enters into direct loans with the borrowers (vendee loans). In addition, the VA has the authority to pool and sell loans to investors. (This authority had expired at the end of 2011, but was reinstated in August 2012 as part of P.L. 112-154). Each of these transactions results in income to the VA, although the income may not be sufficient to counteract losses. For example, because the VA guarantees payment of principal and interest on the loans that it sells, borrower default may result in greater outflows than inflows.

THE SPECIALLY ADAPTED HOUSING PROGRAM

The Specially Adapted Housing Program provides grants to veterans and servicemembers with certain service-connected disabilities to assist them in constructing, purchasing, or remodeling homes to fit their needs.[128] While Specially Adapted Housing loans are available (see discussion in the "The Original Direct Loan for Veterans in Rural Areas, Now Limited to Veterans with Disabilities" section of this report), the majority of funds are distributed as grants that veterans and servicemembers need not pay back.

The Specially Adapted Housing Program, which was introduced in 1948 in P.L. 80-702, initially targeted veterans with a total service-connected disability causing paralysis in the legs or lower body. Over the years, Congress amended the law to expand the range of disabilities eligible for assistance, to make family members' homes eligible for adaptation (P.L. 109-233), to include active duty servicemembers with service-connected disabilities (P.L. 110-289), to expand benefits to individuals residing outside the United States (P.L. 110-289), and to include loans as well as grants (P.L. 96-526).

Within the Specially Adapted Housing Program are two grant programs for veterans and active duty servicemembers, which are discussed in separate subsections, below.[129] The first, sometimes referred to as the Specially Adapted Housing Grant (or Section 2101(a) grant, after the section of the U.S. Code), is targeted to veterans with mobility impairments, while the second, sometimes referred to as the Special Housing Adaptation Grant (or Section 2101(b) grant) assists veterans who are blind or who have lost the use of their hands. The grant limits for the first category of adapted housing are higher than for the second, and both types of adapted housing are available to veterans with severe burn injuries.

Specially Adapted Housing Grants, 38 U.S.C. Section 2101(a)

The original law authorizing the Specially Adapted Housing Program was enacted to assist veterans who had lost use of their legs due to either spinal cord disease or injury. The law originally provided for grants of up to $10,000 for veterans to build homes with features adapted to their disabilities, to purchase homes that were already adapted, or to purchase homes without adaptations and then modify them. Since the program was introduced, the grant limit has increased (see "Grant Limits") and the original disability requirement was modified and expanded to include veterans and servicemembers with a broader range of mobility impairments resulting from service-connected disabilities:

- Those who have lost or lost the use of *both* lower extremities and require the aid of braces, crutches, canes, or a wheelchair for locomotion (P.L. 86-239).
- Veterans and servicemembers who have lost or lost the use of *one or more* lower extremities where the loss so affects balance and propulsion as to require the aid of braces, crutches, canes, or a wheelchair for ambulating (P.L. 112-154). The disability must have occurred on or after September 11, 2001, and eligible individuals must be approved for assistance under this provision by the end of FY2013.

- Veterans and servicemembers with blindness in both eyes and who have lost or lost the use of at least one lower extremity (P.L. 86-239).
- Those who have lost or lost the use of one lower extremity together with one of two conditions resulting in the requirement that the veteran or servicemember use a cane, crutches, braces, or wheelchair for locomotion:
  - residuals of an organic disease or injury (P.L. 91-22), or
  - the loss or loss of use of one upper extremity (P.L. 95-117);
- Veterans and servicemembers who have lost or lost the use of both upper extremities such that they cannot use their arms at or above the elbows (P.L. 108- 454).
- Veterans and servicemembers with severe burn injuries (P.L. 110-289). VA regulations define this to mean "full thickness or subdermal burns" reducing mobility in two or more extremities or at least one extremity and the trunk of the body.[130]

Special Housing Adaptation Grants, 38 U.S.C. Section 2101(b)

In the Veterans' Disability Compensation and Housing Benefits Amendments of 1980 (P.L. 96- 385), Congress expanded the Specially Adapted Housing Program to include veterans who may need to modify their homes, but not to the degree required for veterans eligible for the Section 2101(a) grant. This portion of the program is sometimes referred to as the "Special Housing Adaptation Grant."

The impetus to expand the Specially Adapted Housing Program grew out of the concern that the needs of totally blind veterans were not being met.[131] Unless blind veterans were also without use of a lower extremity, they did not qualify for the Specially Adapted Housing Program, and while they could receive home modifications through VA's home health program, the modifications were limited to $2,500. Congress was concerned that the health program's home modifications were not sufficient to serve veterans who were blind, so it requested a study of the needs of blind veterans as part of P.L. 96-22, the Veterans' Health Care Amendments of 1979.[132] While the report did not contain definitive data about the modification needs of blind veterans, the same year that the report was released, Congress enacted the Veterans' Disability Compensation and Housing Benefits Amendments of 1980 (P.L. 96-385), which created a new category in the Specially Adapted Housing Program for veterans who had blindness in both eyes with 5/200 visual acuity or less, as well as those who had lost or lost use of both hands. The Senate Veterans' Affairs Committee noted that home adaptation needs for these veterans might not be as extensive as those with mobility issues, and they did not warrant grant amounts at the same level.[133] At the time the law was enacted, Specially Adapted Housing Grants were limited to $30,000; the portion of the program to assist blind veterans and those without use of their hands was limited to $5,000 in 1980.

Since enactment, the Special Housing Adaptation Grant has been expanded to include veterans with severe burn injuries (P.L. 110-289). According to VA regulations, a veteran qualifies for the grant if (1) the burns are considered "deep partial thickness burns" and result in limitation in motion of two or more extremities or at least one extremity and the trunk of the body, (2) the burns are considered "full thickness or subdermal burns" and result in limitation in motion of one or more extremities or the trunk of the body, or (3) the veteran has residuals of an inhalation injury.[134] In addition, as part of P.L. 112-154, the visual acuity standard was modified to be in line with the VA visual impairment standard for disability compensation, which was changed from 5/200 to 20/200 as part of the Dr. James Allen Veteran Vision Equity Act (P.L. 110-157).

Use of Grants to Modify the Home of a Family Member

The law provides that veterans may use the Special Housing Adaptation grant (§2101(b)) to modify homes of family members in cases where a veteran or servicemember plans to continue living there. In addition, a separate provision in the law, enacted in 2006, specifically provides the authority to give these grants to veterans or servicemembers living *temporarily* in the homes of family members, whether the individuals meet disability requirements for Section 2101(a) or Section 2101(b).[135] This is sometimes referred to as the Temporary Residence Adaptation (TRA) grant.

The TRA grant was set up as a five-year pilot program and enacted as part of the Veterans' Housing Opportunity and Benefits Improvement Act of 2006 (P.L. 109-233). There was concern that many injured veterans returning from Operation Iraqi Freedom and Operation Enduring Freedom did not have homes of their own and were instead returning to family members' homes.[136] The grants for veterans and servicemembers living temporarily in the homes of family members allow individuals to access a portion of the full grant to which they are entitled. The program is authorized through December 31, 2022 (P.L. 112-154).

Grant Limits

When the Specially Adapted Housing and Special Housing Adaptation grant programs were created, the Section 2101(a) grant had a limit of $10,000, while the Section 2101(b) limit was set at $5,000. Over the years, Congress increased the statutory limits, most recently to $63,780 and $12,756, respectively (P.L. 112-154); the new limits take effect one year after enactment of P.L. 112-154, in August 2013. In addition, the Housing and Economic Recovery Act of 2008 (P.L. 110-289) provided that the VA Secretary shall annually adjust the levels based on a residential home cost-of-construction index, to be established by the Secretary.[137] Most recently, in 2013, as a result of this index adjustment, the levels were set at $64,960 for Section 2101(a) grants and $12,922 for Section 2101(b).[138]

The limits for the TRA grants were initially set at $14,000 for Section 2101(a)-eligible recipients and $2,000 for Section 2101(b)-eligible recipients. In August 2012, as part of P.L. 112-154, the limits were increased to $28,000 and $5,000, respectively. The law also provided that the maximum TRA grants be increased using the same cost of construction index that is used to increase the maximum grants for a veteran's or servicemember's own home. Prior to enactment of P.L. 112-154, the TRA grants were not subject to annual adjustment. Pursuant to the cost of construction index adjustment, the limits for 2013 are $28,518 and $5,092.[139]

A veteran may qualify for more than one housing grant under the Specially Adapted Housing Program. For example, a veteran or servicemember could make some improvements to his or her home using a Section 2101(a) grant, and receive an additional grant later, as long as the total of all grants did not exceed the $64,960 cap. However, grants used in one component of the program count against the maximum grant for another component. For example, if a veteran received a TRA grant to improve the home of a parent with whom he was residing temporarily, the amount of that grant would reduce the total Section 2101(a) grant he would be eligible to receive if he later purchased his own home. Similarly, a veteran or servicemember who receives a Section 2101(b) grant, and who later qualifies for a Section 2101(a) grant, would have the maximum grant reduced by the amount already used.

As part of the Honoring America's Veterans and Caring for Camp Lejeune Families Act of 2012 (P.L. 112-154), a provision was added to the law to protect veterans where a previously adapted home is "destroyed or substantially damaged in a natural or other disaster." The law provides that, where a damaged home was being used and occupied by a veteran or servicemember, he or she may receive funds to acquire another suitable home. It makes assistance available as if a veteran or servicemember had not already received assistance, and the assistance does not count toward a veteran's maximum benefit. The law sets the maximum benefit at the lesser of (1) the cost (as determined by VA) to repair or replace the property that is in excess of any insurance coverage; or (2) the statutory grant maximums for Section 2101(a), Section 2101(b), or the TRA grants, whichever is applicable.

Table 7. Specially Adapted Housing Grant Limits, 2012

Location	§2101(a) Specially Adapted Housing Grant	§2101(b) Special Housing Adaptation Grant
Veteran's or Servicemember's Own Home	$64,960	$12,992
Family Member's Home (indefinite)	NA	$12,992
Family Member's Home (temporary)	$28,518	$5,092

Source: 38 U.S.C. §2102, 38 U.S.C. §2102A, P.L. 112-154, and Department of Veterans Affairs, "Annual Increase in Construction Cost Index and Specially Adapted Housing Grants."

The number and amount of Section 2101(a) and Section 2101(b) grants made in recent years are in Table 8, below. Funding for the Specially Adapted Housing Program is mandatory funding provided through the Readjustment Benefits portion of the Veterans Benefits Administration budget. Grants are available to veterans and servicemembers based on eligibility rather than amounts appropriated. The appropriation does not contain a specific allocation for Specially Adapted Housing grants. Instead, the VA estimates the amount that will be obligated as part of its Congressional Budget Justifications, which is subsumed in the total for Readjustment Benefits.

The number and dollar amount of Specially Adapted Housing (§2101(a)) grants nearly doubled from FY2007 to FY2008, and have remained higher than in previous years since that time. In addition to an increase in need due to veterans returning from the wars in Iraq and Afghanistan, VA cited broadened eligibility as a factor contributing to the increases in grants distributed.[140] The Housing and Economic Recovery Act of 2008 (P.L. 110-289) made a number of changes to the grants, among them making active duty servicemembers eligible for the grants, including severe burn injuries as an eligible disability, and increasing maximum grants from $50,000 to $60,000 for Section 2101(a) grants, and from $10,000 to $12,000 for Section 2101(b) grants. The increases applied to veterans who had previously received grant assistance.

Table 8. Specially Adapted Housing and Special Housing Adaptation Grants FY2000-FY2011

	Specially Adapted Housing Grants		Special Housing Adaptation Grants	
Fiscal Year	Number of Grants	Amount of Grants in Year ($ in millions)	Number of Grants	Amount of Grants in Year ($ in millions)
2000	509	21.308	65	0.507
2001	456	19.600	49	0.510
2002	475	23.365	56	0.459
2003	435	20.467	58	0.518
2004	450	22.008	51	0.484
2005	526	25.742	61	0.580
2006	503	24.176	45	0.412
2007	585	24.235	68	0.675
2008	1,058	36.000	70	0.760
2009	1,189	51.547	81	0.750
2010	1,421	64.972	128	1.165
2011	1,135	54.833	100	0.897

Source: U.S. Department of Veterans Affairs, *Annual Benefits Reports*, FY1999-FY2011, available at http://www.vba.va.gov/REPORTS/abr/index.asp.

Special Considerations on Trust Lands

In order to qualify for the maximum available assistance through the Section 2101(a) grant, a veteran or servicemember must have an ownership interest in the property being purchased or modified.[141] Until recently, the allowable forms of ownership were somewhat limited. An ownership interest, defined in regulation, included a fee simple interest, a lease or interest in a cooperative of at least 50 years, or a life estate through a revocable trust. As mentioned in the section about the VA direct loan program, individuals living on Native American trust land may not have a traditional interest in property, and individuals living in American Samoa and the Commonwealth of the

Northern Mariana Islands may not own property unless they meet nativity requirements.

In 2010, the VA, recognizing the limitations facing veterans or servicemembers living on trust land or in the territories, issued a final rule that updated the regulations defining an ownership interest (among other changes).[142] Individuals may now qualify for the Section 2101(a) grant if they have a life estate (without the limitation of a revocable trust), the functional equivalent of a life estate (such as a long-term lease or land installment contract), a lease pursuant to a memorandum of understanding between a tribe and the VA, or a beneficial interest in property located outside of the United States, defined as "an interest deemed by the Secretary as one that provides (or will provide) an eligible individual a meaningful right to occupy a housing unit as a residence."[143]

Veterans or servicemembers using the Section 2101(b) grants may qualify for the full grant if they live in the home of a family member, so ownership interests may not be as important. For example, a veteran who does not meet the nativity requirements for property ownership in the territories may have a spouse who does.

VA Actions in Event of Delinquency, Default, and Foreclosure

Delinquencies and foreclosures for all categories of loans, including VA-guaranteed loans, have increased in recent years. Beginning about the same time that the country entered recession (December 2007),[144] the housing market began to experience difficulties, with the percentage of all loans past due and the percentage of loans in foreclosure both beginning to grow. In the first quarter of 2007, the overall foreclosure rate was 1.28%; by the third quarter of 2012, the rate was 4.07%.[145] During the same period, the percentage of loans 90 days or more past due increased from 0.98% to 2.96%. The peak for loans 90 days or more past due was 5.02% in the first quarter of 2010, and foreclosures reached 4.64% in the fourth quarter of 2010.

While foreclosures for all categories of loans have increased since the beginning of the recession, the foreclosure and delinquency rates for VA-guaranteed loans have been lower than the rates for FHA loans, as well as lower than the overall rates.[146] During the period from the first quarter of 2007 through the third quarter of 2012, the foreclosure rate for VA-guaranteed loans increased from 1.05% to 2.21%, and for FHA loans from 2.19% to 4.08%.[147] The rate for loans 90 days or more past due for VA loans increased from 1.52% to 2.21%, and for FHA loans from 3.34% to 4.37%. Foreclosure and delinquency rates for VA loans have not always been lower than FHA loans or loans in general.[148] The VA has suggested a number of factors that could contribute to the recently exhibited lower default rates, including underwriting practices, oversight of lenders, and a robust default servicing program where the VA gets directly involved with borrowers and servicers, if necessary.[149] The increased popularity of subprime loans leading up to the recession may also have contributed to comparably lower rates for VA loans by moving veterans away from VA loans.

Options to Prevent Foreclosure

A number of options may exist for veterans who entered into mortgages through the VA Loan Guaranty Program and find themselves facing delinquency or foreclosure.

Servicer Workouts

One way in which the VA Loan Guaranty Program attempts to prevent properties from going to foreclosure is to encourage servicers to work out agreements with borrowers. In cases where veterans are delinquent on VA-guaranteed loans, the VA may make incentive payments to servicers that are able to work out arrangements with borrowers to prevent foreclosure.[150] These arrangements, or loss mitigation efforts, include repayment plans, forbearance agreements, loan modifications, sales for less than the amount owed ("compromise sales"), or deeds in lieu of foreclosure. Most of these efforts were introduced when VA revised its regulations in 2008.[151]

Under existing VA regulations, a lender may enter into a loan modification with a borrower without prior VA approval in circumstances where the borrower is in default, the reasons for loan default have been resolved and are not expected to recur, the borrower is a "reasonable" credit risk, at least 12 payments have been made since the loan closed, and a loan modification would reinstate the loan.[152] On February 7, 2011, the VA published an interim final rule in the Federal Register modifying these regulations to further help encourage modifications.[153] In cases where the conditions listed above have not been met, lenders will be able to request approval from the VA to modify loans nonetheless. In addition, maximum interest rates for modified loans will be tied to the Freddie Mac weekly maximum interest rate (to make it easier to re-pool and securitize modified loans with loans having similar interest rates), and legal fees and foreclosure costs can now be added to the principal balance of a modified loan.

VA Servicing

The VA may intervene to assist with loss mitigation efforts if the servicer has been unwilling or unable to work with the borrower, or if the VA has determined that the loan servicing is inadequate.[154] If loss mitigation is unsuccessful, the VA may purchase the loan and take over servicing; however, this occurs rarely, and only if the circumstances causing delinquency were temporary and the veteran is able to resume payments.[155]

"HAMP-Style" Modifications

In 2009, the Obama Administration introduced the Home Affordable Modification Program (HAMP), an initiative to help borrowers who are behind on their mortgage payments.[156] Through HAMP, homeowners whose mortgage payments exceed 31% of their incomes (in general),[157] and who face additional hardships that make it difficult to remain current on their mortgages, may work with their loan servicers to modify their loans so that they are affordable. Technically, VA loans are not included as part of the HAMP program, but the VA has issued guidance requiring loan servicers to determine whether borrowers are eligible for "HAMP-style" modifications before proceeding with foreclosure or similar alternatives.[158]

Where a borrower has missed payments and loss mitigation efforts have been unsuccessful, loan servicers are to evaluate the borrower to see if the loan could be modified through methods such as reduced interest rates or forebearance on principal payments to a point where the payments are at or below 31% of borrower income. If necessary, the VA will adjust its guaranty for larger loan amounts. Unlike HAMP (where loans must have originated on or before January 1, 2009), any VA-guaranteed loan is potentially eligible. If a lender and borrower enter into a modified loan, unlike HAMP, there is no trial period, and any reduced interest rate lasts for the life of the loan.

Mortgages That Are Underwater, But Current

In addition to increased foreclosures, the downturn in the economy has resulted in situations where some borrowers may have mortgages that exceed the value of their homes, sometimes referred to as being "underwater." This makes it difficult to refinance mortgages to take advantage of lower interest rates because lenders generally do not want to lend more than a home's appraised value. In cases where borrowers are current on their mortgage payments, but owe more than their homes are worth, they may qualify for an interest rate reduction refinancing loan (IRRRL) through the VA, despite the fact that their debt exceeds their homes' values.[159] Because an IRRRL does not require an appraisal, it is possible that some lenders may be willing to enter into a refinancing loan even where the loan exceeds the current property value.

Agreement between State Attorneys General and Large Mortgage Servicers

VA borrowers who are delinquent and/or underwater may also be eligible for assistance through an agreement reached between 49 state attorneys general,[160] the attorney general for the District of Columbia, and five large mortgage servicers in March 2012. Under the agreement, $25 billion is to be made available to assist certain borrowers.[161] In order to qualify for assistance, loans cannot have been purchased by Fannie Mae or Freddie Mac (and VA loans are not purchased by Fannie Mae or Freddie Mac), and they must be serviced by Bank of America, JPMorgan Chase, Wells Fargo, Citigroup, or Ally Financial. Pursuant to the settlement, the servicers must commit a minimum of $17 billion for foreclosure prevention, including principal reduction, and they must commit another $3 billion to assist underwater homeowners. Another $5 billion is to be awarded to the states, some of which, about $1.5 billion, will consist of payments to borrowers who lost their homes to foreclosure.[162]

Servicemembers Civil Relief Act

Another potential protection for borrowers may come through the Servicemembers Civil Relief Act (SCRA), which provides financial protections for active duty servicemembers, including home mortgage protections.[163] The act may assist veterans who entered into mortgages (including VA loans) prior to being called to active duty, and who are having trouble making their mortgage payments. In cases where a lender brings an action against a borrower for a mortgage obligation during a period of active duty, or within nine months after, the SCRA gives courts the authority to stay the proceedings.[164] In addition, the SCRA also generally declares invalid any foreclosure or home sale that takes place during this time period.

VA Actions in the Event of Foreclosure

If arrangements cannot be worked out to avoid foreclosure and properties proceed to sale, in most instances, loan servicers acquire the property at foreclosure sale and, in turn, sell it to the VA.[165] Whether a transfer to the VA occurs depends on the property value and the amount owed by the veteran borrower; each of these values is determined prior to the foreclosure sale.[166] The procedures that the VA goes through in order to determine when it will acquire a property, and for how much, were set up to ensure that the VA would not spend more than the amount for which the loan was guaranteed.[167] When a property goes to foreclosure, the VA will also pay the lender's claim against the guaranty. If the total indebtedness has been reduced over the life of the loan, then the guaranty is prorated,[168] and the guaranty is limited to the borrower's total indebtedness minus the VA's purchase price.[169]

Veterans who default on guaranteed loans are liable to the VA for losses suffered, and, in general, cannot have entitlement restored and obtain a new loan unless the loss is repaid to the VA.[170] The VA may waive the debt in cases where it determines collection "would be against equity and good conscience."[171] A veteran must request a waiver within one year of being notified about the debt. Circumstances that might result in a waiver could include job loss, disability, or other financial hardship. The VA may also accept a compromise payment and settle a debt for less than the amount owed.[172]

Table 9, below, shows the number of properties with VA-guaranteed loans that are at some point in the foreclosure process, as well as foreclosed properties held in the VA inventory over the past decade. Since 2008, when the housing market began to experience difficulties, the number of homes with VA loans in foreclosure has increased, growing from about 4,700 homes in foreclosure in FY2007 to more than 9,000 in FY2008, 17,000 in FY2009, and exceeding 20,000 in each year from FY2010 through FY2012. Once the VA has acquired properties through the process of foreclosure, it attempts to resell them. In doing so, purchasers need not be veterans. In FY2012, the average time between VA acquisition of a foreclosed property and sale was eight months.[173] For more information about disposition of property, see the earlier section of this report entitled "Direct Loans Resulting from Borrower Delinquency or Default (Acquired and Vendee Loans)."

Table 9. VA Loans in Foreclosure Process and Foreclosed Properties in VA Inventory, FY2001-FY2012

Fiscal Year	Foreclosed Properties Held in VA Inventory[a]	Properties in the Foreclosure Process[b]
2001	14,543	8,425
2002	11,981	10,986
2003	11,832	10,513
2004	15,539	10,355
2005	7,288	6,597
2006	6,490	4,703
2007	6,975	4,696
2008	7,605	9,077
2009	8,464	17,000
2010	10,835	20,500
2011	7,322	22,000
2012	10,400	23,400

Source: VA *Performance and Accountability Reports*, FY2002-FY2012. The reports are available on the VA website, http://www.va.gov/budget/report/index.asp.

[a] Properties as of the end of the fiscal year.

[b] The Performance and Accountability Reports do not indicate exactly what the "foreclosure process" entails.

End Notes

[1] 38 C.F.R. §36.4301.

[2] U.S. Congress, House Veterans' Affairs Committee, *The Historical Development of Veterans' Benefits in the United States, A Report on Veterans' Benefits in the United States*, committee print, prepared by The President's Commission on Veterans' Pensions, 84th Cong., 2nd sess., May 9, 1956, H.Prt. 84-244 (Washington: GPO, 1956), p. 161.

[3] Ibid.

[4] U.S. Congress, House Committee on World War Veterans' Legislation, *Providing Federal Government Aid for the Readjustment in Civilian Life of Returning World War II Veterans*, report to accompany S. 1767, 78th Cong., 2nd sess., May 5, 1944, H.Rept. 1418, p. 2.

[5] U.S. Congress, House Conference Committee, *Providing Federal Government Aid for the Readjustment to Civilian Life of Returning World War II Veterans*, report to accompany S. 1767, 78th Cong., 2nd sess., June 12, 1944, H.Rept. 1624, pp. 162-163.

[6] 38 U.S.C. §101(2). For more information about who is a veteran, see CRS Report R42324, *"Who is a Veteran?"— Basic Eligibility for Veterans' Benefits*, by Christine Scott.

[7] Reservists were made eligible as part of the Veterans Home Loan Program Amendments of 1992 (P.L. 102-547).

[8] The disability must meet one of three duration requirements: (1) it was continuously rated totally disabling for 10 or more years immediately preceding death; (2) it was continuously rated totally disabling for at least five years from the date of discharge from active duty; or (3) it was continuously rated totally disabling for not less than one year immediately preceding death, and the veteran had been a prisoner of war who died after September 30, 1999.

[9] 38 U.S.C. §3702(a)(2).

[10] See 38 U.S.C. §3710(g) and 38 C.F.R. §36.4340. Further guidance is at U.S. Department of Veterans Affairs, *Lenders Handbook – VA Pamphlet 26-7*, revised June 28, 2010, chapter 4, http://www.benefits pam26_7.asp (hereinafter *VA Lenders Handbook*).

[11] 38 C.F.R. §36.4340(d).

[12] 38 C.F.R. §36.4340(f).

[13] *VA Lenders Handbook*, p. 4-55.

[14] 38 C.F.R. §36.4340(e).

[15] 38 C.F.R. §36.4340(g).

[16] Ibid.

[17] 38 U.S.C. §3710.

[18] 38 C.F.R. §36.4301.

[19] Ibid. There is an exception for a dwelling owned by more than one veteran—in that case there may be an extra unit for each additional veteran owner. For example, if three veterans owned a property together, it could consist of six units as long as three of the six units were occupied by the veteran owners.

[20] *VA Lenders Handbook*, p. 3-14.

[21] Ibid.

[22] 38 U.S.C. §3704(c). P.L. 112-154 amended the law to allow dependent children to satisfy the occupancy requirement.

[23] 38 C.F.R. §36.4301.

[24] Ibid., definition of "residential property."

[25] 38 U.S.C. §3710(a)(9)(A)(ii).

[26] *VA Lenders Handbook*, Chapter 12.

[27] See VA response to questions for the record, U.S. Congress, House Committee on Veterans' Affairs, Subcommittee on Economic Opportunity, *Hearing on the Loan Guaranty Program*, 111th Cong., 2nd sess., May 20, 2010, p. 66.

[28] For a complete list of acceptable improvements, see 38 U.S.C. §3710(d).

[29] During the 1990s, the VA insured a decreasing number of manufactured housing units per year as reported in the VA Annual Reports. From FY1971 through FY1990, the VA guaranteed 112,786 manufactured home loans. U.S. Department of Veterans Affairs, *FY1990 Annual Report of the Secretary of Veterans Affairs*, March 1991, p. 29. In FY1991, the VA insured 313 loans, with this number decreasing to 126 in FY1992, 67 in FY1993, 24 in FY1994, 23 in FY1995, and 9 in FY1996, the last year in which manufactured home loans were separately noted in either the VA Annual Reports or the VA Annual Benefits Reports.

[30] This definition is from the manufactured housing portion of the regulations at 38 C.F.R. §36.4202. The definition of manufactured housing for the regular home loan guaranty at 38 C.F.R. §36.4301 is substantially the same.

[31] *VA Lenders Handbook*, p. 12-20.

[32] For state laws governing the titling of manufactured housing as well as the conversion of housing titled as a motor vehicle to real property, see the Fannie Mae website, https://www.efanniemae.com/sf/guides/ssg/relatedsellinginfo/manufachousing/titling manufhsing.jsp.

[33] U.S. Census Bureau, *Selected Characteristics of New Manufactured Homes Placed: By Region - 2010*, p. 1, http://www.census.gov/const/mhs/char10.pdf.

[34] U.S. Congress, Senate Labor and Public Welfare Committee, *Extension of Veterans' Home Loan Entitlements and Inclusion of Mobile Home Purchases*, report to accompany S. 3656, 91st Cong., 2nd sess., September 23, 1970, S.Rept. 91-1230, p. 13. When the Veterans' Housing Act (H.R. 16710) was considered and passed by the Senate, the bill was amended by and replaced with S. 3656, the companion bill to H.R. 16710, which contained a similar version of the loan guaranty program. See "Veterans' Housing Act of 1970," Senate debate, *Congressional Record*, vol. 116 (September 25, 1970), pp. 33781-33783.

[35] *Report of the President's Committee on the Vietnam Veteran*, Washington, DC, 1970, p. 33.

[36] Ibid.

[37] 38 U.S.C. §3712(d). The maximum loan terms are: single-wide, about 20 years for home and lot; double-wide, a maximum of 25 years for home and lot; or lot purchase, approximately 15 years.

[38] 38 U.S.C. §3712(c)(5).

[39] Email communication from the VA, May 17, 2012. Regarding appraisals, manufactured housing dealers often sold manufactured homes with furniture included, but beginning in the 1980s, the furniture could no longer be included in appraised value.

[40] 38 U.S.C. §3710(a)(8) and (a)(9)(i).

[41] 38 U.S.C. §3710(a)(5).

[42] 38 U.S.C. §3710(e).

[43] Ibid.

[44] 38 U.S.C. §3710(e)(1)(C).

[45] U.S. Congress, House Committee on Veterans' Affairs, *Veterans' Housing Rehabilitation and Program Improvement Act of 1987*, report to accompany H.R. 2672, 100th Cong., 1st sess., July 30, 1987, H.Rept. 100-257, p. 15.

[46] *VA Lenders Handbook*, p. 6-2.

[47] Ibid., p. 3-3.

[48] Ibid., p. 10-10.

[49] Ibid., p. 6-18.

[50] U.S. Department of Housing and Urban Development and U.S. Department of Commerce, *American Housing Survey for the United States: 2009*, March 2011, p. 65, http://www.census.gov/prod/2011pubs/h150-09.pdf. See p. A-23 for the way in which "primary mortgage" status is determined.

[51] Statement of Tim S. Embree, Iraq and Afghanistan Veterans of America, U.S. Congress, House Committee on Veterans' Affairs, Subcommittee on Economic Opportunity, *Hearing on the Loan Guaranty Program*, 111th Cong., 2nd sess., May 20, 2010, pp. 51-52.

[52] For more information about Freddie Mac and the conforming loan limits, see CRS Report RS22172, *The Conforming Loan Limit*, by N. Eric Weiss and Sean M. Hoskins.

[53] P.L. 91-351, §305. The FHA statute was amended in 1969 to raise the limit to $33,000 (P.L. 91-152).

[54] P.L. 93-383, §805. The federal savings and loan limits on mortgage lending were codified at 12 U.S.C. §1464(c) (1976).

[55] P.L. 96-399, §313.

[56] Federal Housing Finance Agency, *History of Conforming Loan Limits*, http://www.fhfa.gov/webfiles/860/ loanlimitshistory07.pdf. Limits were increased in each year with the exception of 1990.

[57] P.L. 111-5 returned the limit for high-cost areas to the level first instituted in 2008 as part of the Economic Stimulus Act of 2008 (P.L. 110-185).

[58] 38 U.S.C. §3703.

[59] 38 U.S.C. §3703(a)(1)(C).

[60] 12 U.S.C. §1454.

[61] This is based on the provision in the Freddie Mac statute for areas where 115% of median home prices exceed the conforming loan limit. 12 U.S.C. §1454(a)(2)(C). See the text box for more information.

[62] U.S. Department of Veterans Affairs, *VA Circular 26-08-19, Implementation of Loan Guaranty Provisions of P.L. 110-389* , October 16, 2008, p. 2, http://www.benefits.va.gov /homeloans/docs/26_08_19.pdf.

[63] 2013 VA County Loan Limits, http://www.benefits 2013_county_loan_limits.pdf.

[64] U.S. Department of Veterans Affairs, *FY2011 Annual Benefits Report*, p. 66, http://www.vba.va.gov/REPORTS /abr/ 2011_abr.pdf.

[65] 12 U.S.C. §1454(a)(2)(C).

[66] The higher conforming loan limit for Alaska, Hawaii, and Guam was introduced in 1980 (P.L. 96-399). The U.S. Virgin Islands was added to the list in 1992 (P.L. 102-550). See also, U.S. Congress, Conference Report, report to accompany S. 2719, 96th Cong., 2nd sess., September 26, 1980, H.Rept. 96-1420, p. 117.

[67] 2013 VA County Loan Limits, http://www.benefits 2013_county_loan_limits.pdf.

[68] *The Ginnie Mae Mortgage Backed Securities Guide*, August 1, 2011, p. 9-1, http://www.ginniemae.gov/guide/pdf / chap09.pdf.

[69] *VA Lenders Handbook*, p. 3-9.

[70] 38 U.S.C. §3703(a).

[71] *VA Lenders Handbook*, pp. 3-12 and 3-14.

[72] 38 U.S.C. §3702(b).

[73] Ibid. See also *VA Lenders Handbook*, p. 2-15.

[74] *VA Lenders Handbook*, p. 2-15.

[75] Ibid., p. 3-9.

[76] See CRS Report RS20530, *FHA-Insured Home Loans: An Overview*, by Katie Jones.

[77] See CRS Report R42875, *The FHA Single-Family Mortgage Insurance Program: Financial Status and Related Current Issues*, by Katie Jones.

[78] Ibid.

[79] 38 C.F.R. §36.4313.

[80] See *VA Lenders Handbook*, p. 8-7.

[81] U.S. Department of Housing and Urban Development, *Handbook 4155.2, Lender's Guide to the Single Family Mortgage Insurance Process*, p. 6-A-12, http://portal.hud.gov /hudportal/documents/huddoc?id=4155-2_6_secA.pdf.

[82] CRS Report R42875, *The FHA Single-Family Mortgage Insurance Program: Financial Status and Related Current Issues*, by Katie Jones.

[83] 38 U.S.C. §3731 requires the VA Secretary to set up a process for approving appraisers that includes a testing process and recommendations from other appraisers, and to develop and maintain a list of approved appraisers.

[84] *VA Lenders Handbook*, chapter 15.

[85] See Section 2(1)(B)(ii)(I). Just prior to the enactment of P.L. 107-326, veteran borrowers qualified for a principle balance of 100% of the first $25,000 of the appraised value, compared to 97% for non-veteran borrowers. In addition, the maximum principle balance on amounts above $125,000 was 90% for non-veteran borrowers, compared to 95% for veteran borrowers.

[86] See Section 2113 of P.L. 110-289.

[87] U.S. Congress, Senate Committee on Banking and Currency, *Housing Act of 1950*, report to accompany S. 2246, 81st Cong., 2nd sess., February 24, 1950, S.Rept. 81-1286, p. 92.

[88] The old U.S. Code Section, 38 U.S.C. §694*l* (1952), was replaced by 38 U.S.C. §1811 (1958). See the table of contents for Title 38 of the U.S. Code 1958 version.

[89] U.S. Congress, House Committee on Veterans' Affairs, Subcommittee on Housing, *Bills to Provide for Purchase of Mobile Homes Under Veterans' Administration Guaranty and Other Bills Related to Veterans' Housing*, 91st Cong., 2nd sess., July 14 and 16, 1970, pp. 3461-3462.

[90] 38 U.S.C. §3711.

[91] U.S. Veterans Administration, *Annual Report 1981*, May 1982, p. 71.

[92] For example, the language in the FY2012 Consolidated Appropriations Act (P.L. 112-74) was "not to exceed $500,000 in gross obligations for direct loans are authorized for specially adapted housing loans." According to the Conference Committee Report, the law "limits obligations for direct loans to not more than $500,000." See H.Rept. 111-366.

[93] U.S. Department of Veterans Affairs, *FY2013 Congressional Budget Submission, Volume III, Benefits and Burial Programs and Departmental Administration*, pp. 2E-1 and 2E-6, http://www.va.gov/budget/docs/summary/Fy2013_Volume_III-Benefits_Burial_Dept_Admin.pdf (hereinafter FY2013 VA Budget Justifications).

[94] See U.S. Department of Veterans Affairs, *M26-1 Guaranteed Loan Processing Manual*, p. 10-15, http://www.benefits

[95] 38 U.S.C. §3765(3). The statute refers to "Pacific Islander" as one who is "who is indigenous to a United States territory or possession located in the Pacific Ocean," as defined by the Native American Programs Act of 1974, 42 U.S.C. §2992c(7). The three U.S. territories in the Pacific are American Samoa, Guam, and the Commonwealth of the Northern Mariana Islands.

[96] U.S. Congress, Senate Committee on Veterans' Affairs, *Veterans Benefits and Health Care Act of 1989*, report to accompany S. 13, 101st Cong., 1st sess., September 13, 1989, S.Rept. 101-126 (Washington: GPO, 1989), pp. 290-291. The Senate amended H.R. 901 (which would ultimately become P.L. 101-237) with provisions from S. 13.

[97] U.S. Department of the Interior, *DOI Trust Reform: As-Is Trust Business Model Report*, March 21, 2003, p. 2-1, http://www.ost.doi.gov/trust_reform

[98] U.S. Department of Agriculture, *Lending on Native American Lands: A Guide for Rural Development Staff*, June 2006, p. 24, http://www.rurdev.usda.gov/rd/aian/LendingOnNativeLands_RD.pdf.

[99] See U.S. Congress, Senate Committee on Veterans' Affairs, *Native American Veterans Home Loan Equity Act of 1992*, report to accompany S. 2528, 102nd Cong., August 12, 1992, S.Rept. 102-378, p. 11. Quoting from an evaluation of VA lending on tribal land, the report stated that "The inability to use tribal land as security for a mortgage loan is the most significant factor in limiting access to the VA loan guaranty benefit that can be affected by VA." S. 2528 was incorporated into P.L. 102-547. See "Veterans Home Loan Program Revitalization Act of 1992," House debate, *Congressional Record*, vol. 138, part 22 (October 5, 1992), p. 32374.

[100] See the Department of the Interior website, "Insular Area Summary for American Samoa," http://www.doi.gov/oia/ Islandpages/asgpage.htm.

[101] AM. SAMOA CODE ANN. §37.0204.

[102] N.M.I. Const., Art. XII, Sec. 1.

[103] Congress, in response to the concerns of the Advisory Committee on Native American Veterans, directed the Departments of Veterans Affairs and Interior to look into the extent to which Native American veterans on trust land participated in the loan guaranty program and release a report (see the Veterans' Benefits Amendments of 1989 (P.L. 101-237)). The findings of the report are summarized in S.Rept. 102-378, p. 10.

[104] The MOU is available at http://www.benefits

[105] U.S. Department of Veterans Affairs, *Annual Benefits Report FY2011*, p. 63, http://www.vba.va.gov/REPORTS /abr/2011_abr.pdf.

[106] Ibid.

[107] U.S. Congress, Senate Committee on Veterans' Affairs, *Pending Benefits-Related Legislation*, 109th Cong., 1st sess., June 23, 2005, S.Hrg. 109-243, p. 27.

[108] Ibid., p. 28.

[109] E-mail communication from the VA, April 13, 2012.

[110] U.S. Department of Veterans Affairs, *FY2011 Performance and Accountability Report*, November 15, 2011, p. III-13, http://www.va.gov/budget/docs/report/2011-VAPAR_FullWeb.pdf (hereinafter *FY2011 Performance and Accountability Report*).

[111] 38 U.S.C. §§3733(a)(1) and (a)(7).

[112] See *FY2011 Performance and Accountability Report*, pp. III-30 to III-31. Congress authorized the VA to guarantee principal and interest payments on these certificates as part of P.L. 102-291, which is codified at 38 U.S.C. §3720(h).

[113] *FY2011 Performance and Accountability Report*, p. III-31.

[114] E-mail communication from the VA, April 13, 2012.

[115] The FCRA was part of the Omnibus Reconciliation Act of 1990. It is found under Title XIII, Budget Enforcement, as Title V, Credit Reform.

[116] Ibid.

[117] The reestimates are part of the Supplemental Materials on the OMB Budget website. There are tables for reestimates of direct loan subsidy rates and loan guarantee subsidy rates. See Office of Management and Budget, *FY2013 Federal Credit Supplement*, pp. 73-74 for guaranteed loans and pp. 49-50 for direct loans, http://www.whitehouse.gov/sites/default/files/omb/budget/fy2013/assets/cr_supp.pdf.

[118] 38 U.S.C. §3722. The fund was instituted in 1998 as part of P.L. 105-368, the Veterans Programs Enhancement Act. Prior to this, the loan guaranty and direct loan programs had been funded through three accounts, the Guaranty and Indemnity Fund, and two liquidating accounts.

[119] 38 U.S.C. §3729.

[120] 38 U.S.C. §3729(c) and P.L. 112-154.

[121] 38 U.S.C. §3729(a). See also, *VA Lenders Handbook*, p. 3-11.

[122] The Veterans' Readjustment Benefits Act of 1966 (P.L. 89-358) imposed a fee of 0.5% on veterans who served during the post-Korean War era, but this fee was withdrawn four years later as part of the Veterans' Housing Act of 1970 (P.L. 91-506).

[123] The letter and draft legislation were made part of the House Veterans' Affairs Committee report for H.R. 6782, a bill where the section regarding loan fees was eventually incorporated into the Omnibus Budget Reconciliation Act of 1982 (P.L. 97-253). See CQ Almanac 1982, 38th ed., *Reconciliation Savings: $130 Billion by 1985*, 1983, pp. 199-204,

http://library.cqpress.com/cqalmanac/cqal82-1164004. The VA administrator letter is at U.S. Congress, House Committee on Veterans' Affairs, *Veterans' Disability Compensation and Survivors' Benefits Amendments of 1982*, report to accompany H.R. 6782, 97th Cong., 2nd sess., July 23, 1982, H.Rept. 97-660, pp. 49-50.

124 Ibid.

125 See, for example, U.S. Congress, House Committee on Veterans' Affairs, Subcommittee on Housing and Memorial Affairs, *VA Home Loan Guaranty Program*, 97th Cong., 2nd sess., March 23, 1982.

126 Note that prior to the extension of existing fees in P.L. 108-183, in August 2011 the Restoring GI Bill Fairness Act of 2011 (P.L. 112-26) changed fees for subsequent loans with less than 5% down payment for both active duty veterans and reservists.

127 See U.S. Department of Veterans Affairs, *VA Circular 26-11-15, Updated Funding Fee Changes*, October 6, 2011, http://www.benefits and *VA Circular 26-11-19, Funding Fee Update as of November 22, 2011*, November 22, 2011, http://www.benefits.va.gov/ homeloans /circulars/26_11_19.pdf.

128 The Specially Adapted Housing Program is codified at 38 U.S.C. §§2101-2107.

129 The first is addressed in 38 U.S.C. §2101(a) and the second in 38 U.S.C. §2101(b).

130 38 C.F.R. §3.809.

131 See U.S. Congress, Senate Committee on Veterans' Affairs, *Veterans' Disability Compensation and Housing Benefits Amendments of 1980*, report to accompany S. 2649, 96th Cong., 2nd sess., July 30, 1980, S.Rept. 96-876, pp. 24-26.

132 The resulting report was published as a committee print, U.S. Congress, House Committee on Veterans' Affairs, *The Needs of Veterans Who Are Totally Blind from Service-Connected Causes for Home Modifications*, committee print, prepared by Veterans' Administration, 96th Cong., 2nd sess., January 11, 1980, H.Prt. 96-56.

133 U.S. Congress, Senate Committee on Veterans' Affairs, *Veterans' Disability Compensation and Housing Benefits Amendments of 1980*, report to accompany S. 2649, 96th Cong., 2nd sess., July 30, 1980, S.Rept. 96-876, pp. 25-26.

134 38 C.F.R. §3.809a.

135 38 U.S.C. §2102A.

136 U.S. Congress, House Committee on Veterans' Affairs, *Veterans Housing and Employment Improvement Act of 2005*, report to accompany H.R. 3665, 109th Cong., 1st sess., November 1, 2005, H.Rept. 109-263, p. 13.

137 The cost of construction index is to reflect the average change in construction costs from year to year. The VA chose an existing index, the Turner Building Cost Index. See U.S. Department of Veterans Affairs, "Loan Guaranty: Assistance to Eligible Individuals in Acquiring Specially Adapted Housing; Cost-of-Construction Index," 74 *Federal Register* 48658, September 24, 2009.

138 See VA Circular 26-12-8, "Annual Increase in Construction Cost Index and Specially Adapted Housing Grants," October 2, 2012, http://www.benefits

139 Ibid.

140 U.S. Department of Veterans Affairs, *FY2009 Performance and Accountability Report*, November 16, 2009, p. II-4, http://www.va.gov/budget/report/index.asp.

141 38 C.F.R. §36.4405.

142 U.S. Department of Veterans Affairs, "Loan Guaranty: Assistance to Eligible Individuals in Obtaining Specially Adapted Housing ," 75 *Federal Register* 56875-56880, September 17, 2010. In advance of the final rule, the VA had issued guidance broadening property ownership categories. See U.S. Department of Veterans Affairs, *Circular 26-08-5,*

Expansion of the Types of Ownership Interests Permissible Under the Specially Adapted Housing (SAH) Grant Program, March 10, 2008, http://www.benefits

[143] 38 C.F.R. §36.4401.

[144] National Bureau of Economic Research, *Determination of the December 2007 Peak in Economic Activity*, December 11, 2008, http://www.nber.org/cycles

[145] Mortgage Bankers Association, *National Delinquency Survey, First Quarter 2007*, data as of March 31, 2007, p. 3, and *National Delinquency Survey, Third Quarter 2012*, data as of September 30, 2012, p. 3.

[146] The Mortgage Bankers Association releases quarterly National Delinquency Surveys with delinquency and foreclosure data that includes subprime loans, prime loans, FHA loans, and VA loans. From 2002 to the present, the VA foreclosure rate has been lower than the FHA foreclosure rate; since 2007, the VA foreclosure rate has been lower than the rate for all loans; and since the end of 2010, the VA loan foreclosure rate has been lower than fixed-rate prime loans.

[147] Mortgage Bankers Association, National Delinquency Surveys, see footnote 145.

[148] See, for example, Historical Statistics of the United States, *Table Dc1255-1270, Mortgage foreclosures and delinquencies: 1926-1979*, http://hsus.cambridge.org/HSUS Web/toc/tableToc.do?id=Dc1255-1270, and Mortgage Bankers Association Historical National Delinquency Survey Data.

[149] Statement of Thomas J. Pamperin, VA Associate Deputy Under Secretary for Policy and Program Management, U.S. Congress, House Committee on Veterans' Affairs, Subcommittee on Economic Opportunity, *Hearing on the Loan Guaranty Program*, 111th Cong., 2nd sess., May 20, 2010, pp. 22-23.

[150] 38 C.F.R. §36.4319.

[151] U.S. Department of Veterans Affairs, "Loan Guaranty: Loan Servicing and Claims Procedures Modifications," 73 *Federal Register* 6294-6368, February 1, 2008.

[152] 38 C.F.R. §36.4315.

[153] U.S. Department of Veterans Affairs, "Loan Guaranty Revised Loan Modification Procedures," 76 *Federal Register* 6555-6559, February 7, 2011.

[154] U.S. Department of Veterans Affairs, *VA Loan Electronic Reporting Interface VA Servicer Guide*, July 31, 2009, p. 87, http://www.benefits

[155] 38 C.F.R. §36.4320.

[156] For more information about HAMP and other foreclosure prevention initiatives, see CRS Report R40210, *Preserving Homeownership: Foreclosure Prevention Initiatives*, by Katie Jones.

[157] Until June 1, 2012, in order to participate in HAMP, borrowers were required to have mortgage payments that exceeded 31% of their income. However, the Obama Administration announced "HAMP Tier II" on March 9, 2012, in order to try to assist additional borrowers. Beginning June 1, 2012, borrowers may have mortgage payments that make up less than 31% of their income and still qualify for HAMP. See *Making Home Affordable Supplemental Directive 12- 02*, March 9, 2012, https://www.hmpadmin.com /portal/programs /docs/hamp_servicer/sd1202.pdf.

[158] U.S. Department of Veterans Affairs, *Circular 26-10-6, Revised VA Making Home Affordable Program*, May 24, 2010, http://www.benefits

[159] VA Circular 26-10-6 states that veterans who are current on their VA-guaranteed loans should be evaluated for the IRRRL.

[160] Oklahoma was not a party to the agreement.

[161] U.S. Department of Justice, "Federal Government and State Attorneys General Reach $25 Billion Agreement with Five Largest Mortgage Servicers to Address Mortgage Loan Servicing and Foreclosure Abuses," press release, February 9, 2012, http://www.justice.gov/opa/pr/2012/February/12-ag-186.html.

[162] For more information, see the website devoted to the settlement, http://www.nationalmortgagesettlement.com/.

[163] For more information, see CRS Report RL34575, *The Servicemembers Civil Relief Act (SCRA): An Explanation*, by R. Chuck Mason.

[164] 50 U.S.C. Appendix §533.

[165] Veterans Benefits Administration Powerpoint Presentation, "Loan Guaranty Program Overview."

[166] 38 U.S.C. §3732(c) gives the VA the authority to purchase property from the loan servicer where the net value of the property exceeds the unguaranteed portion of the loan. Further, pursuant to 38 C.F.R. §36.4323(b), the VA may acquire properties even where the net value does not exceed the unguaranteed portion of the debt. However, in these cases, the servicer must waive the amount of the indebtedness that exceeds the net value (i.e., the servicer will not pursue the veteran borrower for the deficiency) for the VA to be able to accept the transfer.

[167] See U.S. Congress, conference report to accompany H.R. 4170, 98th Cong., 2nd sess., June 23, 1984, H.Rept. 98-861, pp. 1374-1375.

[168] See 38 U.S.C. §3703(b): "The liability of the United States under any guaranty, within the limitations of this chapter, shall decrease or increase pro rata with any decrease or increase of the amount of the unpaid portion of the obligation." But "[i]n no event may the liability of the United States under a guaranteed loan exceed the amount guaranteed with respect to that loan under section 3703 (b) of this title." 38 U.S.C. §3732(c)(9).

[169] 38 U.S.C. §3732(c)(5). The VA pays the "net value" for the property—its fair market value minus costs the VA would incur while holding the property.

[170] 38 U.S.C. §3702(b).

[171] 38 U.S.C. §5302(b).

[172] 38 U.S.C. §3720(a).

[173] *FY2012 Performance and Accountability Report*, November 15, 2012, p. III-35, http://www.va.gov/budget/docs/ report/2012-VAPAR_FullWeb.pdf.

In: Veterans
Editor: Timothy C. Roberts
ISBN: 978-1-63321-722-5

Chapter 2

THE NUMBER OF VETERANS THAT USE VA HEALTH CARE SERVICES: A FACT SHEET*

Erin Bagalman

INTRODUCTION

It's a simple question—how many veterans use services at the Veterans Health Administration (VHA)? It's a question being asked a lot these days, and it is important, baseline information to know when changes are being contemplated[1] to the way in which VA delivers health care to veterans.

In the course of an investigation into allegations[2] that veterans seeking health care services from the VHA experienced long delays in treatment, the Department of Veterans Affairs (VA) Office of Inspector General (OIG) released an interim report[3] that substantiated the delays. Final determinations by the OIG of the full scope and impact of the problems, including whether delays in treatment resulted in harm to or the death of any veterans, will not be available until the OIG completes its investigation and issues a final report.

The issue of wait times for VA health care is not new. Approaches to providing timely access to care for veterans enrolled in VA health care have included the use of non-VA care reimbursed by the VA. The need to rely on non-VA care in some cases has raised questions about the VA's capacity to

* This is an edited, reformatted and augmented version of a Congressional Research Service publication R43579, prepared for Members and Committees of Congress, dated June 3, 2014.

provide services to the veteran population now and in the future. Knowing how many veterans there are is essential to answering those questions.

Number of Veterans and VA Health Care Users

Veterans Total Population: Annual estimates of the total population of living veterans[4] are based in part on a U.S. Census Bureau definition of veterans as "men and women who have served (even for a short time), but are not currently serving, on active duty in the U.S. Army, Navy, Air Force, Marine Corps, or the Coast Guard, or who served in the U.S. Merchant Marine during World War II."[5]

VA Enrollees: Eligibility for federal veterans' benefits begins with a statutory definition of a veteran as a "person who served in the active military, naval, or air service, and who was discharged or released therefrom under conditions other than dishonorable."[6] To receive VA health care, veterans generally must enroll in the system after meeting eligibility requirements (which for most veterans are based on previous military service, presence of service-connected disabilities, and/or other factors).[7]

VA Patients (Veterans): In a given year, not every VA-enrolled veteran receives VA health care services. Some veterans may opt not to seek care during the year, while others may receive care outside the VA system, paying for care using private health insurance, Medicare, Medicaid, the military health system (TRICARE), or other means. Thus not every VA-enrolled veteran is counted as a VA patient during a given year.

VA Patients (Non-veterans): The VA also provides health care services to certain non-veteran patients, including "active duty military and reserve, spousal collateral, consultations and instruction, CHAMPVA workload, reimbursable workload with affiliates, humanitarian care, and employees receiving occupational immunizations such as Hepatitis A&B and flu vaccinations."[8]

Table 1 provides the total veteran population, VA-enrolled veterans, and VA patients (including both veteran and non-veteran patients) for each year from FY2001 through FY2014. These data allow several observations, including the following:

- The total veteran population has decreased by 17% from FY2001 to FY2014.

- The VA-enrolled veteran population has increased by 78% from FY2001 to FY2014.
- As a proportion of the total veteran population, the VA-enrolled veterans have increased from 20% in FY2001 to 42% in FY2014.
- Since FY2003, 63%–65% of VA enrolled veterans have used VA health care each year. (In FY2001, 76% of enrolled veterans used VA health care, but this is anomalous within the time period. In FY2002 it was 69%.)
- The number of non-veteran VA patients has increased faster than the number of veteran patients; as of FY2014, non-veteran patients represent 11% of all VA patients.

Table 1.Veteran Population, VA Enrollees, and VA Patients, FY2001–FY2014

Year	Total Veteran Population	VA-Enrolled Veterans	Patients Using VA Health Care During the Year		
			Veterans	Non-Veterans	Total Patients
FY2001	26,092,046	5,124,168	3,890,871	356,333	4,247,204
FY2002	25,627,596	6,248,949	4,290,717	380,320	4,671,037
FY2003	25,217,342	7,186,643	4,544,430	417,023	4,961,453
FY2004	24,862,857	7,419,851	4,713,583	453,250	5,166,833
FY2005	24,521,247	7,655,562	4,862,992	445,322	5,308,314
FY2006	24,179,183	7,872,438	5,030,582	435,488	5,466,070
FY2007	23,816,018	7,833,445	5,015,689	463,240	5,478,929
FY2008	23,442,489	7,834,763	5,078,269	498,420	5,576,689
FY2009	23,066,965	8,048,560	5,221,583	523,110	5,744,693
FY2010	23,031,892	8,343,117	5,441,059	559,051	6,000,110
FY2011	22,676,149	8,574,198	5,582,171	584,020	6,166,191
FY2012	22,328,279	8,762,548	5,680,374	652,717	6,333,091
FY2013	21,972,964	8,926,546	5,803,890	680,774	6,484,664
FY2014	21,619,731	9,111,955	5,908,042	708,921	6,616,963

Sources: Total Veterans numbers are from VetPop2011 (FY2010–FY2014), available at http://www.va.gov/ vetdata/Veteran_Population.asp, and an archived copy of an earlier version no longer available on the website (FY2000–FY2009). VA-Enrolled Veterans numbers and Patients Using VA Health Care During the Year numbers are from VA budget submissions for FY2002–FY2015; the number for each fiscal year is taken from the budget submission two years later (e.g., the FY2000 number is from the FY2002 budget submission).

Notes: FY2014 numbers for VA-Enrolled Veterans and Patients Using VA Health Care during the Year are estimates.

End Notes

[1] United States Senate Committee on Veterans' Affairs, Press Release, "Chairman Sanders Lays Out Legislative Action Plan for Veterans," June 1, 2014, http://www.veterans.senate.gov /newsroom/majority-news/chairman-sanders-lays-outlegislative-action-plan-for-veterans, website accessed June 2, 2014. Senator McCain has indicated he will present an alternative. See Michael C. Bender, "Reid-Backed Veterans Care Plan Draws Repubilcan Alternate," Bloomberg, June 3, 2014, http://www.bloomberg.com/news/2014-06-02/reid-backed-veterans-care-plan-draws-republican-alternate.html, website accessed June 3, 2014.

[2] CNN, "Shinseki resigns, but will that improve things at VA hospitals?," May 31, 2014, http://www.cnn.com/2014/05/30/politics/va-hospitals-shinseki/index.html?hpt=hp_inthenews, website accessed June 2, 2014.

[3] Veterans Health Administration, "Interim Report: Review of Patient Wait Times, Scheduling Practices, and Alleged Patient Deaths at the Phoenix Health Care System," May 28, 2014, http://www.va.gov/ oig/pubs/VAOIG-14-02603- 178.pdf, website accessed June 2, 2014.

[4] United States Department of Veterans Affairs, National Centers for Veterans Analysis and Statistics, "Veteran Population," website accessed June 2, 2014, http://www.va.gov/ vetdata/Veteran_Population.asp.

[5] United States Census Bureau, "Definitions and Concepts: Who are veterans?," http://www.census.gov/hhes/ veterans/ about/definitions.html, website accessed June 2, 2014.

[6] 38 U.S.C. Section 101(2), http://uscode.house.gov/view.xhtml?req=%28title:38%20section: 101%282%29% 20edition:prelim, website accessed June 2, 2014.

[7] CRS Report R42747, Health Care for Veterans: Answers to Frequently Asked Questions, by Sidath Viranga Panangala and Erin Bagalman.

[8] Department of Veterans Affairs, "Volume II, Medical Programs and Information Technology Programs, Congressional Submission, FY 2015 Funding and FY 2016 Advance Appropriations," p. VHA-32, http://www.va.gov/ budget/docs/summary/Fy2015-VolumeII-MedicalProgramsAndInformationTechnology. pdf#page=34, website accessed June 2, 2014.

In: Veterans
Editor: Timothy C. Roberts

ISBN: 978-1-63321-722-5

Chapter 3

VETERANS' MEDICAL CARE: FY2015 APPROPRIATIONS*

Sidath Viranga Panangala

SUMMARY

The Department of Veterans Affairs (VA) provides benefits to veterans who meet certain eligibility criteria. Benefits to veterans range from disability compensation and pensions to hospital and medical care. The VA provides these benefits through three major operating units: the Veterans Health Administration (VHA), the Veterans Benefits Administration (VBA), and the National Cemetery Administration (NCA). This report focuses on funding for the VHA. The VHA is primarily a direct service provider of primary care, specialized care, and related medical and social support services to veterans through the nation's largest integrated health care system. Eligibility for VA health care is based primarily on previous military service, disability, and income.

The President's FY2015 budget request was submitted to Congress on March 4, 2014. The President's budget is requesting $158.6 billion in budget authority for the VA as a whole. This includes $93.5 billion in mandatory funding and $65.1 billion in discretionary funding. For FY2015, the Administration is requesting $56.6 billion for VHA. This includes $45.4 billion for the medical services account, $5.9 billion for

* This is an edited, reformatted and augmented version of a Congressional Research Service publication, No. R43547, dated May 15, 2014.

the medical support and compliance account, $4.7 billion for the medical facilities account, and nearly $589 million for the medical and prosthetic research account. Furthermore, as required by the Veterans Health Care Budget Reform and Transparency Act of 2009 (P.L. 111-81), the President's budget is requesting $58.6 billion in advance appropriations for the three medical care accounts (medical services, medical support and compliance, and medical facilities) for FY2016.

On April 3, 2014, the House Military Construction and Veterans Affairs Subcommittee approved its version of a Military Construction and Veterans Affairs and Related Agencies Appropriations bill for FY2015 (MILCON-VA Appropriations bill). The full House Appropriations Committee approved a draft measure by voice vote on April 9, 2014, and the House passed MILCON-VA Appropriations bill for FY2015 (H.R. 4486; H.Rept. 113-416) on April 30, 2014. The House-passed version of the MILCON-VA Appropriations bill for FY2015 proposes a total of $158.2 billion for the VA as whole. For FY2015, H.R. 4486 proposes $56.2 billion for VHA. This includes $45 billion for the medical services account, $5.9 billion for the medical support and compliance account, $4.7 billion for the medical facilities account, and nearly $589 million for the medical and prosthetic research account. H.R. 4486 (H.Rept. 113-416) includes $58.6 billion in advance FY2016 funding for the medical services, medical support and compliance, and medical facilities accounts—the same level included in the President's request.

INTRODUCTION

The Department of Veterans Affairs (VA) provides a range of benefits and services to veterans[1] who meet certain eligibility rules; these benefits include medical care, disability compensation and pensions,[2] education,[3] vocational rehabilitation and employment services,[4] assistance to homeless veterans,[5] home loan guarantees,[6] administration of life insurance as well as traumatic injury protection insurance for servicemembers,[7] and death benefits that cover burial expenses.[8]

The VA carries out its programs nationwide through three administrations and the Board of Veterans Appeals (BVA).[9] The Veterans Benefits Administration (VBA) is responsible for, among other things, providing compensation, pensions, and education assistance. The National Cemetery Administration (NCA)[10] is responsible for maintaining national veterans' cemeteries; providing grants to states for establishing, expanding, or improving state veterans' cemeteries; and providing headstones and markers for the graves of eligible persons, among other things.

The Veterans Health Administration (VHA) is responsible for health care services and medical and prosthetic research programs.[11] The VHA is primarily a direct service provider of primary care, specialized care, and related medical and social support services to veterans through the nation's largest integrated health care system. Inpatient and outpatient care are also provided in the private sector to eligible dependents of veterans under the Civilian Health and Medical Program of the Department of Veterans Affairs (CHAMPVA).[12] The VHA is also a provider of health care education and training for physician residents and other health care trainees.[13] The other statutory missions of VHA are to serve as a contingency backup to the Department of Defense (DOD) medical system during a national security emergency,[14] and to provide support to the National Disaster Medical System and the Department of Health and Human Services as necessary.[15]

In general, eligibility for VA health care is based on previous military service,[16] presence of service-connected disabilities,[17] and/or other factors.[18] Veterans generally must enroll in the VA health care system to receive medical care. Once enrolled, veterans are assigned to one of eight categories (see the **Appendix**).[19] It should be noted that in any given year, not all enrolled veterans obtain their health care services from the VA. While some veterans may rely solely on the VA for their care, others may receive the majority of their health care services from other sources, such as Medicare, Medicaid, private health insurance, and the military health system (TRICARE).[20] VA-enrolled veterans do not pay premiums or enrollment fees to receive care from the VA; however, they may incur out-of-pocket costs for VA care related to conditions that are not service-connected.[21]

THE VETERAN PATIENT POPULATION

In FY2014, there were approximately 21.9 million living veterans in the nation whose service ranged from World War II, Korea, Vietnam, the Gulf War (which includes Operation Enduring Freedom/Operation Iraqi Freedom/Operation New Dawn (OEF/OIF/OND)) and the intervening periods. Of this number approximately 9.1 million were estimated to be enrolled in the VA health care system (see Table 1). From FY2011 through FY2014 the total number of enrollees has increased by 6.3%. Of the total number of enrolled veterans in FY2014, VA anticipated treating approximately 5.9 million unique veteran patients (see Table 2).[22] For FY2015, VHA estimates that it will treat about 6 million unique veteran patients, and of these, VA anticipates treating more than 757,000 Operation Enduring Freedom (OEF), Operation Iraqi Freedom (OIF), and Operation New Dawn (OND) veterans.[23] In FY2015, OEF, OIF, and OND patients would represent approximately 11.2% of the overall patients served by the VA.

VHA also provides medical care to certain non-veterans; in FY2015 this population is expected to increase by more than 14,000 patients over the FY2014 level.[24] In total, including non-veterans, it is estimated the VHA will treat nearly 6.7 million patients in 2015, a slight increase of 1.9% over the number of patients treated in FY2014 (see Table 2). Between FY2011 and FY2015, the number of patients treated by VA has grown by 9.3%.

The total number of outpatient visits, including visits to Vet Centers, reached 91.7 million during FY2013 and is projected to increase to approximately 94.6 million in FY2014 and 97.2 million in FY2015.[25]

Table 1. VHA Unique Enrollees, FY2011-FY2015

Priority Groups	FY2011 Actual	FY2012 Actual	FY2013 Actual	FY2014 Estimate	FY2015 Estimate
1	1,385,482	1,539,632	1,712,369	1,755,002	1,857,218
2	656,828	680,339	704,737	719,218	736,422
3	1,154,954	1,173,673	1,200.952	1,208,263	1,224,544
4	242,385	241,626	242,257	236,709	234,797
5	2,243,148	2,215,449	2,147,686	2,238,782	2,251,917
6	569,400	593,478	610,414	603,393	603,818
Subtotal Priority Groups 1-6	*6,252,197*	*6,444,197*	*6,618,415*	*6,761,367*	*6,908,717*
7	188,823	171,031	196,593	234,115	242,999
8	2,133,178	2,147,320	2,111,538	2,116,473	2,135,577
Subtotal Priority Groups 7-8	*2,322,001*	*2,318,351*	*2,308,131*	*2,350,588*	*2,378,575*
Total Enrollees	8,574,198	8,762,548	8,926,546	9,111,955	9,287,292

Source: Table prepared by the Congressional Research Service based on data from the Department of Veterans Affairs and data from Department of Veterans Affairs, *FY2015 Budget Submission, Medical Programs and Information Technology Programs*, Volume 2 of 4, March 2014, pp.VHA-32.

Note: For a description of Priority Groups see the Appendix.

The rest of this report focuses on appropriations for VHA. It begins with a brief overview of VHA's budget formulation, a description of the accounts that fund the VHA, and a summary of the FY2014 VHA budget. The report ends with a section discussing recent legislative developments pertaining to the FY2015 VHA budget.

Table 2. VHA Unique Patients, FY2011-FY2015

Priority Groups	FY2011 Actual	FY2012 Actual	FY2013 Actual	FY2014 Estimate	FY2015 Estimate
1	1,179,333	1,307,750	1,451,707	1,537,467	1,648,369
2	442,665	456,050	473,841	482,363	491,612
3	687,284	697,548	721,576	727,075	735,975
4	191,177	191,521	192,241	189,436	188,883
5	1,487,637	1,464,198	1,409,341	1,407,554	1,390,365
6	266,374	272,043	275,799	272,927	274,137
Subtotal Priority Groups 1-6	*4,254,470*	*4,389,110*	*4,524,505*	*4,616,822*	*4,729,341*
7	170,690	155,093	167,538	180,357	179,561
8	1,157,011	1,136,171	1,111,487	1,110,863	1,109,638
Subtotal Priority Groups 7-8	*1,327,701*	*1,291,264*	*1,279,385*	*1,291,220*	*1,289,119*
Subtotal Unique Veteran Patients	5,582,171	5,680,374	5,803,890	5,908,042	6,018,540
OEF/OIF/OND veterans included in the above total	*470,755*	*539,970*	*616,487*	*689,974*	*757,674*
Non-veterans[a]	584,020	652,717	680,774	708,921	723,393
Total Unique Veteran and non-Veteran	6,166,191	6,333,091	6,484,664	6,616,963	6,741,933
Patients					

Source: Table prepared by the Congressional Research Service based on data from the Department of Veterans Affairs and data from Department of Veterans Affairs, *FY2015 Budget Submission, Medical Programs and Information Technology Programs*, Volume 2 of 4, March 2014, pp.VHA-32. OEF/OIF/OND data from Department of Veterans Affairs, *FY2015 Budget Submission, Medical Programs and Information Technology Programs*, Volume 2 of 4, March 2014, p.VHA-7.

Notes: For a description of Priority Groups see the Appendix. Unique patients are those that receive at least one episode of care from the VA or whose treatment is paid for by the VA and is counted only once in a given fiscal year.

a. Non-veterans include Civilian Health and Medical Program of the Department of Veterans Affairs (CHAMPVA) patients (certain dependents of veterans), reimbursable patients with VA affiliated hospitals and clinics, care provided on a humanitarian basis, veterans of World War II allied nations, and employees receiving preventative occupational immunizations such as Hepatitis A&B and flu vaccinations.

Advance Appropriations[26]

In order to understand annual appropriations for the Veterans Health Administration (VHA), it is essential to understand the role of advance appropriations. In 2009, Congress enacted the Veterans Health Care Budget Reform and Transparency Act of 2009 (P.L. 111-81) authorizing advance appropriations for three of the four accounts that comprise VHA: medical services, medical support and compliance, and medical facilities.[27] The fourth account, the medical and prosthetic research account, is not funded with an advance appropriation. P.L. 111-81 also required the Department of Veterans Affairs to submit a request for advance appropriations for VHA with its budget request each year. Congress first provided advance appropriations for the three VHA accounts in the FY2010 appropriations cycle; the Consolidated Appropriations Act, 2010 (P.L. 111-117), provided advance appropriations for FY2011. Subsequently, each successive appropriation measure has provided advance appropriations for the VHA accounts: the Department of Defense and Full-Year Continuing Appropriations Act, 2011 (P.L. 112-10), provided advance appropriations for FY2012; the Consolidated Appropriations Act, 2012 (P.L. 112-74), provided advance appropriations for FY2013; the Consolidated and Further Continuing Appropriations Act, 2013 (P.L. 113-6), provided advance appropriations for FY2014; and the Consolidated Appropriations Act, 2014 (P.L. 113-76) provided advance appropriations for FY2015. The Military Construction, Veterans Affairs, and Related Agencies Appropriations Bill, 2015 (H.R. 4486) as reported by the House Appropriations Committee provides advance appropriations for FY2016.

Under current budget scoring guidelines, advance appropriations of budget authority are scored as new budget authority in the fiscal year in which the funds become newly available for obligation, and not in the fiscal year the appropriations are enacted.[28] Therefore, throughout the funding tables of this report, advance appropriations numbers are shown under the label "memorandum" and in the corresponding fiscal year column. For example, the Consolidated Appropriations Act, 2014 (P.L. 113-76) provided advance appropriations for FY2015. Funding shown for FY2014 does not include advance appropriations provided in FY2014 by P.L. 113-76 for use in FY2015. Instead, the advance appropriation provided in FY2014 for use in FY2015 is shown in the memorandum in the FY2015 column.

DEPARTMENT OF VETERANS AFFAIRS BUDGET

The VA budget includes both mandatory[29] and discretionary funding.[30] Mandatory accounts fund disability compensation, pensions, vocational rehabilitation and employment, education, life insurance, housing, and burial benefits (such as graveliners, outer burial receptacles, and headstones), among other benefits and services. Discretionary accounts fund medical care, medical research, construction programs, information technology, and general operating expenses, among other things.

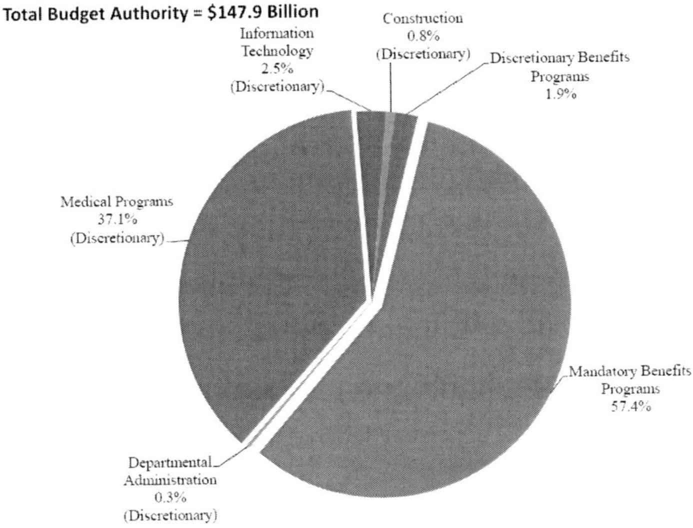

Source: Chart prepared by the Congressional Research Service based on U.S. Congress, House Committee on Appropriations, Subcommittee on Military Construction, Veterans Affairs, and Related Agencies, *Military Construction, Veterans Affairs, And Related Agencies Appropriations Bill, 2015,* report to accompany H.R. 4486, 113th Congress, 2nd session, April 17, 2014, H.Rept. 113-416, pp. 6-10.

Notes: Discretionary budget authority includes medical programs; information technology; construction; other discretionary benefits, such as operation and maintenance of VA's national cemeteries; and departmental administration. Mandatory benefits include disability compensation, pensions, education, vocational rehabilitation and employment services, among other benefits and services. Totals may not add due to rounding.

Figure 1. FY2014 VA Budget Allocations.

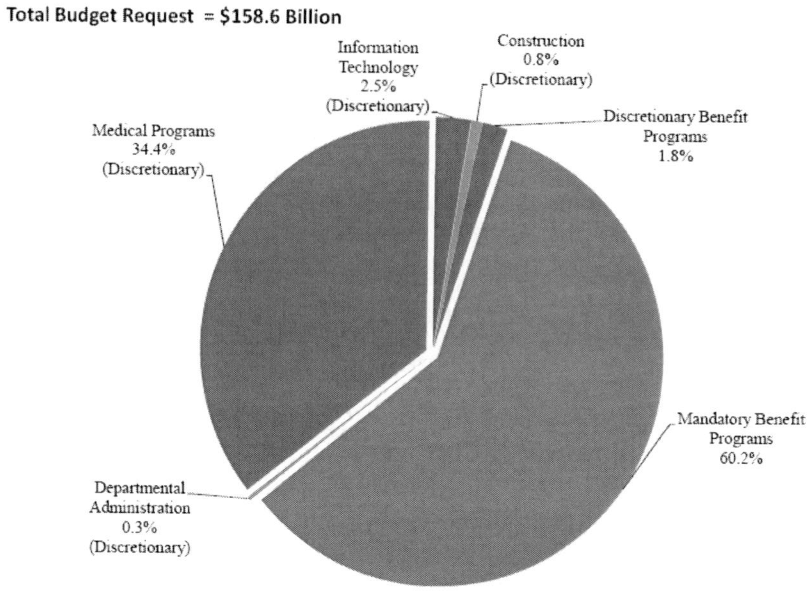

Source: Chart prepared by the Congressional Research Service based on U.S. Congress, House Committee on Appropriations, Subcommittee on Military Construction, Veterans Affairs, and Related Agencies, *Military Construction, Veterans Affairs, And Related Agencies Appropriations Bill, 2015,* report to accompany H.R. 4486, 113th Congress, 2nd session, April 17, 2014, H.Rept. 113-416, pp. 6-10.

Notes: Discretionary budget authority includes medical programs; information technology; construction; other discretionary benefits, such as operation and maintenance of VA's national cemeteries; and departmental administration. Mandatory benefits include disability compensation, pensions, education, vocational rehabilitation and employment services, among other benefits and services. Totals may not add due to rounding.

Figure 2. FY2015 VA Budget Request.

Figure 1 provides a breakdown of FY2014 budget allocations for both mandatory and discretionary programs. In FY2014, the total VA budget authority was approximately $147.9 billion; discretionary budget authority accounted for about 42.8% ($63.2 billion) of the total, with about 86.9% ($54.9 billion) of this discretionary funding going toward supporting VA health care programs, including medical and prosthetic research. The VA's mandatory budget authority accounted for about 57.4% ($84.7 billion) of the total VA budget authority, with about 84.4% ($71.4 billion) of this mandatory funding going toward disability compensation and pension programs.

Figure 2 provides a breakdown of the FY2015 President's budget request for both mandatory and discretionary programs. For FY2015, the Administration requested approximately $158.6 billion. This includes approximately $65.1 billion in discretionary funding and $93.5 billion in mandatory funding. A major portion of the mandatory benefits will be for compensation and pension benefits for veterans and surviving spouses, dependent children, and dependent parents.

Overview of Veterans Health Administration's Budget Formulation[31]

Similar to most federal agencies, the VA begins formulating its budget request approximately 10 months before the President submits the budget to Congress, generally in early February. VHA's budget request to Congress begins with the formulations of the budget based on the Enrollee Health Care Projection Model (EHCPM), [32] and the Civilian Health and Medical Program Veterans Administration (CHAMPVA) Model. The two models collectively estimate the amount of budgetary resources VHA will need to meet the expected demand for most of the health care services it provides.

The EHCPM's estimates are based on three basic components: the projected number of veterans who will be enrolled in VA health care, the projected utilization of VA's health care services—that is, the quantity of health care services enrollees are expected to use—and the projected unit cost of providing these services. Each component is subject to a number of adjustments to account for the characteristics of VA health care and the veterans who access VA's health care services. The EHCPM makes projections three or four years into the future. Each year, VHA updates the EHCPM estimates to "incorporate the most recent data on health care utilization rates, actual program experience, and other factors, such as economic trends in unemployment and inflation."[33] For instance, in 2013, VHA used data from FY2012 to develop its health care budget estimate for the FY2015 request, including the advance appropriations request for FY2016.[34]

The CHAMPVA Model is a more recent model adopted by VHA in 2010. The CHAMPVA model projects the cost of providing medical coverage to CHAMPVA eligible beneficiaries.[35] The CHAMPVA Model is composed of two major components: the enrollment model and the claims cost model. The enrollment model projects the number of beneficiaries enrolled in

CHAMPVA, and the claims cost model projects expenditures for providing care to beneficiaries. According to the VHA, the "2013 CHAMPVA Model was developed using data from fiscal years 2005 to 2012, publically available research, and input from a development team (including subject matter experts from VHA and VHA's CHAMPVA program)."[36]

Table 3 provides a detailed timeline for formulating the FY2015 budget request and the FY2016 advance appropriations request.

Table 3. Department of Veterans Affairs, Budget Formulation Time Line (FY2015 budget request)

Month, Year	Activity
April, 2013	VA issues internal call letter for FY2015/FY2016 budget proposals.
May, 2013	VA Administrations (VBA; VHA; and NCA) develop FY2015 budget, program, and legislative proposals; VHA also develops the FY2016 Advance Appropriations request for medical care.
June, 2013	VA construction budget proposals for FY2015 prioritized through Strategic Capital Investment Planning (SCIP) process.
July, 2013	VA leadership considers the FY2015/FY2016 budget proposals.
August, 2013	VA prepares the budget submission to Office of Management and Budget (OMB)
September, 2013	VA submits 2015 budget to OMB and the FY2016 Advance Appropriations request for medical care.
November, 2013	VA receives OMB Passback of 2015/2016 budget decisions.
December, 2013	VA and OMB reach agreement on budget amounts.
January, 2014	VA prepares the FY2015 Congressional Budget Submissions.
February, 2014[a]	President's FY2015 Budget Request and the Advance Appropriations request for medical care for FY2016 Submitted to Congress.

Source: Table prepared by CRS based on U.S. Congress, House Committee on Veterans' Affairs, *U.S. Department of Veterans Affairs Budget Request For Fiscal Year 2013*, 112th Congress, 2nd session, February 15, 2012, p. 143.

Note: a. The President's FY2014 budget request was submitted in March 2014.

Funding for the VHA

As noted previously, VHA is funded through four appropriations accounts. These are supplemented by other sources of revenue. Although the appropriations account structure has been subject to change from year to year, the appropriation accounts used to support the VHA traditionally include medical care, medical and prosthetic research, and medical administration.

Congress also appropriates funds for construction of medical facilities through a larger appropriations account for construction for all VA facilities. In FY2004, "to provide better oversight and [to] receive a more accurate accounting of funds," Congress changed the VHA's appropriations structure.[37]

Specifically, the Department of Veterans Affairs and Housing and Urban Development and Independent Agencies Appropriations Act, 2004 (P.L. 108-199, H.Rept. 108-401), funded VHA through four accounts: (1) medical services, (2) medical administration (currently known as medical support and compliance), (3) medical facilities, and (4) medical and prosthetic research. Brief descriptions of these accounts are provided below.

Medical Services

The medical services account covers expenses for furnishing inpatient and outpatient care and treatment of veterans and certain dependents, including care and treatment in non-VA facilities; outpatient care on a fee basis; medical supplies and equipment; salaries and expenses of employees hired under Title 38, United States Code (U.S.C.); cost of hospital food service operations;[38] aid to state veterans' homes; and assistance and support services for family caregivers of veterans authorized by the Caregivers and Veterans Omnibus Health Services Act of 2010 (P.L. 111-163). For FY2013, the President's budget request proposed the transfer of funding for biomedical engineering services from the medical facilities account to this account.[39]

The Consolidated and Further Continuing Appropriations Act, 2013 (P.L. 113-6), approved this transfer. The President's budget request for FY2014 proposed to continue funding for biomedical engineering services in the medical services account. The Military Construction and Veterans Affairs, and Related Agencies Appropriations bill for FY2014 (H.R. 2216; H.Rept. 113-90) that was passed by the House of Representatives June 4, 2013, and the Senate Appropriations Committee reported version of H.R. 2216 (S.Rept. 113-48) continued this transfer for FY2014. The Military Construction, Veterans Affairs, and Related Agencies Appropriations Bill, 2015 (H.R. 4486) continues to fund bioengineering services under the medical services account.

Medical Support and Compliance (Previously Medical Administration)

This account provides for expenses related to the management, security, and administration of the VA health care system through the operation of VA medical centers, and other medical facilities such as community-based outpatient clinics (CBOCs) and Vet Centers.[40] It also funds 21 Veterans Integrated Service Network (VISN)[41] offices and facility director offices; chief of staff operations; public health and environmental hazard programs; quality and performance management programs; medical inspection; human research oversight; training programs and continuing education; security; volunteer operations; and human resources management.

Medical Facilities

The medical facilities account funds expenses pertaining to the operations and maintenance of the VHA's capital infrastructure. These expenses include utilities and administrative expenses related to planning, designing, and executing construction or renovation projects at VHA facilities. It also funds leases, laundry services, grounds maintenance, trash removal, housekeeping, fire protection, pest management, and property disposition and acquisition.

Medical and Prosthetic Research

As required by law, the medical and prosthetic research program (medical research) focuses on research into the special health care needs of veterans.[42] This account provides funding for many types of research, such as investigator-initiated research; mentored research; large-scale, multi-site clinical trials; and centers of excellence. VA researchers receive funding not only through this account but also from the Department of Defense (DOD), the National Institutes of Health (NIH), and private sources.

In general, VA's research program is intramural; that is, research is performed by VA investigators at VA facilities and approved off-site locations. Unlike other federal agencies, such as NIH and DOD, VA does not have the statutory authority to make research grants to colleges and universities, cities and states, or any other non-VA entities.

Medical Care Collections Fund (MCCF)

In addition to the appropriations accounts mentioned above, the Committees on Appropriations include medical care cost recovery collections when considering funding for the VHA.

Congress has provided VHA the authority to bill some veterans and most health care insurers for nonservice-connected care provided to veterans enrolled in the VA health care system, to help defray the cost of delivering medical services to veterans.[43] Funds collected from first and third party (copayments and insurance) bills are retained by the VA health care facility that provided the care for the veteran. VA is expecting MCCF total collections to be approximately $2.5 billion in 2015.

FY2014 BUDGET SUMMARY[44]

Consolidated Appropriations Act, 2014 (P.L. 113-76)

House and Senate Action

Congress was unable to complete action on any of the FY2014 appropriation acts prior to the beginning of the new fiscal year. Lawmakers also failed to agree on language in a FY2014 continuing resolution (CR).

With no agreement in place on October 1, 2013, the resulting lapse in funding led to a partial shutdown of government operations. Congress finally reached agreement on a temporary CR on October 16, 2013, and the President signed the Continuing Appropriations Act, 2014 (P.L. 113-46) the following day to reopen the government. That CR (P.L. 113-46) funded most of the VA (excluding the three medical care accounts: medical services, medical support and compliance, and medical facilities) through January 15, 2014. P.L. 113-73 extended the CR through January 18, allowing extra time for legislative consideration of an omnibus appropriation bill.

On January 17, 2014, the President signed into law the Consolidated Appropriations Act, 2014 (P.L. 113-76). Division J of this act included the Military Construction and Veterans Affairs, and Related Agencies Appropriations Act, 2014 (MILCON-VA Appropriations Act, 2014).

In total the MILCON-VA Appropriations Act, 2014 provides a total of $147.9 billion in budget authority for VA programs in FY2014. Of this amount $54.9 billion is provided for VHA which comprises four accounts: medical services, medical support and compliance, medical facilities, and medical and prosthetic research accounts. P.L. 113-76 provides $40 million for FY2014 for the medical services account in addition to the advance appropriation of $43.6 billion which was provided in P.L. 113-6 (see Table 5).

Furthermore, the MILCON-VA Appropriations Act, 2014 provides $85 million for FY2014 for the medical facilities account in addition to the advance appropriation of $4.9 billion provided in P.L. 113-6. This additional funding will be used to address the backlog of non-recurring maintenance needs at existing VA hospitals and clinics.

As required by the Veterans Health Care Budget Reform and Transparency Act of 2009 (P.L. 111-81), the MILCON-VA Appropriations Act, 2014 provides advance appropriations of $55.6 billion for FY2015 for three VHA accounts (medical services, medical support and compliance, and medical facilities).

Furthermore, P.L. 113-76 rescinds $229 million from the FY2014 VHA accounts (see Table 5).[45]

FY2015 VHA Budget

President's Request

The President submitted his FY2015 budget request to Congress in March 2014. The FY2015 President's Budget is requesting $158.6 billion for the VA as a whole (see Table 4).

For VA medical services, the Administration's budget is requesting $367.8 million in additional funding above the FY2015 advance appropriations of $45 billion provided in FY2014.

In total, the President is requesting $56.6 billion for VHA for FY2015. This includes $45.4 billion for the medical services account, $5.9 billion for the medical support and compliance account, $4.7 billion for the medical facilities account, and nearly $589 million for the medical and prosthetic research account (see Table 5). As required by the Veterans Health Care Budget Reform and Transparency Act of 2009 (P.L. 111-81), the President's budget is requesting $58.6 billion in advance appropriations for the three medical care appropriations (medical services, medical support and compliance, and medical facilities) for FY2016 (see Table 5). This request for advance appropriations would provide care for over 6.8 million unique patients in FY2016.

House Action

On April 3, 2014, the House Military Construction and Veterans Affairs Subcommittee approved its version of a Military Construction and Veterans Affairs and Related Agencies Appropriations bill for FY2015 (MILCON-VA Appropriations bill). The full House Appropriations Committee approved a draft version of the measure by voice vote in an April 9, 2014, and the House passed the MILCON-VA Appropriations bill for FY2015 (H.R. 4486; H.Rept. 113-416) on April 30, 2014. H.R. 4486 proposes a total of $158.2 billion for the VA (see Table 4). The total includes $93.5 billion for mandatory programs, and $64.7 billion for discretionary programs (see Table 4).

H.R. 4486 (H.Rept. 113-416) as passed by the House proposes $56.2 billion for VHA for FY2015 (see Table 5), which comprises four accounts: medical services, medical support and compliance, medical facilities, and medical and prosthetic research. The House-passed measure does not include the additional funding amount of $367.8 million (above the FY2015 advance appropriations) for the medical services account that was requested by the President for FY2015.

According to H.Rept. 113-416, "with $450 million in unobligated, balances expected to be available and a drop of $690 million in projected medical services expenditures, the Committee believes that the identified need can be absorbed within existing resources."[46] H.R. 4486 proposes $58.6 billion in advance FY2016 funding for the medical services, medical support and compliance, and medical facilities accounts—the same level as the President's request (see Table 5).

Table 4. VA and VHA Appropriations, FY2014-FY2015, and Advance Appropriations, FY2016 ($ in thousands)

	Consolidated Appropriations Act, 2014 (P.L. 113-76)		President's Request		House (H.R. 4486; H.Rept. 113-416)	
	FY2014	FY2015	FY2015	FY2016	FY2015	FY2016
Total Department of Veterans Affairs (VA)	$147,934,261	—	$158,639,938	—	$158,220,762	—
Total Mandatory	$84,869,569	—	$93,512,828	—	$93,512,828	—
Total Discretionary	$63,244,692	—	$65,127,110	—	$64,707,934	—
Total Veterans Health Administration (VHA)[a]	$54,943,664	—	$56,591,034	—	$56.223,149	—
Memorandum:[b] Advance appropriations VHA	—	$55,634,227	—	$58,662,202	—	$58,662,202

Source: Table prepared by the Congressional Research Service based on U.S. Congress, House Committee on Appropriations, Subcommittee on Military Construction, Veterans Affairs, and Related Agencies, *Military Construction, Veterans Affairs, And Related Agencies Appropriations Bill, 2015*, report to accompany H.R. 4486, 113th Congress, 2nd session, April 17, 2014, H.Rept. 113-416, pp. 6-10.

Notes:

[a] Includes funding for medical services, medical support and compliance, medical facilities, and medical and prosthetic research accounts, and excludes collections deposited into the Medical Care Collections Fund (MCCF).

[b] The Veterans Health Care Budget Reform and Transparency Act 2009 (P.L. 111-81; codified at 38 U.S.C. §117) provided for advance appropriations (appropriations that become available one fiscal year after the fiscal year for which the appropriations act was enacted) for VA's medical services, medical support and compliance, and medical facilities appropriations accounts, and requires the VA to submit a request for advance appropriation with its annual congressional budget submission. Under current budget scoring guidelines new budget authority for an advance appropriation is scored in the fiscal year in which the funds become available for obligation. Therefore, in this table the advance appropriations budget authority for FY2015 is recorded in the FY2015 column. Likewise, the Administration's advance appropriations request for FY2016 and advance appropriations budget authority for FY2016 proposed in the Military Construction and Veterans Affairs, and Related Agencies Appropriations bill, 2015 are recorded in the FY2016 column.

Table 5. VHA Appropriations by Account, FY2014-FY2015, and Advance Appropriations, FY2016 ($ in thousands)

Account	Consolidated Appropriations Act, 2014 (P.L. 113-76)		President's Request		House (H.R. 4486; H.Rept. 113-416)	
	FY2014	FY2015	FY2015	FY2016	FY2015	FY2016
Medical Services	$43,557,000	—	$45,015,527	—	$45,015,527	—
Additional funding over FY2014 Advance Appropriation	40,000	—	—	—	—	—
Additional funding over FY2015 Advance Appropriation	—	—	367,885		—	—
Rescission	(179,000)	—	—	—	—	—
Subtotal Medical Services	43,418,000	—	45,383,412	—	45,015,527	—
Medical Support and Compliance	6,033,000	—	5,879,700	—	5,879,700	—
Subtotal Medical Support and Compliance	6,033,000	—	5,879,700	—	5,879,700	—
Medical Facilities	4,872,000	—	4,739,000	—	4,739,000	—
Additional funding over FY2014 Advance Appropriation	85,000	—	—	—	—	—
Subtotal Medical Facilities	4,957,000	—	4,739,000	—	4,739,000	—
Medical and Prosthetic Research	585,664	—	588,922	—	588,922	—
Subtotal Medical and Prosthetic Research	585,664	—	588,922	—	588,922	—
Across-the-Board Administrative Rescission	(50,000)	—	—	—	—	—

Table 5. (Continued)

Account	Consolidated Appropriations Act, 2014 (P.L. 113-76)		President's Request		House (H.R. 4486; H.Rept. 113-416)	
	FY2014	FY2015	FY2015	FY2016	FY2015	FY2016
Total VHA Appropriations (without collections)	54,943,664	—	56,591,034	—	56,223,149	—
Medical Care Collection Fund (MCCF)	2,485,000	—	2,456,000	—	2,456,000	—
Total VHA Appropriations (with collections)	$57,428,664	—	$59,047,034	—	$58,679,149	—
Memorandum:[a] Advance Appropriations	FY2014	FY2015	FY2015	FY2016	FY2015	FY2016
Medical Services	—	$45,015,527	—	$47,603,202	—	$47,603,202
Account	Consolidated Appropriations Act, 2014 (P.L. 113-76)		President's Request		House (H.R. 4486; H.Rept. 113-416)	
	FY2014	FY2015	FY2015	FY2016	FY2015	FY2016
Medical Support and Compliance	—	5,879,7000	—	6,144,000	—	6,144,000
Medical Facilities	—	4,739,000	—	4,915,000	—	4,915,000
Total VHA Advance Appropriations	—	$55,634,227	—	$58,662,202	—	$58,662,202

Source: Table prepared by the Congressional Research Service based on U.S. Congress, House Committee on Appropriations, Subcommittee on Military Construction, Veterans Affairs, and Related Agencies, *Military Construction, Veterans Affairs, And Related Agencies Appropriations Bill, 2015*, report to accompany H.R. 4486, 113th Congress, 2nd session, April 17, 2014, H.Rept. 113-416, pp. 6-10.

Note:

a. The Veterans Health Care Budget Reform and Transparency Act 2009 (P.L. 111-81; codified at 38 U.S.C. §117) provided for advance appropriations (appropriations that become available one fiscal year after the fiscal year for which the appropriations act was enacted) for VA's medical services, medical support and compliance, and medical facilities appropriations accounts, and requires the VA to submit a request for advance appropriation with its annual congressional budget submission. Under current budget scoring guidelines new budget authority for an advance appropriation is scored in the fiscal year in which the funds become available for obligation. Therefore, in this table the advance appropriations budget authority for FY2015 is recorded in the FY2015 column. Likewise, the Administration's advance appropriations request for FY2016 and advance appropriations budget authority for FY2016 proposed in the Military Construction and Veterans Affairs, and Related Agencies Appropriations bill, 2015 are recorded in the FY2016 column.

APPENDIX. PRIORITY GROUPS

Table A-1. Priority Groups and Their Eligibility Criteria

Priority Group 1
Veterans with service-connected disabilities rated 50% or more disabling
Veterans determined by VA to be unemployable due to service-connected conditions
Priority Group 2
Veterans with service-connected disabilities rated 30% or 40% disabling
Priority Group 3
Veterans who are former POWs a
Veterans awarded the Purple Heartb
Veterans in receipt of the Medal of Honorc
Veterans whose discharge was for a disability that was incurred or aggravated in the line of duty
Veterans with service-connected disabilities rated 10% or 20% disabling
Veterans awarded special eligibility classification under Title 38, U.S.C., Section 1151, "benefits for individuals disabled by treatment or vocational rehabilitation"
Priority Group 4
Veterans who are receiving aid and attendance or housebound benefits
Veterans who have been determined by VA to be catastrophically disabled
Priority Group 5
Nonservice-connected veterans and noncompensable service-connected veterans rated 0% disabled whose annual income and net worth are below the established VA means test thresholds
Veterans receiving VA pension benefits
Veterans eligible for Medicaid benefits
Priority Group 6
Compensable 0% service-connected veterans
Mexican Border War veterans
Veterans solely seeking care for disorders associated with:
—exposure to herbicides while serving in Vietnam; or
—ionizing radiation during atmospheric testing or during the occupation of Hiroshima and Nagasaki; or
—for disorders associated with service in the Gulf War; or
—for any illness associated with service in combat in a war after the Gulf War or during a period of hostility after November 11, 1998, as follows:

—Veterans discharged from active duty on or after January 28, 2003, who were enrolled as of January 28, 2008, and veterans who apply for enrollment after January 28, 2008, for five years post discharge
—Veterans discharged from active duty before January 28, 2003, who apply for enrollment after January 28, 2008, until January 27, 2011
Veterans who served on active duty at Camp Lejeune in North Carolina for not less than 30 days during the period beginning on January 1, 1957, and ending on December 31, 1987, for any of the 15 medical conditions specified in 38 U.S.C. 1710(e)(1)(F). d
Priority Group 7
Veterans who agree to pay specified copayments with income and/or net worth above the VA means test threshold and income below the VA national geographic income thresholds
Priority Group 8
Veterans who agree to pay specified copayments with income and/or net worth above the VA means test threshold and the VA national geographic threshold
Subpriority a: Noncompensable 0% service-connected and enrolled as of January 16, 2003, and who have remained enrolled since that date and/or placed in this subpriority due to changed eligibility status
Subpriority b: Noncompensable 0% service-connected and enrolled on or after June 15, 2009, whose income exceeds the current VA means test threshold or VA national geographic income thresholds by 10% or less
Subpriority c: Nonservice-connected veterans enrolled as of January 16, 2003, and who have remained enrolled since that date and/or placed in this subpriority due to changed eligibility status
Subpriority d: Nonservice-connected veterans enrolled on or after June 15, 2009, whose income exceeds the current VA means test threshold or VA national geographic income thresholds by 10% or less
Subpriority e: Noncompensable 0% service-connected veterans not meeting the above criteria (Currently not eligible for enrollment)
Subpriority g: Nonservice-connected veterans not meeting the above criteria (Currently not eligible for enrollment)

Source: Department of Veterans Affairs.

Notes: Service-connected disability means, with respect to disability, that such disability was incurred or aggravated in the line of duty in the active military, naval or air service.

[a] Veterans who are former Prisoners of War (POWs) are placed in Priority Group 3. This change occurred with the enactment of the Former Prisoner of War Benefits Act of 1981(P.L. 97-37) on August 14, 1981.

[b] Veterans in receipt of a Purple Heart are in Priority Group 3. This change occurred with the enactment of the Veterans Millennium Health Care and Benefits Act (P.L. 106-117) on November 30, 1999.

[c] Veterans in receipt of the Medal of Honor are in Priority Group 3. This change occurred with the enactment of the Caregiver and Veterans Omnibus Health Services Act of 2010 (P.L. 111-163) on May 5, 2010.

[d] Veterans who served on active duty at Camp Lejeune in North Carolina between January 1, 1957 and December 31, 1987 are placed in Priority Group 6. These veterans are eligible to receive free medical care for the following fifteen illnesses or conditions: esophageal cancer; lung cancer; breast cancer; bladder cancer; kidney cancer; leukemia; multiple myeloma; myleodysplasic syndromes; renal toxicity; hepatic steatosis; female infertility; miscarriage; scleroderma; neurobehavioral effects; and non-Hodgkin's lymphoma. This change occurred with the enactment of the Honoring America's Veterans and Caring for Camp Lejeune Families Act of 2012 (P.L. 112-154) on August 6, 2012.

End Notes

[1] In general, payments of benefits made to, or on account of, a beneficiary under any law administered by the VA are exempt from federal taxation. Furthermore, benefits are exempt, in most cases, from "attachment, levy, or seizure by or under any legal or equitable process whatever, either before or after receipt by the beneficiary" (38 U.S.C. §5301(a)(1)).

[2] For a detailed description of disability compensation and pension programs, see CRS Report R42324, *"Who is a Veteran?"—Basic Eligibility for Veterans' Benefits*, by Umar Moulta-Ali; CRS Report RL34626, *Veterans' Benefits: Disabled Veterans*, by Umar Moulta-Ali et al.; and CRS Report RS22804, *Veterans' Benefits: Pension Benefit Programs*, by Umar Moulta-Ali and Carol D. Davis.

[3] For a discussion of education benefits see, CRS Report R42785, *GI Bills Enacted Prior to 2008 and Related Veterans' Educational Assistance Programs: A Primer*, by Cassandria Dortch; and CRS Report R42755, *The Post-9/11 Veterans Educational Assistance Act of 2008 (Post-9/11 GI Bill): Primer and Issues*, by Cassandria Dortch.

[4] For details on VA's vocational rehabilitation and employment see, CRS Report RL34627, *Veterans' Benefits: The Vocational Rehabilitation and Employment Program*, by Benjamin Collins; and CRS Report R42790, *Employment for Veterans: Trends and Programs*, coordinated by Benjamin Collins.

[5] For detailed information on homeless veterans programs see, CRS Report RL34024, *Veterans and Homelessness*, by Libby Perl.

[6] For details on guaranteed loans, direct loans, and specially adapted housing grants see, CRS Report R42504, *VA Housing: Guaranteed Loans, Direct Loans, and Specially Adapted Housing Grants*, by Libby Perl.

[7] For details on insurance programs see, CRS Report R41435, *Veterans' Benefits: Current Life Insurance Programs*, by Christine Scott.

[8] For details on death benefits, see CRS Report R41386, *Veterans' Benefits: Burial Benefits and National Cemeteries*, by Christine Scott.

[9] The BVA is part of the Department of Veterans Affairs, located in Washington, DC, and makes the final determination on an appeal within the VA. The BVA reviews all appeals for entitlement to veterans' benefits, including claims for service connection, increased disability ratings, pension, insurance benefits, educational benefits, home loan guaranties, vocational rehabilitation, dependency and indemnity compensation, health care services, and fiduciary matters. For more information see CRS Report R42609, *Overview of the Appeal Process for Veterans' Claims*, by Daniel T. Shedd.

[10] Established by the National Cemeteries Act of 1973 (P.L. 93-43).

[11] 38 U.S.C. §7301 and 38 U.S.C. §7303.

[12] For more information on CHAMPVA see, CRS Report RS22483, *Health Care for Dependents and Survivors of Veterans*, by Sidath Viranga Panangala.

[13] 38 U.S.C. §7302.

[14] 38 U.S.C. §8111A.

[15] 38 U.S.C. §1785.

[16] Veteran status is established by active-duty status in the U.S. Armed Forces and a discharged or released there from under conditions other than dishonorable (38 U.S.C.§ 101(2); 38 C.F.R. § 3.1(d)). Generally, persons enlisting in one of the Armed Forces after September 7, 1980, and officers commissioned after October 16, 1981, must have completed two years of active duty or the full period of their initial service obligation to be eligible for VA health care benefits. An exception may be granted if the servicemember was discharged or released because of an early out or hardship (10 U.S.C. §§ 1171 or 1173); was discharged or released for a service-connected disability directly due to service; or, has a compensable service-connected disability (38 U.S.C. § 5303A; 38 C.F.R. § 3.12a).

[17] A service-connected disability is a disability that was incurred or aggravated in the line of duty in the U.S. Armed Forces (38 U.S.C. §101 (16). VA determines whether veterans have service-connected disabilities, and for those with such disabilities, assigns ratings from 0% to 100% based on the severity of the disability. Percentages are assigned in increments of 10 (38 C.F.R. §§4.1-4.31).

[18] For information on eligibility for VA health care see, CRS Report R42747, *Health Care for Veterans: Answers to Frequently Asked Questions*, by Sidath Viranga Panangala and Erin Bagalman.

[19] Ibid.

[20] TRICARE provides medical care to active duty servicemembers and other eligible beneficiaries (such as military retirees) through a combination of direct care in military clinics and hospitals and civilian-purchased care. For more information on TRICARE see, CRS Report RL33537, *Military Medical Care: Questions and Answers*, by Don J. Jansen.

[21] For more information on VA cost-sharing requirements see, CRS Report R42747, *Health Care for Veterans: Answers to Frequently Asked Questions*, by Sidath Viranga Panangala and Erin Bagalman.

[22] In a given year not all enrolled veterans receive care from the VA, either because they are not sick or they have other sources of care such as the private sector.

[23] On September 1, 2010, the combat mission in Iraq (Operation Iraqi Freedom, OIF) formally ended and transitioned to Operation New Dawn (OND), which ended on December 15, 2011. VA considers OND to be part of the same contingency operation that was formerly called OIF. Therefore, VA considers participants in OND to be eligible for health care under the legal authorities pertaining to OIF. OEF/OIF/OND data from Department of Veterans Affairs, *FY2015 Budget Submission, Medical Programs and Information Technology Programs,* Volume 2 of 4, March 2014, p.VHA-7.

[24] Non-veterans include Civilian Health and Medical Program of the Department of Veterans Affairs (CHAMPVA) patients (certain dependents of veterans), reimbursable patients in VA affiliated hospitals and clinics, care provided on a humanitarian basis, veterans of World War II allied nations, and employees receiving preventative occupational immunizations such as Hepatitis A&B and flu vaccinations.

[25] Department of Veterans Affairs, *FY2015 Budget Submission, Medical Programs and Information Technology Programs,* Volume 2 of 4, March 2014, p.VHA-33.

[26] In general, an appropriations act makes budget authority available beginning on October 1 of the fiscal year for which the appropriations act is passed ("budget year"). However, there are some types of appropriations that do not follow this pattern; among them are advance appropriations. An advance appropriation means appropriation of new budget authority that becomes available one or more fiscal years beyond the fiscal year for which the appropriations act was passed (i.e., beyond the budget year). For more information on advance appropriations, see CRS Report R43482, *Advance Appropriations, Forward Funding, and Advance Funding: Concepts, Practice, and Budget Process Considerations*, by Jessica Tollestrup

[27] Codified at 38 U.S.C. §117.

[28] Executive Office of the President, Office of Management and Budget (OMB), *Appendix A-Scorekeeping Guidelines*, OMB Circular No. A–11, PART 7, July 2013, p. 2.

[29] Mandatory programs funded through the annual appropriations process are commonly referred to as appropriated entitlements. In general, appropriators have little control over the amounts provided for appropriated entitlements; rather, the authorizing statute establishes the program parameters (e.g., eligibility rules, benefit levels) that entitle certain recipients to payments. If Congress does not appropriate the money necessary to meet these commitments, entitled recipients (e.g., individuals, states, or other entities) may have legal recourse. For an overview of mandatory spending see, CRS Report RL33074, *Mandatory Spending Since 1962*, by Mindy R. Levit and D. Andrew Austin.

[30] Funding for discretionary programs are provided and controlled through the annual appropriations process. For more information see, CRS Report R41726, *Discretionary Budget Authority by Subfunction: An Overview*, by D. Andrew Austin.

[31] A major part of this discussion was drawn from U.S. Government Accountability Office, *Veterans' Health Care: VA Uses a Projection Model to Develop Most of Its Health Care Budget Estimate to Inform the President's Budget Request*, GAO-11-205, January 2011, pp. 4-8; and U.S. Government Accountability Office, V*eterans' Health Care Budget: Better Labeling of Services and More Detailed Information Could Improve the Congressional Budget Justification*, GAO-12-908, September 2012, pp. 5-6.

[32] The Veterans' Health Care Eligibility Reform Act of 1996 (P.L. 104-262) required the VHA to manage the provision of hospital care and medical services through an enrollment system based on a system of priorities.

[33] Department of Veterans Affairs, *FY2014 Budget Submission, Medical Programs and Information Technology Programs*, Volume 2 of 4, February 2013, p. 1A-6.

[34] VHA uses methodologies other than the EHCPM to develop estimates of the amount of resources needed for state-based long-term care programs, readjustment counseling, legislation recently enacted, expansions to homeless veterans programs, and care provided to non-veterans patients.

[35] For more information on CHAMPVA see, CRS Report RS22483, *Health Care for Dependents and Survivors of Veterans*, by Sidath Viranga Panangala.

[36] Department of Veterans Affairs, *FY2015 Budget Submission, Medical Programs and Information Technology Programs*, Volume 2 of 4, March 2014, p. VHA-46.

[37] U.S. Congress, Conference Committees, *Consolidated Appropriations Act, 2004*, conference report to accompany H.R. 2673, 108th Cong., 1st sess., H.Rept. 108-401, p. 1036.

[38] In its FY2008 budget request to Congress, the VA requested the transfer of food service operations costs from the medical facilities appropriations to the medical services appropriations. The House and Senate Appropriations Committees concurred with this request. The cost of food service operations support hospital food service workers, provisions, and supplies related to the direct care of patients.

[39] Biomedical engineering services include the maintenance and repair of all medical equipment used in the treatment, monitoring, diagnosis, or therapy of patients.

[40] Vet Centers are community-based counseling centers that provide a wide range of social and psychological services such as professional readjustment counseling to veterans who have served in a combat zone, military sexual trauma (MST) counseling, bereavement counseling for families who experience an active duty death, substance abuse assessments and referral, medical referral, veterans' benefits explanation and referral, and employment counseling, among other services.

[41] VISN offices provide management and oversight to the medical centers and clinics within their assigned geographic areas. Each VISN office is responsible for allocating funds to facilities, clinics, and programs within its region and coordinating the delivery of health care to veterans.

[42] 38 U.S.C. §7303(a)(3). The Office of Research and Development (ORD) within the Veterans Health Administration (VHA) manages the medical research program. The medical research program encompasses, among other things, biomedical laboratory research, clinical trials, health services research, and rehabilitation research.

[43] The Consolidated Omnibus Budget Reconciliation Act of 1985 (P.L. 99-272), enacted into law in 1986 established means testing for veterans seeking care for nonservice-connected conditions. The Balanced Budget Act of 1997 (P.L. 105-33) established the Department of Veterans Affairs Medical Care Collections Fund (MCCF) and gave the VHA the authority to retain these funds in the MCCF. Instead of returning the funds to the Treasury, the VA can use them, without fiscal year limitations, for medical services for veterans. In FY2004, the Administration's budget requested consolidating several existing medical collections accounts into one MCCF. The conferees of the Consolidated Appropriations Act of 2004 (H.Rept. 108-401) recommended that collections that would otherwise be deposited in the Health Services Improvement Fund (former name), Veterans Extended Care Revolving Fund (former name), Special Therapeutic and Rehabilitation Activities Fund (former name), Medical Facilities Revolving Fund (former name), and the Parking Revolving Fund (former name) should be deposited in MCCF. The Consolidated Appropriations Act of 2005 (P.L. 108-447, H.Rept. 108-792) provided the VA with permanent authority to deposit funds from these five accounts into the MCCF.

[44] For a detailed discussion of the VHA appropriations for FY2014, see CRS Report R43179, *Veterans' Medical Care: FY2014 Appropriations*, by Sidath Viranga Panangala.

[45] Section 226 of Division J of P.L. 113-76 rescinds FY2014 medical account funding and re-appropriates it to be available for two years. The provision rescinds and re-appropriates $1,400,000,000 for the medical services account, rescinds $150,000,000 for the medical support and compliance account and re-appropriates $100,000,000 for that account, and rescinds and re-appropriates $250,000,000 for medical facilities account (Explanatory Statement Regarding the House Amendment to the Senate Amendment on H.R. 3547,

Consolidated Appropriations Act, 2014," House, *Congressional Record*, vol. 160, Book II (January 15, 2014), p. H1150.).

[46] U.S. Congress, House Committee on Appropriations, Subcommittee on Military Construction, Veterans Affairs, and Related Agencies, *Military Construction, Veterans Affairs, And Related Agencies Appropriations Bill, 2015*, report to accompany H.R. 4486, 113th Cong., 2nd sess., April 17, 2014, H.Rept. 113-416, p. 31.

In: Veterans
Editor: Timothy C. Roberts

ISBN: 978-1-63321-722-5

Chapter 4

VA HEALTH CARE: ADDITIONAL STEPS NEEDED TO STRENGTHEN BENEFICIARY TRAVEL PROGRAM MANAGEMENT AND OVERSIGHT*

United States Government Accountability Office

WHY GAO DID THIS STUDY

VHA's Beneficiary Travel Program is designed to encourage eligible veterans to seek medical care by reducing travel costs to medical appointments. Veterans are eligible to receive reimbursement for some travel expenses, such as mileage, through the program that is administered by VA medical centers. In February 2013, the VA Office of Inspector General identified issues with inadequate management and oversight. VHA has identified the program as susceptible to significant improper payments and has estimated $71 million in improper payments for fiscal year 2012.

GAO was asked to examine VHA's Beneficiary Travel Program. In this report, GAO examined recent efforts VHA has developed or implemented to improve the program. GAO reviewed documents and interviewed VHA officials about these efforts; and determined whether VHA applied the

* This is an edited, reformatted and augmented version of a United States Government Accountability Office publication, No. GAO-13-632, dated July 2013.

appropriate internal controls. GAO also reviewed documents and interviewed officials from six VA medical centers, which vary on the basis of fiscal year 2012 mileage reimbursement spending, geographic location, and other factors.

WHAT GAO RECOMMENDS

GAO recommends that VA identify and apply internal controls in its efforts to improve management and oversight of the Beneficiary Travel Program, including ensuring compliance with the Dashboard, evaluating performance indicators for the Beneficiary Travel Analytics Tool, and providing effective communication tools to medical centers for EFT. VA generally agreed with GAO's conclusions and concurred with the recommendation.

WHAT GAO FOUND

The Department of Veterans Affairs' (VA) Veterans Health Administration (VHA) has developed efforts to improve the Beneficiary Travel Program, but lack of internal controls may impede their effectiveness. Specifically, VHA has developed multiple efforts to improve the management and oversight of its process for reimbursing veterans' travel expenses for medical appointments, as well as the timeliness and accuracy of payments, including the following:

- **Dashboard**. Web-based software that determines a veteran's eligibility for travel reimbursement, the amount of any deductibles, and the number of miles from the veteran's residence to the closest VA medical facility. The software is designed to enable VA medical center staff to quickly and consistently calculate veterans' mileage reimbursement.
- **Beneficiary Travel Analytics Tool**. Tool that provides each medical center with reports identifying questionable veteran reimbursement patterns, such as frequently changing addresses on reimbursement claims, which may be done to inappropriately increase travel reimbursement amounts. The reports are intended to help medical

centers define and implement facility-level internal controls to reduce improper payments.

- **Electronic Funds Transfer (EFT)**. Process to transfer travel reimbursement funds electronically into veterans' bank accounts. This effort implements a Department of the Treasury requirement for federal agencies to convert cash payments to electronic funds payments, and aims to improve efficiency, increase oversight, and reduce the amount of cash on hand.

These efforts are expected to increase the consistency of how the program is administered by medical centers. However, GAO found that internal controls were lacking for some of the efforts, including the following:

- **Monitoring Compliance.** VHA has not developed a plan to ensure medical centers' compliance with the efforts or existing policies. For example, although medical centers are required to use the Dashboard, VHA officials told us they do not have a plan in place to ensure that each medical center is using this new software.
- **Evaluating Performance Indicators**. VHA has not developed a plan for evaluating VHA-wide performance indicators for at least one of its efforts, the Beneficiary Travel Analytics Tool.
- **Providing Effective Communication**. VHA did not provide a communication plan for sharing information on EFT with medical centers and veterans in a timely manner.

Without necessary internal controls in place, VHA cannot ensure that its new efforts will meet its goals, such as improved management and oversight, or that the Beneficiary Travel Program, which has seen spending more than double in the past 5 years—approaching $1 billion annually—is operating effectively.

ABBREVIATIONS

EFT	electronic funds transfer
IPERA	Improper Payments Elimination and Recovery Act of 2010
OIG	Office of Inspector General
VA	Department of Veterans Affairs

VHA	Veterans Health Administration
VISN	Veterans Integrated Service Network

July 15, 2013
Congressional Requesters

The Department of Veterans Affairs' (VA) Veterans Health Administration (VHA) Beneficiary Travel Program is designed to encourage eligible veterans to seek needed medical care by reducing travel costs to medical appointments. Veterans are eligible to receive reimbursement for some travel expenses associated with medical appointments, such as mileage, if they meet certain criteria, generally related to whether they have a service-connected disability or low income level.

Concerns have been raised about the program's efficacy and management, including VHA's oversight of VA medical centers that are responsible for implementing the program at the local level. Specifically, findings from a recent audit conducted by the VA Office of Inspector General (OIG) identified problems with the Beneficiary Travel Program, including inadequate management and oversight, and inaccurate payments to veterans.[1] Members of Congress also have raised concerns about the program, particularly regarding veterans' difficulties receiving travel reimbursement, including reports of veterans waiting in long lines to receive cash reimbursement for travel expenses, or facing delays receiving reimbursement checks by mail. Furthermore, VHA has identified the Beneficiary Travel Program as a program that is susceptible to significant improper payments, and has estimated $71 million in improper payments for fiscal year 2012.[2] Spending for the Beneficiary Travel Program comes out of individual medical center medical care funds—the same funds that are used for patient care—and has increased from about $370 million in fiscal year 2008 to about $860 million in fiscal year 2012.

Congressional requesters expressed interest in obtaining information on VHA's Beneficiary Travel Program. In this report, we examine the efforts, if any, VHA has identified to improve the process for reimbursement of veterans' travel expenses to medical appointments within the Beneficiary Travel Program.

To determine whether VHA has developed efforts to improve the Beneficiary Travel Program, we asked officials from VHA's Chief Business Office and Office of Finance—the offices that have responsibility for setting policies and procedures related to the Beneficiary Travel Program—to identify national efforts to improve the program. We focused on efforts, including policies, processes, and initiatives, that were developed or implemented from October 2011 to May 2013. For each effort VHA identified, we reviewed VHA documentation describing its purpose, development or implementation status, and any issues encountered in the development and implementation of the effort. We also collected documentation and interviewed officials from VHA about any communication VHA provided for veterans about the effort. To identify local perspectives on any efforts VHA is deploying nationally and local officials' experiences with the program generally, we reviewed documents and interviewed officials from six VA medical centers: (1) Kansas City VA Medical Center (Mo.); (2) Malcolm Randall VA Medical Center (Gainesville, Fla.); (3) Minneapolis VA Health Care System (Minn.); (4) Maine VA Medical Center (Augusta, Maine); (5) Veterans Health Care System of the Ozarks (Fayetteville, Ark.); and (6) West Los Angeles VA Medical Center (Calif.). These medical centers vary in terms of fiscal year 2012 total mileage reimbursement spending; participation as a pilot or early implementation site for any of VHA's efforts to improve its travel reimbursement program; VA region; rural/urban location; and VA-assigned facility complexity level.[3] We also interviewed officials from selected veteran service organizations—Blinded Veterans Association, Disabled American Veterans, and Paralyzed Veterans of America—to get their perspectives on VHA's Beneficiary Travel Program, including challenges veterans may face in seeking reimbursement, and VHA's efforts to improve the program. Using strategic planning and performance measures consistent with the Government Performance and Results Act and GAO's related internal control standards,[4] we determined whether VHA applied appropriate internal controls in the development and implementation of the efforts.

We conducted this performance audit from December 2012 to July 2013 in accordance with generally accepted government auditing standards. Those standards require that we plan and perform the audit to obtain sufficient, appropriate evidence to provide a reasonable basis for our findings and conclusions based on our audit objectives. We believe that the evidence obtained provides a reasonable basis for our findings and conclusions based on our audit objectives.

Background

Under authority first provided by Congress in 1940, VA reimburses eligible veterans for travel expenses associated with medical appointments through VHA's Beneficiary Travel Program.[5] Specifically, travel expenses eligible for reimbursement include mileage, tolls, meals, and lodging. Through the program, VA may also pay for special mode transportation—such as ambulances and wheelchair vans.

Veterans are eligible for travel reimbursement if they have 30 percent or more service-connected disability ratings; are receiving care related to their service-connected disability if their service-connected disability rating is less than 30 percent; receive VA pension benefits; have an annual income below a set annual rate;[6] present clear evidence that they are unable to defray the cost of travel; or are traveling for compensation and pension exams.[7] Certain caregivers also may be eligible for travel reimbursement. Generally, eligible veterans are only reimbursed for round-trip travel costs associated with scheduled appointments, except in the case of emergency care.[8] Since the program's inception, Congress has made several modifications, including adjusting eligibility requirements, types of travel expenses covered, deductible costs,[9] and mileage reimbursement rates. For example, in fiscal years 2008 and 2009, Congress directed VA to increase its mileage reimbursement rate from 11 cents per mile to 28.5 cents per mile and then to 41.5 cents per mile. Committee reports accompanying VA's fiscal years 2008 and 2009 Medical Services appropriations indicated that the committees identified specific amounts to fund these rate increases.[10]

Program Spending

Spending for the Beneficiary Travel Program increased from about $370 million in fiscal year 2008 to about $860 million in fiscal year 2012, with mileage reimbursement accounting for an increased proportion of the spending in this same period. (See fig. 1.) According to VHA officials, the increase in spending was primarily due to the increased number of veterans claiming mileage reimbursement, a rise in the average number of claims per veteran, and higher mileage reimbursement rates. For example, according to VHA, the number of veterans claiming mileage reimbursement increased from about 450,000 in fiscal year 2008 to about 1,450,000 in fiscal year 2012.[11]

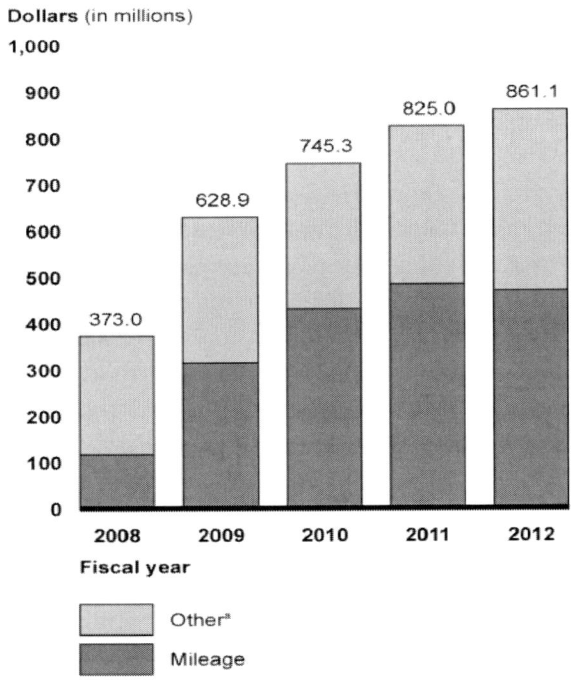

Source: GAO analysis of VHA data.

[a]Other includes expenses other than mileage, such as tolls, meals, lodging, and special mode transportation costs such as ambulance services and wheelchair vans.

Figure 1. Spending for VHA's Beneficiary Travel Program, Fiscal Year 2008 through Fiscal Year 2012.

Program Management and Oversight

VHA's Chief Business Office is responsible for establishing policies and providing guidance to medical centers for the Beneficiary Travel Program. These policies describe, for example, the eligibility requirements and the types of travel expenses that are reimbursable.[12] VHA's Office of Finance is responsible for establishing national policies for the processing of payments for reimbursement and financial quality assurance.[13] Veterans Integrated Service Networks (VISN) have no specific oversight responsibilities for the Beneficiary Travel Program beyond the general responsibility of ensuring compliance with VHA's policies at the medical centers within their region.[14]

Administration of the program is largely handled at the local medical center level.

VHA's policies outline requirements for the Beneficiary Travel Program's reimbursement process, and can be summarized into the following three broad steps:

- **Veteran applies for travel reimbursement**: VHA policies stipulate that veterans must apply for reimbursement within 30 calendar days of the travel. Veterans must provide information on the travel costs incurred to the medical center responsible for the care.
- **Medical center reviews eligibility and determines reimbursement amount**: After the veteran applies for reimbursement, VHA requires medical centers to assess the veteran's eligibility for reimbursement,[15] determine distance traveled, and apply appropriate deductibles. For example, VHA policies stipulate that except under certain circumstances, veterans are reimbursed for mileage between their place of residence and the nearest VA facility where the care could be provided.[16]
- **Medical center reimburses veteran**: After eligibility has been verified and reimbursement amounts determined, medical centers reimburse veterans those amounts.

Medical centers also have local procedures for managing the program. (See app. I for examples of procedures used by some of the medical centers included in our review.)

In February 2013, the VA OIG released a report summarizing findings from its audit of VHA's Beneficiary Travel Program.[17] The audit revealed problems such as inadequate management and oversight, and inaccurate payment amounts. Specifically, the VA OIG reported that it did not have reasonable assurance that Beneficiary Travel Program costs were accurate or were being paid only to eligible veterans. The VA OIG report found that from January 2010 through March 2011 VA paid $89 million more in beneficiary travel reimbursements than facilities approved, including $42.5 million in unexplained payments.[18] On the basis of its findings, the VA OIG recommended that VHA establish and implement procedures to strengthen authorization, payment, and oversight controls for the program. VHA concurred with the OIG's findings and recommendations and reported that it would, among other things, be implementing several initiatives to address the findings.

Additionally, VHA has identified the Beneficiary Travel Program as being susceptible to significant improper payments. The Improper Payments Elimination and Recovery Act of 2010 (IPERA) requires agencies with programs identified as being susceptible to significant improper payments to estimate the annual amount of improper payments for each program and publish these estimates and corresponding corrective actions in an annual report;[19] VA includes this information in its annual Performance and Accountability Report. For VA's 2012 Performance and Accountability Report, VHA estimated that the Beneficiary Travel Program had $71 million in improper payments.[20] IPERA also requires federal agencies' inspectors general to annually determine whether their respective agencies are in compliance with IPERA requirements and to report on their determinations. In March 2013, the VA OIG reported limitations in VHA's methodology for estimating improper payments for the Beneficiary Travel Program and other programs but noted that this was not a matter of noncompliance with IPERA requirements.[21]

VHA Has Developed Efforts to Improve the Beneficiary Travel Program, but Lack of Internal Controls May Impede Their Effectiveness

VHA has developed multiple efforts to improve the management and oversight of its process for reimbursing veterans' travel expenses for medical appointments. However, lack of internal controls for some efforts may hinder VHA's ability to improve the process.

VHA Has Developed Efforts That Aim to Improve the Management and Oversight of the Beneficiary Travel Program

VHA has developed multiple efforts to improve the management and oversight of the Beneficiary Travel Program, as well as the timeliness and accuracy of payments. (See table 1.) These efforts—many of which medical centers are or will be required to implement—are expected to increase the consistency of how the program is administered. For example, the Dashboard, a Web-based software, provides a standardized process that medical centers are required to use to determine a veteran's eligibility for travel reimbursement, the amount of any deductibles, and the number of miles from the veteran's residence to the closest VA medical facility where care could be provided.

Table 1. VHA-Identified Efforts to Improve the Management and Oversight of the Beneficiary Travel Program

Effort	Description	Implementation status, as of May 14, 2013
Beneficiary Travel Analytics Tool (Data Mining Tool)	Tool that provides each medical center with reports identifying questionable veteran reimbursement patterns, such as frequently changing addresses on reimbursement claims, which may be done to inappropriately increase travel reimbursement amounts. The reports are intended to help medical centers define and implement facility-level internal controls to reduce improper payments.	●
Beneficiary Travel Eligibility Review	Web-based tool that identifies cases where previously disbursed travel benefits need to be collected from veterans whose income levels were determined—after final verification—to be above eligibility thresholds.	●
Beneficiary Travel Resource Center	Internal VA Web-based content management system with beneficiary travel information, such as links to fact sheets, trainings, and policy guidance, for VA staff use.	●
Dashboard	Web-based software that determines a veteran's eligibility for travel reimbursement, the amount of any deductibles, and the number of miles from the veteran's residence to the closest VA medical facility where care could be provided. The software is designed to enable VA medical center staff to decrease payment processing time and to eliminate the variability in how medical centers calculate veterans' mileage reimbursement.	●
VistA Enhancements	Software addition to the VistA system—VA's electronic health records system—that helps medical centers conduct electronic reimbursement authorizations and payments by consolidating information needed to determine veterans' eligibility and reimbursement amounts, including income level and any deductibles to be applied.	●

Effort	Description	Implementation status, as of May 14, 2013
	The software is designed to improve efficiency, mitigate risks, and better detect improper payments for the Beneficiary Travel Program.	
Beneficiary Travel Payment and Reconciliation Program Database	Software tool that enables medical centers to reconcile the reimbursements that have been approved for payment with those that have been paid. The tool is designed to help reduce the payment processing workload for medical centers and improve the efficiency of and standardize payment processes. VHA anticipates VHA-wide implementation by May 31, 2013.	◓
Debit Card	A VHA-wide card that veterans can use to receive travel reimbursement funds electronically. This effort implements a Department of the Treasury requirement for federal agencies to provide debit card options for electronic payments by March 1, 2013, and aims to improve efficiency, increase oversight, and reduce the amount of cash on hand. VHA has requested and received an extension from the Department of the Treasury, and anticipates VHA-wide implementation by December 31, 2013.	◓
Electronic Funds Transfer (EFT)	Process to transfer travel reimbursement funds electronically into veterans' bank accounts. This effort implements a Department of the Treasury requirement for federal agencies to convert cash payments to electronic funds payments by March 1, 2013, and aims to improve efficiency, increase oversight, and reduce the amount of cash on hand. VHA has requested and received an extension from the Department of the Treasury, and anticipates VHA-wide implementation by December 31, 2013.	◓
Facility Audit Tool	Standardized audit process tool to provide VA networks the ability to audit their facilities' past travel reimbursement transactions and operations. The tool is designed to help identify opportunities to improve processes that may reduce improper payments. VHA does not have a date for VHA-wide implementation.	○

Table 1. (Continued)

Effort	Description	Implementation status, as of May 14, 2013
Standard Operating Procedures (Revised)	Comprehensive standard operating procedures developed for medical centers to use in the management of the Beneficiary Travel Program that include new or revised processes and documents, such as a revised travel reimbursement application. VHA anticipates VHA-wide implementation of the procedures by June 30, 2013.	O
Travel Reimbursement Regulations (Revised)	Regulations to be revised to incorporate recent legislative changes and clarify identified areas of potential confusion, such as the definition of the closest facility for care. VHA does not have a date for VHA-wide implementation because, according to officials, publication of regulations is a lengthy process and cannot be reliably predicted.	O

Source: GAO analysis of VHA information.

Legend:

● Fully implemented (e.g., rolled out VHA-wide to all medical centers)

◓ Partially implemented (e.g., in pilot phase in selected medical centers)

O In development, but not yet implemented

The efforts are in various stages of development and implementation, with some being fully implemented in all medical centers, while others are in earlier stages. For some of the efforts, VHA has utilized a pilot process in a small number of medical centers to help identify and resolve potential problems before releasing the efforts VHA-wide to all medical centers. For example, in the fall of 2012, VHA piloted the Electronic Funds Transfer (EFT) effort—a process for transferring travel reimbursement funds electronically into veterans' bank accounts—in medical centers in 2 of the 21 VISNs.[22] The EFT effort—along with VHA's Debit Card effort, a VHA-wide card that veterans can use to receive travel reimbursement electronically—implements a Department of the Treasury requirement for federal agencies to convert cash payments to electronic funds payments by March 1, 2013.[23] VHA has requested and received an extension from the Department of the Treasury on the implementation of electronic funds payments to allow VHA to simultaneously implement both the EFT and Debit Card efforts. VHA anticipates VHA-wide implementation of both efforts by December 31, 2013.

Some of VHA's efforts to improve the Beneficiary Travel Program have been developed in response to OIG and IPERA report findings as corrective actions to improve monitoring and oversight of the program and to decrease improper payments.*23F*[24] One such effort is the Facility Audit Tool—a tool used to audit facilities' past travel reimbursement transactions and operations through a more standardized process. Currently this tool is being used by VHA's Office of Finance to annually audit programs identified as susceptible to improper payments under IPERA. VHA officials told us that this tool may ultimately be used by VISNs to audit their facilities' past travel reimbursement transactions and operations, but did not have a time frame for its VHA-wide implementation.

Officials from the six medical centers we interviewed told us the new efforts that have been implemented generally improved or would improve some aspects of the Beneficiary Travel Program. For example, medical center officials reported that the implementation of the Dashboard had increased staff efficiency by decreasing the time needed to determine a veteran's eligibility, as well as increased the accuracy of payments, in line with VHA's goals for this program. In addition, officials said EFT would help improve oversight over the payment process. Compared to the process of paying veterans in cash, EFT provides an opportunity for the medical center staff—in this case the fiscal office staff—to review and audit travel payments before a reimbursement is issued to the veteran. Officials said these reviews could help medical centers reduce improper payments, and that EFT also improves security at medical centers because less cash is on hand for reimbursements.

Although medical center officials provided positive feedback on some of the efforts, they also identified implementation challenges. For example, medical center officials reported difficulty tracking EFT reimbursements, and that staff members had received many calls from veterans who were confused by only limited information transmitted with the EFT direct deposits. In addition, when veterans claimed reimbursements for multiple appointments, they did not know which appointment was associated with which electronic reimbursement payment, or which reimbursements were still pending. According to medical center officials, investigating pending reimbursements is time consuming and takes time away from staff members' reimbursement-processing responsibilities. Medical center officials also said the lack of information transmitted with the payments hinders acceptance of the EFT process in general, as veterans do not have complete confidence that their reimbursements are timely and accurate.

Lack of Internal Controls for Some Efforts May Hinder VHA's Ability to Improve the Beneficiary Travel Program

In our review of VHA's efforts to improve the Beneficiary Travel Program, we found that internal controls were lacking for some of the efforts. The implementation of internal controls is important for ensuring efforts achieve intended outcomes and minimizing operational problems. Without these internal controls in place, VHA cannot ensure that the efforts will meet its goals, such as improved management and oversight.

Plan for Evaluating Performance Indicators

VHA has not developed a plan for evaluating VHA-wide performance indicators for at least one of its efforts, the Beneficiary Travel Analytics Tool (Data Mining Tool), as would be consistent with internal control standards. According to established internal control standards, efforts to improve performance and efficiency should include the evaluation of appropriate performance indicators of the effort to gauge progress and inform decision making in resolving any problems. The Web-based Beneficiary Travel Analytics Tool, implemented March 31, 2013, generates travel reimbursement pattern reports—reports identifying questionable veteran reimbursement patterns that may indicate improper payments, such as frequently changing addresses on reimbursement claims, which may be done to inappropriately increase travel reimbursement amounts. According to VHA officials, medical centers are expected to use the reports generated by the tool to diagnose any problems in their own travel reimbursement processes and to implement appropriate corrective actions. VHA expects medical centers to submit documentation to VHA's Chief Business Office on any resulting corrective actions they have taken. Officials told us that they expect to review the corrective actions; however, as of May 14, 2013, they did not have a documented plan for evaluating travel reimbursement pattern data collected for all medical centers on an aggregated (VHA-wide) basis.

An appropriate evaluation plan consistent with internal controls would include documentation of the frequency of performance indicator evaluations, and an analysis plan for assessing either all, or a portion of, the travel reimbursement pattern data. Officials acknowledged the need to fully develop a plan to ensure that potential weaknesses are identified so that needed program improvements may be made. A plan for evaluating the data on a VHA-wide basis is necessary to ensure that the power of the Beneficiary Travel Analytics Tool is more fully realized.

Timely Guidance

VHA has not provided timely guidance to medical centers on its new EFT effort, as would be consistent with internal control standards. According to these standards, reliable and timely program information should be provided to management and others to ensure that responsibilities are being carried out and VHA goals are being met. Specifically, despite being aware of the March 1, 2013, Department of the Treasury deadline for implementation of EFT in December 2010, VHA did not provide guidance to medical centers on how to implement the effort until February 22, 2013. Had the guidance been provided earlier, it would have provided timely, key information to medical centers on the implementation of EFT, including the process that medical centers should be using to enroll veterans; the procedures for veterans to request a waiver from an electronic payment when they have an immediate need for a cash payment; and VHA's contingency plan for the travel reimbursement process due to its delay in providing policies for implementing EFT VHA-wide. By delaying the issuance of the guidance, VHA failed to ensure that all medical centers were provided with consistent and timely guidance, which, according to medical center officials we spoke with, led to frustration for medical centers, as well as confusion for veterans. For example, most medical centers in our review already had developed their own local procedures for enrolling veterans into EFT and processing payments before VHA's EFT pilot began; officials from some of the medical centers in our review expressed frustration that they would have to revise some of these processes when the VHA-wide effort was eventually implemented.

Effective Communication

VHA also did not provide a communication plan for sharing information on EFT with medical centers and veterans in a timely manner, as would have been consistent with internal control standards. Specifically, VHA did not share information on EFT with medical centers to help them inform veterans of the coming changes until February 22, 2013. VHA officials acknowledged they failed to develop a communications plan in a timely manner, and agreed that this is something they should have done to help ensure the success of the conversion to EFT. By not communicating this information in a timely manner, VHA did not ensure that medical centers had consistent and accurate information for informing veterans of the change in payment options, potentially affecting veterans' enrollment in EFT and their satisfaction with the new reimbursement process. Although officials from some medical centers we spoke with said they have developed their own materials for communicating with veterans about EFT, having communication materials come from VHA headquarters would have carried more weight with veterans and provided more consistency across all medical centers for this VHA-wide effort.

Plan for Monitoring Compliance

VHA has not developed a plan to ensure medical centers' compliance with the efforts or its existing policies, as would be consistent with internal control standards. For example, medical centers are required to use the Dashboard, and VHA officials told us that VHA-wide procedures for using the Dashboard will be included in the program's revised Standard Operating Procedures. However, VHA officials told us they do not have a plan in place to ensure that each medical center is using this new software. Without knowing whether all medical centers are using this required software or using it consistently, VHA cannot ensure that the Dashboard's goals, including standardizing the mileage calculations, will be realized.

Furthermore, because medical centers have the flexibility to develop local procedures for administering the Beneficiary Travel Program, it is important that VHA monitor local procedures to ensure they are consistent with VHA policies. For example, one medical center in our review automatically generates travel reimbursement payments to eligible veterans after each completed appointment. Thus, instead of applying for reimbursement after each medical center appointment, eligible veterans who have a signature on record can simply leave the medical center after their appointment and receive their reimbursement payment by mail or direct deposit. Acknowledging that this automatic payment procedure is different from other medical centers, medical center officials said it has greatly increased the efficiency of their management of the Beneficiary Travel Program and has received positive feedback from veterans and staff. Monitoring compliance with program policies, especially due to differences in local procedures, is an important internal control for ensuring that program goals are being met.

Use Information to Improve Efficiency

VHA does not routinely collect information on medical centers' local procedures for administering the Beneficiary Travel Program to identify and share best practices. According to federal internal control standards, identifying and sharing best practices is an essential part of ensuring an effective and efficient use of resources. For example, officials at one of the medical centers we interviewed said that installing drop boxes at multiple locations around their facility was a simple and efficient way to make the process more convenient for veterans, shorten lines at the Beneficiary Travel Office, and improve staff productivity. Some medical center officials described sharing best practices on an ad hoc basis with colleagues in other medical centers, and said that learning from others' experiences is valuable to their administration of the Beneficiary Travel Program. Although VHA officials described one instance of evaluating a software program for national use that was developed and implemented at one medical center, they have not regularly solicited information on best practices; instead, they have relied on medical center and VISN officials to identify and share information. A more systematic identification and sharing of best practices would enhance medical centers' access to the same information in order to minimize problems and maximize efficiencies within the Beneficiary Travel Program.

CONCLUSION

For more than 70 years, VHA's Beneficiary Travel Program has reimbursed eligible veterans for travel expenses associated with medical appointments. In the past 5 years, spending under the program has more than doubled, from about $370 million in fiscal year 2008 to about $860 million in fiscal year 2012. This increase is of particular note, as travel reimbursements come out of the same VA medical center funds used for patient care. At the same time spending is increasing, concerns have been raised about the accuracy of payments and VHA's management and oversight of the program.

In response to these concerns, VHA has taken steps to improve its process for reimbursing veterans for travel expenses by developing multiple efforts aimed at enhancing management and oversight of the program. However, some of the efforts lack key internal controls that would help VHA better manage and oversee its program. Specifically, VHA has not developed a plan for evaluating VHA-wide performance indicators for the Beneficiary Travel Analytics Tool; provided timely guidance and effective communication tools to medical centers for EFT; ensured compliance with Dashboard and other efforts; and routinely collected information on medical centers' local procedures to identify and share best practices. Without appropriate management and oversight, VHA is unable to ensure that its Beneficiary Travel Program—which is on track to spend nearly $1 billion dollars annually in the next few years—is operating effectively, including assurances that payments made through the program are appropriate.

Recommendation for Executive Action

To improve the management and oversight of the Beneficiary Travel Program, we recommend that the Secretary of Veterans Affairs direct the Under Secretary for Health to ensure appropriate internal controls have been identified and applied in the development and implementation of all of VHA's efforts aimed at improving the program, including

- developing and implementing a plan to evaluate performance indicators for the Beneficiary Travel Analytics Tool,
- providing timely guidance and effective communication tools to medical centers as VHA completes its implementation of EFT,
- ensuring medical centers' compliance with Dashboard and other improvement efforts, and
- routinely collecting information to identify and share best practices across medical centers.

Agency Comments and Our Evaluation

We provided a draft of this report to VA for comment. VA generally agreed with our conclusions and concurred with our recommendation. VA identified the activities that VHA would undertake to ensure appropriate internal controls have been identified and applied related to the four specific efforts we noted: performance indicators for the Beneficiary Travel Analytics Tool, guidance and communication to medical centers regarding EFT, compliance with Dashboard and other improvement efforts, and identification and sharing of best practices across medical centers. VA did not directly address ensuring that appropriate internal controls are identified and applied in the development and implementation of all efforts aimed at improving the program. We continue to emphasize the importance of internal controls to the success of VHA's efforts. VA also provided technical comments, which we have incorporated as appropriate.

Debra A. Draper
Director, Health Care

Appendix I: Examples of VA Medical Center Procedures for Administering the Beneficiary Travel Program

Travel reimbursement policy requirement	Example of medical center procedurea	Medical center rationale
Veteran applies for travel reimbursement	Veteran submits claim for reimbursement at medical center travel office.	Allows medical center to provide same-day claim review, and in some cases reimbursement.
	Veteran puts claim for reimbursement in a designated drop box.	Helps reduce the lines at the medical center's travel office, is more convenient for veterans, andallows medical center staff more time to review the claim.
Medical center reviews eligibility and determines reimbursement amount	Medical center staff check veteran's name against photo identification for each claim submitted in person.	Helps improve accuracy and reduce improper payments by ensuring the appropriate person isreimbursed.
	Medical center staff check veteran's address and name against information maintained in VA's data system for claims not submitted in person, such as for a veteran using a drop box.	Helps improve accuracy and reduce improper payments by ensuring correct addresses are used, and VA has consistent information about the veteran in its data system.

Appendix I: (Continued)

Travel reimbursement policy requirement	Example of medical center procedurea	Medical center rationale
Medical center reimburses veteran	Reimbursement provided primarily through cash.b	Allows for same-day reimbursement.
	Reimbursement provided primarily through a check.b	Limits cash payments, which may shorten veterans' time waiting at the medical center's travel office,
		and reduces security and other risks associated with having large amounts of cash on-hand at medical centers. Also, helps ensure VHA has valid addresses for veterans for calculating travel reimbursements, because these addressesare where the checks are mailed.
	Reimbursement provided primarily through direct deposit or a debit card.	Limits cash payments, which may shorten veterans' time waiting at the medical center's travel office, and reduces security and other risks associated with having large amounts of cash on-hand at medical centers. Also, turn-around time for veterans' receipt of direct deposit or debit card reimbursements is generally shorter than for check reimbursements.

Source: VHA and the VA medical centers included in our review.

[a] VA medical centers may employ one or more of these procedures; for example, a medical center may allow veterans to apply for travel reimbursement by submitting a claim at the travel office, putting a claim in a designated drop box, or both.

[b] This procedure will change with full implementation of the Electronic Funds Transfer and Debit Card efforts.

End Notes

[1] See Department of Veterans Affairs, Office of Inspector General, *Veterans Health Administration: Audit of the Beneficiary Travel Program*, 11-00336-292 (Washington, D.C.: Feb. 6, 2013).

[2] See Department of Veterans Affairs, *Department of Veterans Affairs (VA) 2012 Performance and Accountability Report* (Washington, D.C.: Nov. 15, 2012).

[3] VA assigns each medical center a complexity score derived from multiple variables to measure facility complexity arrayed along four categories, namely patient population served, clinical services offered, education and research complexity, and administrative complexity.

[4] GAO, *Results-Oriented Government: Practices That Can Help Enhance and Sustain Collaboration among Federal Agencies*, GAO-06-15 (Washington, D.C.: Oct. 21, 2005); *Managing for Results: Key Considerations for Implementing Interagency Collaborative Mechanisms*, GAO-12-1022 (Washington, D.C.: Sept. 27, 2012); *Executive Guide: Effectively Implementing the Government Performance and Results Act*, GAO/GGD-96-118 (Washington, D.C.: June 1996); *Agencies' Strategic Plans Under GPRA: Key Questions to Facilitate Congressional Review*, GAO/GGD-10.1.16 (Washington, D.C.: May 1997); *Standards for Internal Control in the Federal Government*, GAO/AIMD-00-21.3.1 (Washington, D.C.: November 1999).

[5] See 38 U.S.C. § 111. Under the statute, VA is authorized but not required to reimburse travel expenses for veterans. However, if VA exercises its authority to reimburse travel expenses, VA must pay travel expenses for specified categories of veterans and may reimburse travel expenses for any other veterans receiving medical care in accordance with regulations. In general, VA's regulations for the Beneficiary Travel Program currently designate as eligible the categories of veterans specifically mentioned in 38 U.S.C. § 111. Persons specifically mentioned in other VA statutes as eligible for payment for beneficiary travel are also eligible, such as certain family members of veterans. See 38 C.F.R. § 70.10. Veterans traveling for certain emergency situations may be eligible for travel reimbursement under separate authority. See 38 U.S.C. § 1725; 38 C.F.R. §§ 17.1000– 17.1008.

[6] For calendar year 2013, the annual income rate for a veteran with no dependents was $12,465.

[7] Compensation and pension exams are physical exams provided to veterans applying for service-connected disability compensation to determine the degree of their disability.

[8] Eligible veterans who do not have scheduled appointments but do receive care from VA are only reimbursed for travel costs associated with their return trip.

[9] Except in some circumstances, such as severe financial hardship, an amount of $3 per one-way trip (with a monthly maximum of $18) is required by law to be deducted from beneficiary travel payments. See 38 U.S.C. § 111(c).

[10] The committees identified $125 million in VA's 2008 Medical Services appropriation and $133 million in VA's 2009 Medical Services appropriation to fund the increases in travel reimbursement rates. See House Comm. on Appropriations, 110th Cong., Committee Print on H.R. 2764 / Public Law 110-161, Division I—Military Construction and Veterans Affairs and Related Agencies Appropriations Act, 2008, at 1957 (2007), accompanying the Consolidated Appropriations Act, 2008 (Pub. L. No. 110-161, 121 Stat. 1844 (2007)); 73 Fed. Reg. 6291 (Feb. 1, 2008); House Comm. on Appropriations, 110th Cong., Committee Print on H.R. 2638 / Public Law 110-329, Division E—Military Construction and Veterans Affairs and Related Agencies Appropriations Act, 2009, at 750-51 (2008), accompanying the Consolidated Security, Disaster Assistance, and Continuing Appropriations Act, 2009 (Pub. L. No. 110-329, 122 Stat. 3574 (2008)); 73 Fed. Reg. 68,498 (Nov. 18, 2008).

[11] According to VHA, the number of veterans claiming mileage reimbursement in fiscal year 2008 is an estimate based on limited national data.

[12] See Veterans Health Administration, *VHA Beneficiary Travel*, VHA Handbook 1601B.05 (July 21, 2010).

[13] See Department of Veterans Affairs, *VA Financial Policies and Procedures*, vol. VIII (September 2010) and Veterans Health Administration, *VHA Finance Quality Assurance Reviews*, VHA Handbook 1730.02 (Washington, D.C.: Mar. 16, 2011).

[14] Each of VA's 21 VISNs is responsible for managing and overseeing medical centers within a defined geographic area.

[15] Eligibility for reimbursement is assessed by reviewing the veteran's eligibility for the program (such as service-connected disability rating or income level) and the veteran's record to ensure an appointment was completed.

[16] Veterans can be reimbursed for travel to VA facilities, including medical centers and community-based outpatient clinics, or to non-VA facilities if VA determines that it is necessary to obtain care at a non-VA facility.

[17] See Department of Veterans Affairs, Office of Inspector General, *Veterans Health Administration: Audit of the Beneficiary Travel Program.*

[18] According to the report, the VA OIG could not determine the reason for $42.5 million in unexplained payments due to the lack of an adequate audit trail and system limitations. The VA OIG found that the remaining $46.5 million of this discrepancy was due to miscoded expenses.

[19] Pub. L. No. 111-204, 124 Stat. 2224 (2010).

[20] See Department of Veterans Affairs, *Department of Veterans Affairs (VA) 2012 Performance and Accountability Report.*

[21] See Department of Veterans Affairs, Office of Inspector General, *Department of Veterans Affairs: Review of VA's Compliance with the Improper Payments Elimination and Recovery Act for FY 2012*, 12-04241-138 (Washington, D.C.: Mar. 15, 2013).

[22] These VISNs were selected because several of their medical centers volunteered to work with VHA on the EFT effort, and were familiar with the effort. VHA officials told us that they did not use set criteria to select the pilot sites for the EFT effort, and did not see a downside of selecting pilot sites based on medical centers' willingness to participate. GAO has reported previously on pilot implementation within VA. See GAO, *VA Dialysis Pilot: Increased Attention to Planning, Implementation, and Performance Measurement Needed to Help Achieve Goals,* GAO-12-584 (Washington, D.C.: May 23, 2012).

[23] See 75 Fed. Reg. 80,315 (Dec. 22, 2010).

[24] See Department of Veterans Affairs, *2012 Performance and Accountability Report.*

In: Veterans
Editor: Timothy C. Roberts

ISBN: 978-1-63321-722-5

Chapter 5

PATRIOT EXPRESS: SBA SHOULD EVALUATE THE PROGRAM AND ENHANCE ELIGIBILITY CONTROLS*

United States Government Accountability Office

WHY GAO DID THIS STUDY

In June 2007, SBA established the Patriot Express Pilot Loan Program within its 7(a) loan guarantee program to provide small businesses owned and operated by veterans and other eligible members of the military community access to capital. Through Patriot Express, SBA guarantees individual small business loans that lenders originate. GAO was asked to evaluate the program. This report examines (1) trends in the volume and performance of Patriot Express and related SBA loan programs; (2) the effect of the program on eligible members of the military community; and (3) SBA internal controls to ensure that only eligible borrowers participate. GAO analyzed data on performance and costs of Patriot Express and other similar SBA loan programs from 2007 through 2012; interviewed selected borrowers, lenders, and veteran service organizations; and reviewed SBA internal control guidance on borrower eligibility.

---

* This is an edited, reformatted and augmented version of a United States Government Accountability Office publication, No. GAO-13-727, dated September 2013.

WHAT GAO RECOMMENDS

SBA should design and implement an evaluation plan to assess how well the Patriot Express pilot is achieving program objectives and goals and serving the needs of veterans and eligible borrowers. Going forward, SBA should include an evaluation plan as part of any pilot programs initiated under its own authority and consider the results of the evaluation when deciding whether to extend or terminate a pilot. Further, SBA should enhance internal controls over borrower eligibility requirements. SBA said that it will consider the findings from this report as it reviewed the extension of the Patriot Express pilot.

WHAT GAO FOUND

Patriot Express loans valued at about $703 million have defaulted at a higher rate than loans under the Small Business Administration's (SBA) other related loan guarantee programs, and losses for Patriot Express have exceeded its income. With the exception of loans approved in 2007, Patriot Express loans have defaulted at a higher rate than loans made under SBA's main 7(a) program or loans made under SBA's streamlined loan guarantee program (SBA Express). The Patriot Express program's overall default rate was significantly higher for smaller loans, especially for loans below $25,000 (20 percent). Additionally, one lender accounted for more than 64 percent of these smaller loans and experienced higher default rates than the remaining lenders. From 2007 through 2012, losses in the Patriot Express program exceeded income by $31.1 million (not accounting for future fee revenues or funds recovered from loans in default).

Selected borrowers and lenders, as well as veteran service organizations GAO met with, reported various benefits and challenges to the Patriot Express program, but SBA has yet to evaluate the effect of this pilot program on eligible members of the military community. Borrowers and lenders said that some benefits of the program were that it helped veterans expand their businesses and allowed them to take advantage of the streamlined application process. Some challenges they identified were low awareness of the program and which lenders participated in the program. In 2010, SBA extended the Patriot Express pilot through 2013 to allow time to evaluate the effect of the program. To date, SBA has not evaluated the program or established a plan of what it intends to do to evaluate it. SBA officials told us that they focused their resources on evaluating 7(a) loans because there are many more of them and, therefore, they pose a greater risk to SBA than Patriot Express loans. In addition to Patriot Express, SBA has previously initiated other pilot programs that it has not evaluated. GAO has found that a program evaluation gives an agency the opportunity to refine program design, assess if program operations have resulted in the desired benefits, and, for pilots, determine whether to make the programs permanent. Without conducting evaluations of pilot programs, SBA lacks the information needed to assess their performance and their effects on eligible participants and decide whether to extend these programs, including Patriot Express.

SBA's internal controls over lenders may not provide reasonable assurance that Patriot Express loans are only made to eligible members of the military community and that only these members benefit from loan proceeds. SBA relies on lenders to verify and document borrower eligibility at the time of loan approval. One of SBA's controls over lenders' compliance with eligibility requirements consists of sampling loan files during examinations of the 7(a) program, but few Patriot Express loans are reviewed. Patriot Express is intended to assist only eligible members of the military community and SBA officials told us that they expect borrowers to maintain eligibility after the loan is disbursed. But SBA has not developed procedures for lenders to provide reasonable assurance that borrowers maintain this eligibility. Federal internal control standards and GAO's fraud-prevention framework indicate that ongoing monitoring is an important component of an effective internal control system. Without enhanced internal controls, particularly with respect to monitoring of borrowers, SBA lacks assurance that Patriot Express loans are serving only eligible borrowers.

ABBREVIATIONS

ARRA	American Recovery and Reinvestment Act of 2009
EBV	Entrepreneurship Bootcamp for Veterans with Disabilities
FICO	Fair Isaac Corporation
GPRA	Government Performance and Results Act of 1993
GPRAMA	GPRA Modernization Act of 2010
NAGGL	National Association of Government Guaranteed Lenders
OEG	Operation Endure and Grow
OIG	Office of Inspector General

OMB	Office of Management and Budget
OVBD	Office of Veterans Business Development
PLP	Preferred Lenders Program
SBA	Small Business Administration
SBDC	Small Business Development Centers
SBLC	small business lending company
SBPS	Small Business Portfolio Solutions
SLA	Small Loan Advantage
VBOC	Veteran Business Outreach Centers
VET	Veteran Entrepreneurship Task Force
V-WISE	Veteran Women Igniting the Spirit of Entrepreneurship
WBC	Women's Business Centers

September 12, 2013

The Honorable Mary L. Landrieu
Chair
Committee on Small Business and Entrepreneurship
United States Senate

The Honorable Mark Pryor
United States Senate

Since the Small Business Administration (SBA) established the Patriot Express Pilot Loan Initiative to provide veterans and other eligible members of the military community access to capital to establish or expand small businesses in June 2007, lenders have made about $703 million in Patriot Express loans. The Patriot Express program, a pilot loan initiative under SBA's 7(a) loan guarantee program, allows lenders to use their own underwriting criteria and loan documents to expedite loan decisions for eligible borrowers.[1] Patriot Express borrowers must have a business that is owned and controlled (51 percent or more) by veterans or other eligible members of the military community.[2] The Patriot Express program provides the same loan guarantee to SBA-approved lenders as the 7(a) program and is available on loan amounts up to $500,000, and the loan proceeds can be used for the same purposes as the 7(a) loan proceeds.[3] SBA announced on December 14, 2010, that it would continue to operate the Patriot Express program through December 31, 2013.

You asked us to evaluate the program. This report examines (1) trends in the Patriot Express program and related SBA guarantee programs, including performance of these loans, and what is known about the costs of the Patriot Express program, (2) the benefits and challenges of the Patriot Express program for members of the military community eligible to participate as well as training and counseling opportunities available to them, and (3) what internal controls SBA has in place to ensure that the Patriot Express program is available only to eligible members of the military community.

To describe how Patriot Express loans approved from 2007 through 2012 have performed, we obtained SBA loan-level data from the second quarter of 2007 through the fourth quarter of 2012 for the Patriot Express program and analyzed them for various performance measures, including default rates.[4] To compare the performance of Patriot Express loans to those of SBA's 7(a) and SBA Express programs, we obtained and analyzed SBA loan-level data for loans approved in these programs from 2007 through 2012 and compared default rates to those of the Patriot Express program.[5] To describe what is known about the costs of the Patriot Express program from 2007 through 2012, we obtained and analyzed SBA cash-flow data on SBA purchases of defaulted loans, as well as data on fees generated by the program and recovery rates of defaulted loans. To assess data reliability, we interviewed SBA representatives about how they collected data and helped ensure data integrity, and we reviewed internal agency procedures for ensuring data reliability. In addition, we conducted reasonableness checks on the data to identify any missing, erroneous, or outlying figures. We determined that the data were sufficiently reliable for our purposes.

To assess the effect of the Patriot Express program on members of the military community eligible to participate in the program, we selected and interviewed a nongeneralizable, stratified random sample of 24 Patriot Express loan recipients. We conducted interviews with these recipients to inquire how the Patriot Express loan affected their businesses and to obtain their views on how the program could be improved. To obtain the perspectives of veteran entrepreneurs who were aware of the Patriot Express program and appeared to meet the eligibility requirements for a Patriot Express loan but instead obtained a 7(a) loan, we selected and interviewed a nongeneralizable stratified random sample of four veteran entrepreneurs who obtained a 7(a) loan. We conducted interviews with these recipients to inquire about their experiences with the 7(a) loan and obtain their views on the Patriot Express program. We also interviewed SBA officials and selected lenders and veteran service organizations. To describe other ways in which veteran entrepreneurs accessed capital, as part of our interviews of Patriot Express and 7(a) loan recipients, we inquired about other ways in which they had gained access to capital. For this purpose, we also interviewed selected lenders and veteran service organizations. To describe the training and counseling efforts SBA has in place for veteran entrepreneurs, we obtained and reviewed SBA annual reports and other documents related to training and counseling efforts. We also interviewed SBA officials responsible for these efforts. To obtain the perspectives of veteran entrepreneurs on the effectiveness of SBA's training and counseling efforts, we interviewed veteran service organizations and selected Patriot Express and 7(a) loan recipients.

To evaluate SBA's internal controls related to ensuring that the Patriot Express program is available only to members of the military community eligible to participate in the program, we reviewed SBA's standard operating procedures related to oversight of lenders, federal internal control standards, and GAO's fraud-prevention framework. We interviewed officials from the Office of Credit Risk Management to inquire about SBA's oversight of its lenders, including how it addresses the program's vulnerability to fraud and abuse. To determine how SBA examiners review lenders for compliance with eligibility requirements for the Patriot Express program, we reviewed examination reports for the top 10 Patriot Express lenders (based on the number of loans made) from 2007 through 2012. Finally, to help assess the extent to which the Patriot Express program could be susceptible to fraud and abuse, we reviewed SBA's internal control standards related to ensuring that Patriot Express loans were made to eligible members of the military community. We also interviewed officials from SBA's Office of Credit Risk Management and Office of Inspector General to learn about scenarios under which the Patriot Express program could be susceptible to fraud and abuse.

We conducted this performance audit from November 2012 to September 2013 in accordance with generally accepted government auditing standards. Those standards require that we plan and perform the audit to obtain sufficient, appropriate evidence to provide a reasonable basis for our findings and conclusions based on our audit objectives. We believe that the evidence obtained provides a reasonable basis for our findings and conclusions based on our audit objectives. Appendix I contains additional information on our scope and methodology.

BACKGROUND

SBA was created in 1953 to assist and protect the interests of small businesses, in part by addressing constraints in the supply of credit for these firms. The 7(a) program, named after the section of the Small Business Act that authorized it, is SBA's largest business loan program.[6] The program is intended to serve creditworthy small business borrowers who cannot obtain credit through a conventional lender at reasonable terms and do not have the personal resources to provide financing themselves. Under the 7(a) program, SBA guarantees loans made by commercial lenders to small businesses for working capital and other general business purposes.[7] These lenders are mostly banks, but some are nondepository lenders, including small business lending companies (SBLC).[8] The guarantee assures the lender that if a borrower defaults on a loan, SBA will purchase the loan and the lender will receive an agreed-upon portion (generally between 50 percent and 85 percent) of the outstanding balance. For a majority of 7(a) loans, SBA relies on lenders with delegated authority to process and service 7(a) loans and to ensure that borrowers meet the program's eligibility requirements. To be eligible for the 7(a) program, a business must be an operating for-profit small firm (according to SBA's size standards) located in the United States and meet the "credit elsewhere" requirement, including the personal resources test.[9]

Within the 7(a) program, there are several delivery methods—including regular 7(a), the Preferred Lenders Program (PLP), and SBA Express. Under the regular (nondelegated) 7(a) programs, SBA makes the loan approval decision, including the credit determination. Under PLP and SBA Express, SBA delegates to the lender the authority to make loan approval decisions, including credit determinations, without prior review by SBA. The maximum loan amount under the SBA Express program is $350,000 (as opposed to $5 million for 7(a) loans). This program allows lenders to utilize, to the maximum extent possible, their respective loan analyses, procedures, and documentation. In return for the expanded authority and autonomy provided by the program, SBA Express lenders agree to accept a maximum SBA guarantee of 50 percent. Regular (nondelegated) 7(a) loans and delegated 7(a) loans made by PLP lenders generally have a maximum guarantee of 75 or 85 percent, depending on the loan amount.[10]

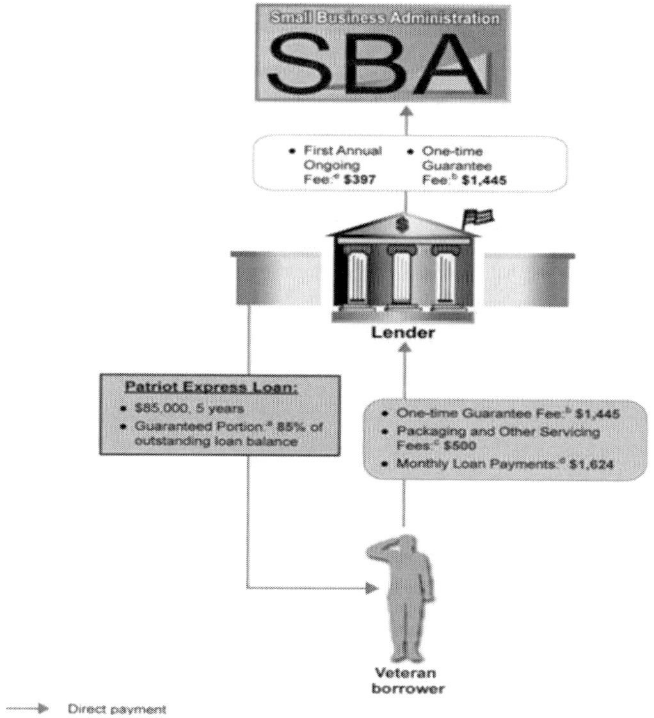

Source: SBA./

[a] The guaranteed portion is the percentage of the loan balance that SBA agrees to cover if the borrower defaults on the loan.

[b]The lender is required to pay SBA a one-time guarantee fee that is a percentage of the guaranteed portion. This fee can be passed on to the borrower and is paid within 90 days of loan approval. For this example, the guarantee fee was 2 percent of the guaranteed amount and was passed on to the borrower.

[c]"Packaging services" include assisting the applicant with completing the application, such as preparing a business plan and cash-flow projections. "Other services" include consulting fees related to the need for financing and the type of financing, as well as broker fees or referral fees. These fees are optional and SBA guidelines state that the fees must be reasonable and customary for the services actually performed and must be consistent with those charged on the lender's similarly-sized, non-SBA-guaranteed loans.

[d] For this example, the payment was calculated by assuming the prime interest rate was 3.25 percent for an $85,000 Patriot Express loan with a term of 60 months (5 years).

[e] The lender is required to pay SBA an annual ongoing fee, and the amount is not to exceed 0.55 percent. Because the fee is applied to the outstanding balance of the guaranteed portion of the loan, the amount of this fee will change every year. This fee cannot be passed onto the borrower.

Figure 1. Patriot Express Loan Origination Process and Costs.

In June 2007, under its own authority, SBA established the Patriot Express pilot loan program, which has features that are similar to those of the SBA Express and other 7(a) loan programs. Like the SBA Express program, the Patriot Express program allows lenders to use their own loan analyses and documents to expedite loan decisions for eligible borrowers. However, the Patriot Express has a different guarantee rate than SBA Express and different eligibility requirements. Patriot Express borrowers must have a business that is owned and controlled (51 percent or more) by the following members of the military community:

- veterans (other than dishonorably discharged),
- service-disabled veterans,
- active duty military participating in the military's Transition Assistance Program,
- reservists or National Guard members,
- spouse of any of these groups,
- a widowed spouse of a service member who died while in service, or
- a widowed spouse of a veteran who died of a service-connected disability.

Like the 7(a) program, the Patriot Express program provides the same loan guarantee to SBA-approved lenders on loan amounts up to $500,000, and the loan proceeds can be used for the same purposes. SBA initially intended to operate the Patriot Express pilot for about 3 years, after which it would evaluate the program. However, SBA announced on December 14, 2010, that it would continue to operate the program for at least 3 more years to allow the agency to evaluate the program. SBA determined that it was premature to assess the results of the pilot because most of the loans were made in the previous 2 years and there had not been enough time to measure their performance. Appendix II compares the key features of the Patriot Express program to those of the regular 7(a) and SBA Express programs. Figure 1 depicts the Patriot Express loan process, including the roles played by the lender and SBA in the transaction and the fees associated with the loans.

A lender may request that SBA honor its guarantee by purchasing the loan if a borrower is in default on an SBA loan for more than 60 calendar days and if the borrower is unable to cure the loan after working with the lender. The lender is required by regulation to liquidate all business personal property collateral before demanding that SBA honor the guarantee. 11 As shown in figure 2, after the lender has liquidated all business personal property collateral, it submits the purchase request to one of SBA's Office of Financial Program Operation's centers, which processes loan guarantee requests. The center reviews the lender's package to determine if it has complied with SBA rules and regulations. If SBA finds that the lender has complied with the agency's rules and regulations and conducted proper due diligence when originating the loan, SBA honors the guarantee and pays the lender the guaranteed portion of the outstanding loan amount.

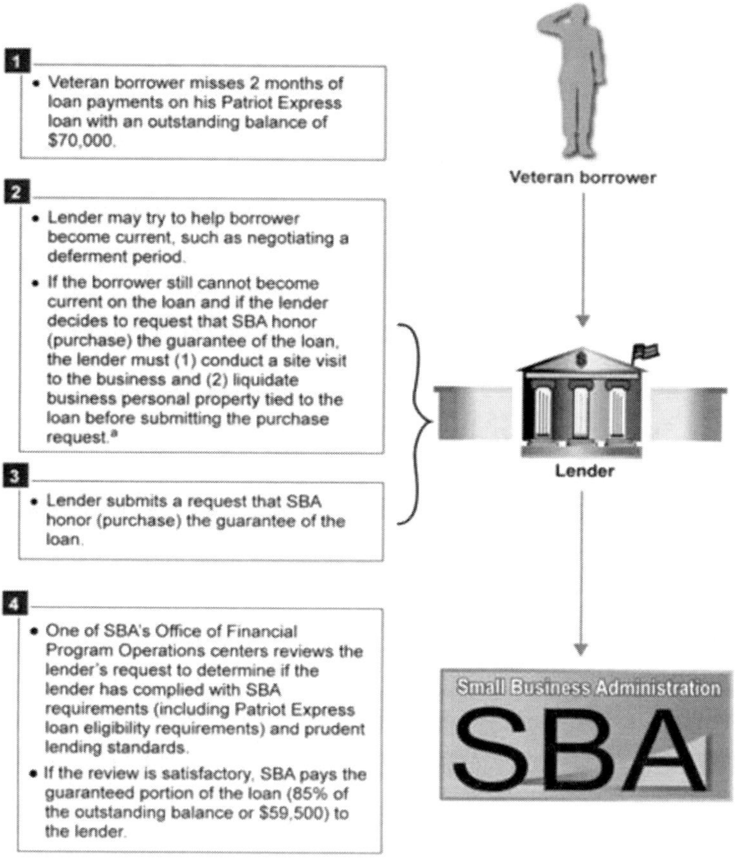

Source: SBA.

[a]According to SBA, for loans approved on or after May 14, 2007, a lender may demand in writing that SBA honor its guarantee if the borrower is in default on any installment for more than 60 calendar days and the default has not been cured, provided all business personal property securing the defaulted SBA loan has been liquidated.

Figure 2. Purchase Process for Patriot Express Loan.

According to SBA officials, the 7(a) program—including its subprograms, such as SBA Express and Patriot Express—is projected to be a "zero subsidy" program in fiscal year 2014, meaning that the program does not require annual appropriations of budget authority for new loan guarantees.[12] To offset some of the costs of the program, such as the costs of purchasing defaulted loans, SBA assesses lenders two fees on each 7(a) loan, including Patriot Express loans. The guarantee fee must be paid by the lender at the time of application for the guarantee or within 90 days of the loan being approved, depending upon the loan term. This fee is based on the amount of the loan and the level of the guarantee, and lenders can pass the fee on to the borrower. The ongoing servicing fee must be paid annually by the lender and is based on the outstanding balance of the guaranteed portion of the loan.

SBA's Office of Credit Risk Management is responsible for overseeing 7(a) lenders, including those with delegated authority. SBA created this office in fiscal year 1999 to better ensure consistent and appropriate supervision of SBA's lending partners. [13] The office is responsible for managing all activities regarding lender oversight, including lender risk ratings and lender activities, and preparing written reports based on such oversight.

Patriot Express Loans Default at a Higher Rate Than Other SBA Loans, and Costs Have Exceeded Overall Program Income Since 2007

From 2007 through 2012, SBA made 8,511 Patriot Express loans. The majority of these loans were valued below $150,000, and close to half were uncollateralized loans valued below $25,000. Although Patriot Express loans represent a fraction of SBA's larger loan portfolio and are concentrated among 11 lenders, these loans have defaulted at higher rates compared to similar SBA loans made in the same time frame. At the current default and recovery rates, the costs of the Patriot Express program will likely continue to exceed overall program income.

Lenders Have Made 8,511 Patriot Express Loans Since 2007

From the start of the program through the fourth quarter of 2012, lenders made a total of 8,511 Patriot Express loans. Taken together, these loans are valued at $702,753,406, with an average of about $82,570 per loan. As shown in figure 3, after a rapid expansion in the first 2 years of the program from 2007 through 2009, the number of Patriot Express loans declined from 2,176 approved in 2009 to 869 approved in 2012. Similarly, the total loan amounts of Patriot Express loans approved each year grew from approximately $67 million in 2007 to over $150 million in 2008 and 2009, but have since decreased. The higher numbers of Patriot Express loans approved in 2009 and 2010 may be attributable, in part, to the American Recovery and Reinvestment Act of 2009 (ARRA)[14] and subsequent legislation, which provided funding to temporarily subsidize the overall 7(a) guarantee program's fees and to increase the maximum loan guarantee percentage from 75 or 85 percent to 90 percent, with the exception of loans approved under the SBA Express 7(a) subprogram.[15] With a 5 to 15 percent increase in the maximum allowed guarantee through ARRA, lenders had a greater incentive to approve SBA loans in general (including Patriot Express loans), knowing that SBA would guarantee a higher percentage of the loan. Figure 3 also shows that average loan amounts have varied over the years. For loans approved in 2007, the average loan amount was for about $100,000, decreasing to about $70,000 in 2009, and increasing since then to just under $100,000 in 2012.

Based on our analysis of SBA data from 2007 through 2012, about 67 percent of borrowers used Patriot Express loans for working capital, and about half of these loans funded businesses that were either new or had been in existence for less than 2 years. The majority of Patriot Express loans approved since the program's inception are valued at 30 percent of the maximum loan limit, and about half are small enough that they do not require collateral. Although SBA allows Patriot Express loans of up to $500,000, about 84.2 percent of the loans made since 2007 (7,166) were below $150,000. Further, 41.2 percent of Patriot Express loans (3,509) were $25,000 or less. More than 64 percent of loans up to $25,000 were provided by one lender and this lender accounted for about 26 percent of total loans in the program. This lender primarily provided loans between $5,000 and $25,000, and its average Patriot Express loan made from 2008 through 2012 was $9,759. As noted previously, loans under the Patriot Express program below $25,000 do not require collateral.

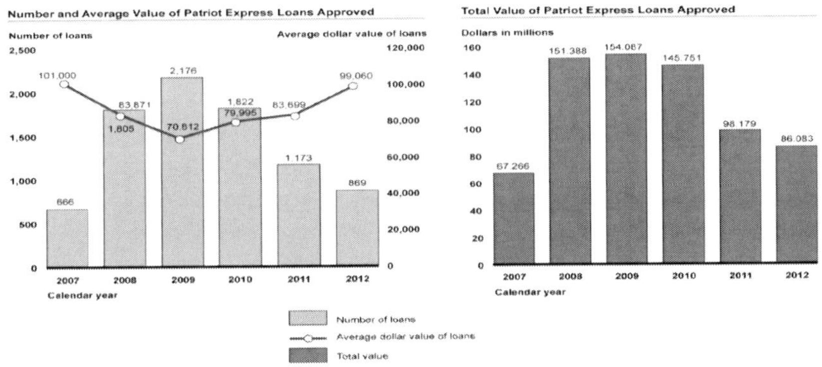

Source: GAO analysis of SBA data.

Figure 3. Number, Average Value, and Total Value of Patriot Express Loans Approved, 2007-2012.

Table 1. Top 11 and Remaining Lenders for Patriot Express Based on Loans Approved, 2007-2012

	Average loan amount	Number of loans	Percentage of total number of loans approved	Total amount approved	Percentage of total amount approved
Lender 1	$9,759	2,248	26.41%	$21,937,500	3.12%
Next 10 lenders	79,154	2,169	25.48	171,684,100	24.43
Remaining lenders (782)	124,360	4,094	48.10	509,131,806	72.45
Total		**8,511**		**$702,753,406**	

Source: GAO analysis of SBA data.

Note: Total percentage may not equal 100% due to rounding.

The Patriot Express program is highly concentrated in a small number of lenders. For example, the top 11 lenders (in terms of number of loans made) represent 52 percent of the Patriot Express loans made since the program's inception (see table 1). These top 11 lenders accounted for 27.55 percent of the total amount approved for the Patriot Express program. This concentration is explained, in part, by one lender that focuses on providing low-dollar loans to veteran-owned businesses and represents about 26 percent of the Patriot Express program, as discussed previously. In contrast, the remaining 782 lenders that participate in Patriot Express have approved fewer loans. For example, 246 of these 782 lenders approved one loan each since the program began in 2007.

The Patriot Express Program Is Much Smaller Than the SBA Express or 7(a) Programs

As previously discussed, in addition to reviewing data on the Patriot Express program from 2007 through 2012, we also reviewed similar data from two other SBA loan programs: the SBA Express program and SBA's 7(a) program. SBA Express and the 7(a) program, which are not limited to borrowers in the military community, are significantly larger than the Patriot Express program. Since 2007, the SBA Express program has surpassed Patriot Express in total number of loans (156,280) and total amount ($10.9 billion) approved, but the average loan amounts for Patriot Express are larger than those for SBA Express. SBA Express has seen a decline in loan numbers and amounts approved since 2007 (see fig. 4). The number of SBA Express loans approved each year declined by about 50 percent from 2007 through 2008, and that number has remained at lower levels since then. SBA officials told us that part of the decline from 2007 through 2008 may have been due to the economic downturn, which prompted lenders to cut back on these loans. Figure 4 also shows the total value of SBA Express loans peaked in 2007 ($2.9 billion) but then decreased by nearly half in 2008 ($1.7 billion). The total value of SBA Express loans then increased to about $2 billion in 2011 before falling to about $1.3 billion in 2012.

The 7(a) program is also significantly larger than the Patriot Express program in all measures, including total numbers of loans approved, average loan amounts, and total loan amounts approved. Annually, the total numbers of 7(a) loans approved have declined since peaking in 2010 at 19,131, while the average loan amount for 7(a) approvals annually has steadily increased from about $470,784 in 2007 to $716,489 in 2012 (see fig. 5). The total value of 7(a) loans approved within each year has been relatively steady, as shown in figure 5, ranging from around $7.7 billion to around $9.2 billion, with the exception of 2010, when the total value of loans approved was around $12 billion.

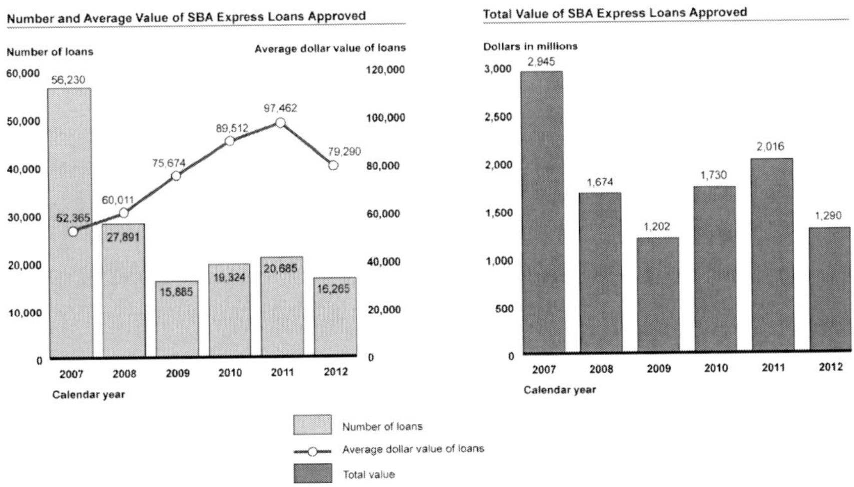

Source: GAO analysis of SBA data.

Figure 4. Number, Average Value, and Total Value of SBA Express Loans Approved, 2007-2012.

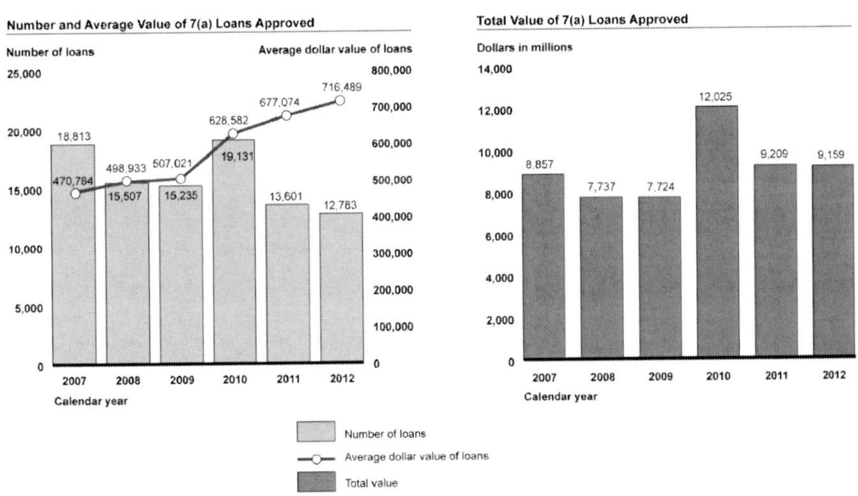

Source: GAO analysis of SBA data.

Figure 5. Number, Average Value, and Total Value of 7(a) Loans Approved, 2007-2012.

Table 2. Average Loan Amounts, Number of Loans, and Total Dollar Amount of Loans for the Patriot Express, SBA Express, and 7(a) Programs, June 2007-2012

	Average loan amount	Number of loans	Percentage of total number of loans approved	Total dollar amount	Percentage of total amount approved
Patriot Express	$82,570	8,511	3.76%	$702,753,406	1.15%
SBA Express	73,194	130,385	57.67	9,543,343,424	15.57
7(a)	585,431	87,192	38.57	51,044,912,552	83.28
Total		**226,088**		**$61,291,009,382**	

Source: GAO analysis of SBA data.

Table 2 shows the total numbers of loans, total dollar values, and average loan amounts approved for Patriot Express, SBA Express, and 7(a) from June 2007 through 2012.

Additionally, the table shows the relative percentage of loans made and dollar values for each program when compared among all three programs. When comparing the three programs since the inception of Patriot Express in June 2007 through the end of 2012, Patriot Express is significantly smaller than SBA Express and 7(a) in terms of number of total loans approved (3.76 percent) and dollar amount (1.15 percent).

However, the average loan amount for Patriot Express is larger than the average loan approved under SBA Express.

Patriot Express Loans Generally Default at a Higher Rate Than SBA Express and 7(a) Loans

When comparing loans approved in each year from the inception of Patriot Express through December 31, 2012, Patriot Express loans (with the exception of 2007) defaulted at a higher rate than SBA Express or 7(a) loans (see fig. 6).[16] For loans approved in 2009, the default rate for Patriot Express was 17 percent, approximately three times that of SBA Express and 7(a) loans. Additionally, the default rate for Patriot Express loans approved in 2010 was 7.4 percent, again more than three times that of SBA Express and 7(a) loans.

Loans approved in more recent years have had a shorter amount of time during which to observe defaults, which may at least partially explain lower default rates in more recent years of the program.[17] The higher default rates for Patriot Express are generally consistent with one of the key measures of creditworthiness that SBA collects, the Small Business Portfolio Solutions (SBPS) scores.[18] For example, 61.6 percent and 52.1 percent of 7(a) and SBA Express loans approved from 2007 through 2012 had SBPS scores of 180 or greater, compared to just 48.3 percent of Patriot Express loans approved in the same time period.

Finally, although the economic downturn may account for some of the overall higher default rates in all three programs from 2007 through 2009, Patriot Express has maintained a higher default rate compared to SBA Express and 7(a) since 2008.

The default rates for the Patriot Express program are generally higher for the smaller loan amounts. For example, as shown in figure 7, loans under $10,000, which represent 21.3 percent of all Patriot Express loans from 2007 through 2012, had an overall 22 percent default rate. Additionally, Patriot Express loans under $25,000, which represent 41.2 percent of loans made in the same period, had a default rate of 20 percent.

Our analysis of SBA data identified a concentration of low-dollar, uncollateralized Patriot Express loans with significantly higher default rates (compared to other Patriot Express loans) that were approved by a single lender. In 2009, the peak year for Patriot Express, this lender accounted for about 39 percent of Patriot Express loans approved, as shown in figure 8. Patriot Express loans approved by this lender have been defaulting at rates as high as 38 percent for loans approved in 2008 and 25 percent for loans approved in 2009, approximately 13 percentage points higher than loans approved by other lenders in the same years, also shown in figure 8. Although overall default rates have decreased since 2008, the default rates for this lender remain significantly higher than those of all other lenders. For example, in 2009, at 25 percent, the default rate of the one lender was more than double that of the remaining lenders, at 12 percent.

In May 2013, SBA decided not to renew this lender's delegated authority to make SBA loans, which includes its authority to make Patriot Express loans.

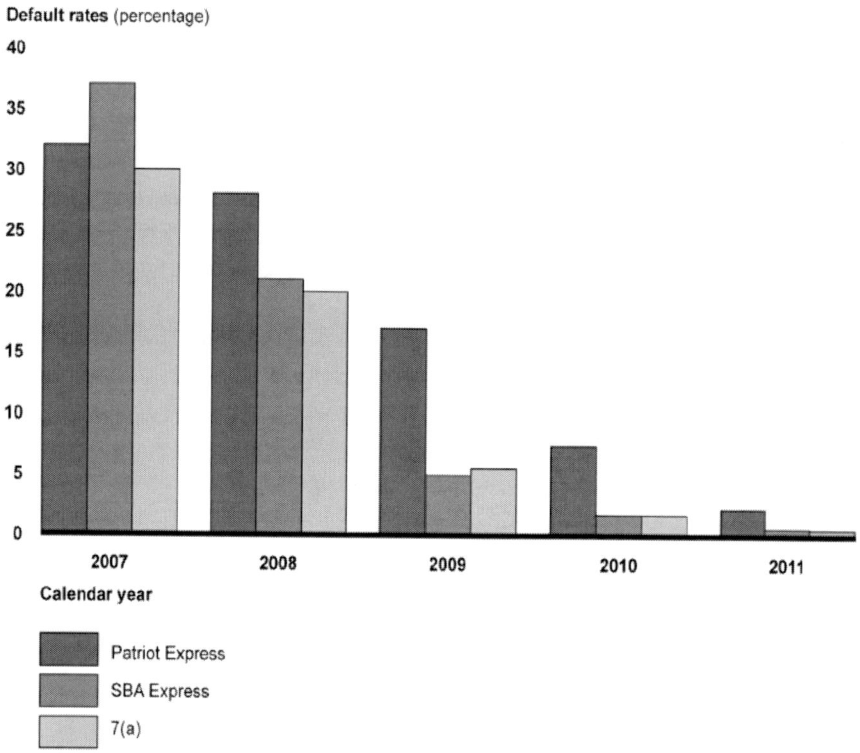

Source: GAO analysis of SBA data.

Note: This figure presents default rates for Patriot Express, SBA Express, and 7(a) as of December 31, 2012. We did not include the default rate for loans approved in 2012 because too little time had passed as of December 31, 2012, to fully assess the default rate for this cohort. The Patriot Express program began on June 28, 2007. In the figure, we present 2007 default rates for the entire year for the 7(a) and SBA Express programs. Limiting our analysis to July 1, 2007, for Patriot Express, SBA Express, and 7(a) produced similar results. Starting in 2008, one lender that specialized in Patriot Express loans valued up to $25,000 began approving loans that defaulted at a higher rate than loans approved by other lenders. A more detailed comparison of this lender to other Patriot Express lenders is shown later in figure 8.

Figure 6. Default Rates for Patriot Express, SBA Express, and 7(a) by Loan Approval Year, as of December 31, 2012.

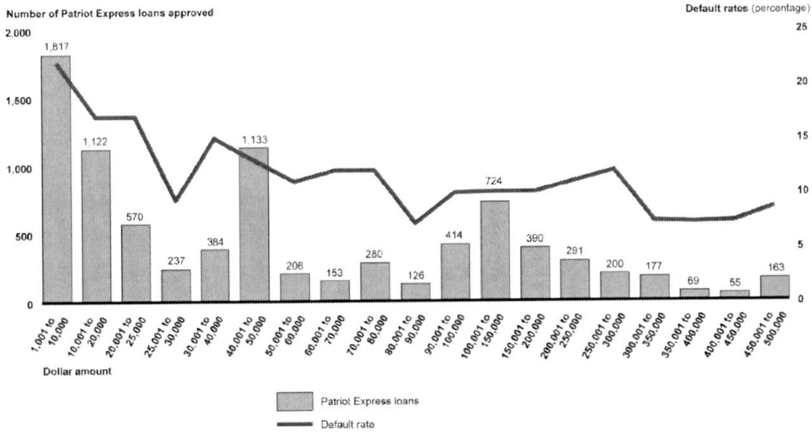

Source: GAO analysis of SBA data.

Note: This figure presents default rates for Patriot Express, from 2007 to 2012. The Patriot Express program began on June 28, 2007.

Figure 7. Default Rates and Number of Loans Approved for Different Loan Amounts for the Patriot Express Program, 2007- 2012.

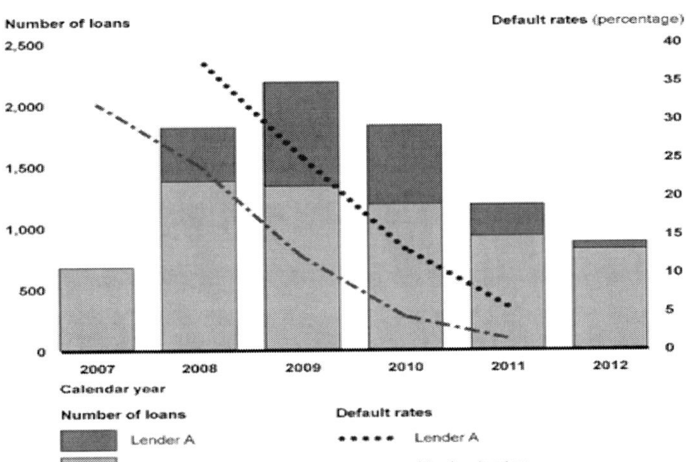

Source: GAO analysis of SBA data.

Note: We did not include the default rate for loans approved in 2012 because too little time has passed as of December 31, 2012, to fully assess the default rate for this cohort. The Patriot Express program began on June 28, 2007.

Figure 8. Total Number of Patriot Express Loans and Default Rates by Lender and Loan Approval Year 2007-2012, as of December 31, 2012.

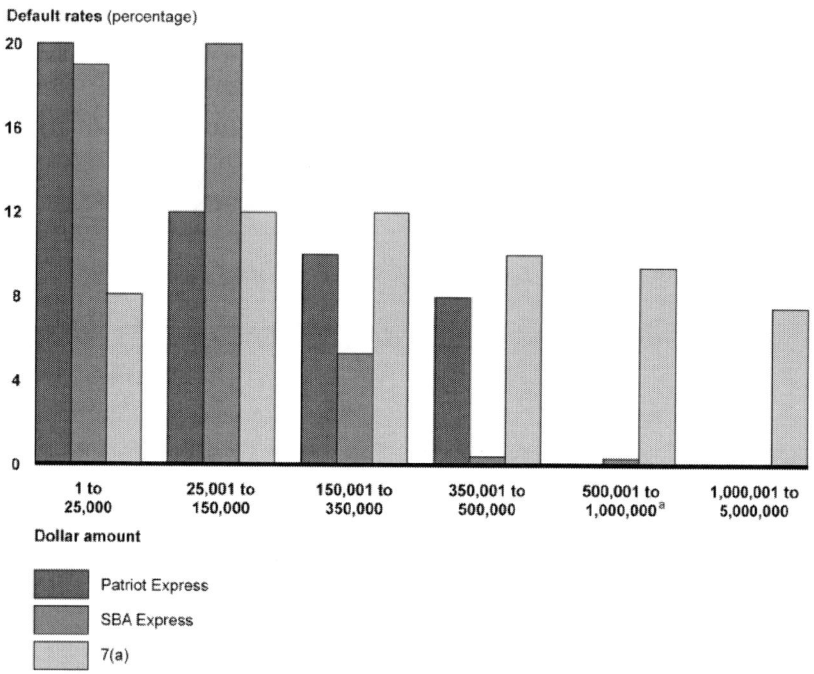

Source: GAO analysis of SBA data.

Note: This figure presents default rates for Patriot Express, SBA Express, and 7(a) from 2007-2012. The Patriot Express program began on June 28, 2007. In the figure, we present 2007 default rates for the entire year for the 7(a) and SBA Express programs. Limiting our analysis to June 1, 2007, for Patriot Express and July 1, 2007, for 7(a) and SBA Express, produced similar results. These loan categories were chosen based on characteristics of each of the programs. For example, the first category was chosen because SBA Express and Patriot Express loans of $25,000 or less do not require collateral. The third and fourth loan categories were chosen because they were the maximum loan limits for SBA Express ($350,000) and Patriot Express ($500,000).

[a]SBA was provided authority under the Small Business Jobs Act of 2010 to raise the limit on SBA Express to $1 million for loans for 1 year following the act's enactment on September 27, 2010.

Figure 9. Default Rates by Loan Amounts Approved for Patriot Express, SBA Express, and 7(a), 2007-2012.

Figure 9 shows the default rates of Patriot Express, SBA Express, and 7(a) by loan amounts. When comparing default rates with different loan amounts based on program requirements, the performance of Patriot Express loans improves as loan amounts increase. For example, the largest improvement in performance for Patriot Express loans was between loans of less than $25,000 and loans valued from $25,000 to $150,000; for loans in this range, the default rate drops by almost half, from 20 percent to 12 percent. As mentioned earlier, more than 64 percent of loans up to $25,000 were provided by one lender. However, even when loans approved by this one lender were excluded, the default rate for loans up to $25,000 did not change significantly.

Loans to Veterans through Patriot Express, SBA Express, and 7(a) Have Declined over Time

Consistent with overall SBA lending through Patriot Express, SBA Express, and 7(a), available data suggest that the number of loans made to veterans through these programs are currently at similar levels, but overall lending to veterans through these programs has decreased over the past 8 years. Although some SBA loans made to veterans may not be identified, the available data using the veteran status field in SBA's database show that the differences in levels of lending to veterans across the 7(a), SBA Express, and Patriot Express programs have been lower over the last 2 years, as shown in figure 10. For example, in 2012, 664 loans were made to veterans through the Patriot Express program, 551 loans through the SBA Express program, and 391 loans through the 7(a) program. In comparison, there were more than twice as many Patriot Express loans made to veterans compared to SBA Express loans and 7(a) loans in 2009.[19] The trends shown in figure 10 are consistent with overall lending from 2007 through 2012 in terms of total loans made under Patriot Express, SBA Express, and 7(a).

Although veterans have been able to access capital through the Patriot Express, SBA Express, and 7(a) loan programs, overall lending to veterans peaked in 2004—at which time only the 7(a) and SBA Express programs existed—and has continued to decrease since then, even after the Patriot Express program started in 2007. Between 2004 and 2012, the number of loans made to veterans decreased 77 percent, from about 7,000 loans in 2004 to 1,600 loans in 2012. Further, even with the introduction of the Patriot Express program in 2007, the overall levels of lending to veterans through all three SBA programs has remained lower than the overall level of lending to veterans before the program's inception. A number of factors could have contributed to this decrease in overall lending to veterans through SBA programs, including more conservative lender credit standards and the economic downturn in 2008.

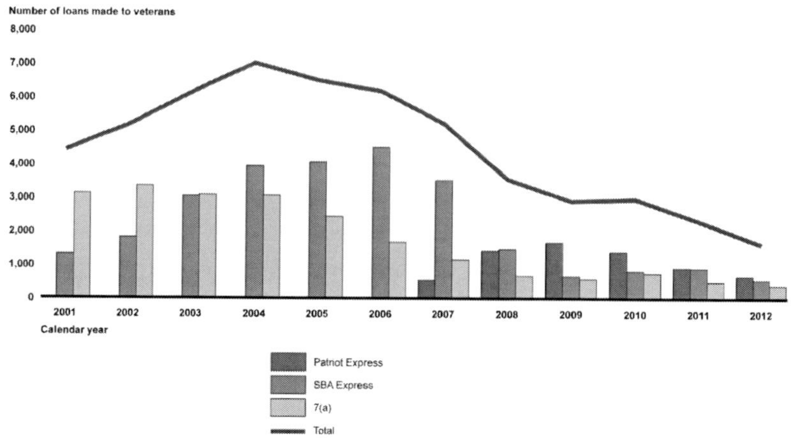

Source: GAO analysis of SBA data.

Note: The Patriot Express program began on June 28, 2007. Because this information is self-reported, SBA officials indicated that the veteran status field in its database for 7(a) and SBA Express borrowers may not be accurately or consistently capturing all veterans who have received a loan through these programs. The numbers for 2001-2006 are based on data provided by SBA, while the numbers for 2007-2012 are based on our analysis of SBA data.

Figure 10. Number of Patriot Express, SBA Express, and 7(a) Loans Made to Veterans, 2001-2012.

In addition, as mentioned previously, veteran status information is self-reported by 7(a) and SBA Express borrowers, and the veteran status field may not accurately and consistently capture all veterans who have received a loan through these programs.

In addition to a decrease in the total number of loans, the total dollar amount of loans made to veterans through Patriot Express, SBA Express, and 7(a) and also decreased from 2007 through 2012. As shown in figure 11, the overall dollar amount of loans to veterans through these three programs decreased from 2007 through 2009 before spiking in 2010 and continuing to decline again through 2012.[20] The trends shown in figure 11 are consistent with overall lending in terms of total value of loans made under the Patriot Express, SBA Express, and 7(a) programs from 2007 through 2012. In May 2013, SBA announced a new initiative to increase lending to veteran entrepreneurs by $475 million over the next 5 years across all SBA loan programs.

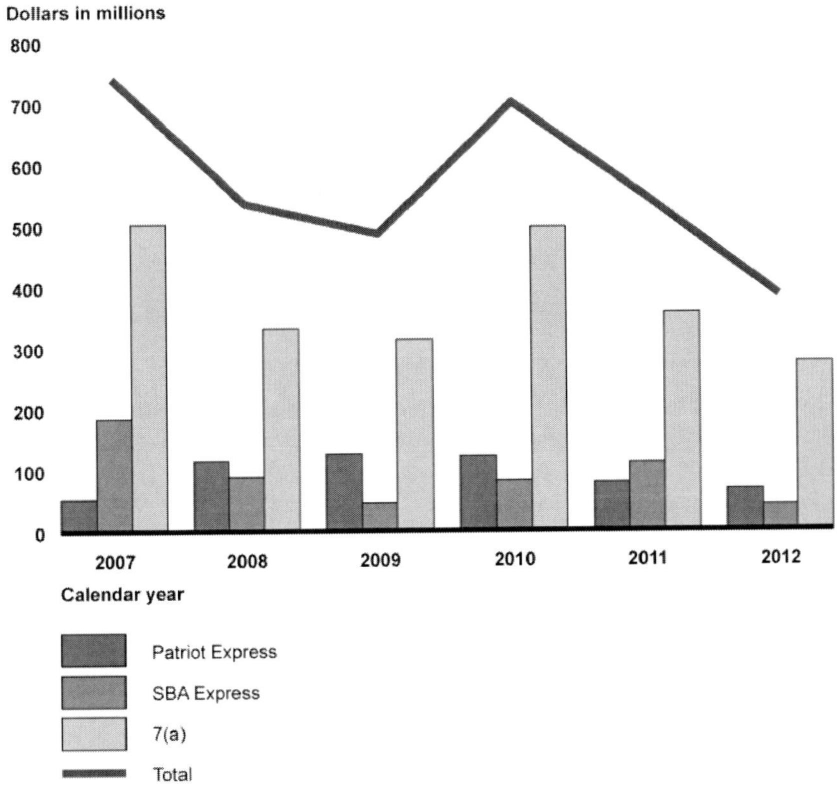

Source: GAO analysis of SBA data.
Note: The Patriot Express program began on June 28, 2007.

Figure 11. Dollar Amounts Approved for Patriot Express, SBA Express, and 7(a) Loans Made to Veterans, 2007-2012.

Figure 12 shows the default rates of Patriot Express, SBA Express, and 7(a) loans made to veterans by approval year. Loans made to veterans through these programs in 2007 and 2008 had higher default rates than those in more recent years, which may be at least partially explained by the longer time periods these loans have had in which to observe defaults. While the default rates for veteran loans for SBA Express and 7(a) have decreased for more recent loan cohorts, the Patriot Express default rates for veteran loans remained relatively high. For example, Patriot Express loans made to veterans in 2009 and 2010 defaulted more than twice as often as loans made to veterans through SBA Express and 7(a).

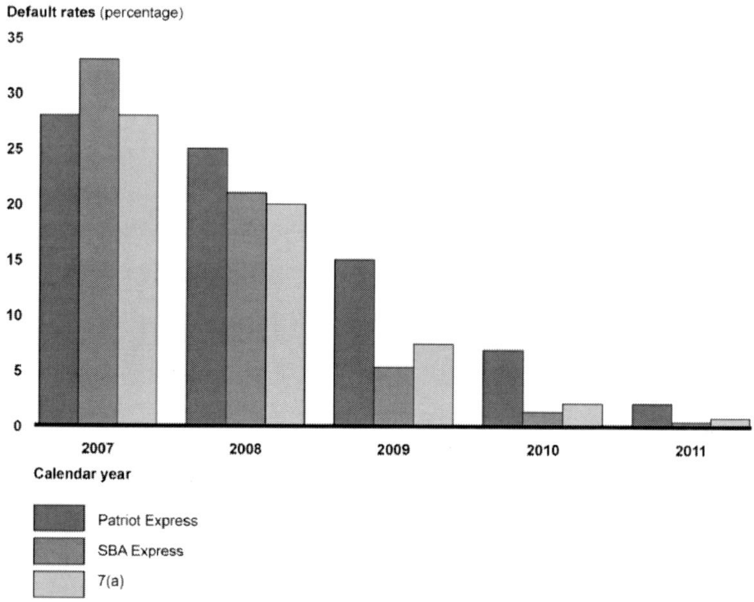

Source: GAO analysis of SBA data.

Note: We did not include the default rate for loans approved in 2012 because too little time has passed as of December 31, 2012, to fully assess the default rate for this cohort. The Patriot Express program began on June 28, 2007. In the figure, we present 2007 default rates for the entire year for the 7(a) and SBA Express programs. Limiting our analysis to July 1, 2007, for Patriot Express, SBA Express, and 7(a) produced similar results.

Figure 12. Default Rates of Loans Made to Veterans through Patriot Express, SBA Express, and 7(a) by Year of Approval, as of December 31, 2012.

Patriot Express Costs Exceed Fees Collected and Recoveries

According to our analysis of SBA's data on Patriot Express, program costs exceed the fees collected, funds recovered from borrowers in default, and other funds collected by SBA to offset the costs of the program. SBA's costs for the Patriot Express program are primarily based on the guaranteed portion of the purchased loan. As described earlier, when a loan defaults, the lender asks SBA to honor the guarantee (that is, purchase the loan). For the Patriot Express program, as indicated previously, the guaranteed portion is 85 percent for loans of $150,000 or less and 75 percent for loans over $150,000.[21] The exact amount that SBA purchases is offset by any proceeds of sale of collateral prior to purchase. Following default, if SBA determines that it will honor the guarantee, SBA purchases these loans from the lender at either 85 percent or 75 percent, depending on the approved value of the loan.[22] These costs are partially offset by guarantee fees that SBA collects at origination and annual fees it collects from lenders. Additional offsets are based on recoveries in the form of borrower payments following purchase or from proceeds from the liquidation of collateral that was not liquidated within 60 days following default of the loan.[23] According to SBA officials, Patriot Express lenders are required to liquidate non-real-estate collateral prior to purchase, unless situations arise that would prevent them from liquidating, such as a bankruptcy or stay on liquidation.[24] In these situations, SBA will purchase a loan prior to full liquidation.

Table 3. Patriot Express Program Fees, Recoveries, Purchases, and Net Cash Flows, Fiscal Years 2007-2012

Fiscal year	Up-front fee	Annual fee	Recovery	Purchase	Net cash flow[a]
2007	$338,274	$122	N/A	N/A	$338,397
2008	2,621,719	218,692	$4,077	- $275,603	2,568,884
2009	1,083,855	661,610	4,058	- 3,589,587	- 1,840,063
2010	657,255	1,124,399	219,147	- 12,800,709	- 10,799,908
2011	1,273,529	1,495,612	439,620	- 15,626,195	- 12,417,434
2012	1,903,299	1,518,379	631,337	- 13,004,418	- 8,951,403
Total	$7,877,931	$5,018,815	$1,298,239	- $45,296,512	-$31,101,527

Source: SBA.
Note: Totals for each column may not add up exactly due to rounding.
[a]Net cash flow is equal to the sum of all fees and recoveries minus purchases.

As shown in table 3, from fiscal years 2007 through 2012, SBA purchased $45.3 million in Patriot Express loans. These default costs were offset by $12.9 million in collected fees and $1.3 million in recoveries, resulting in $31.1 million in losses for this period (excluding future revenues from fees and potential additional recoveries). Based on these cash flows, the Patriot Express program has had an overall recovery rate of 2.87 percent since 2008—that is, of $45.3 million in Patriot Express loans that SBA purchased from 2008 through 2012, SBA has recovered almost $1.3 million (2.87 percent) of the funds.[25] The low recovery rate for Patriot Express makes it more likely that the program will continue operating at a loss. In addition, SBA provided projected cash flows for the Patriot Express program, which show projected losses of $36 million including future revenues from fees and potential recoveries.

Figure 13 shows SBA's loan purchases compared to the funds collected to offset those costs, including both fees and recoveries. Purchases peaked in 2011 and then declined slightly, but have remained significantly higher than the offsets.

Given the losses in the Patriot Express program since inception, if the program continues on its current trend, Patriot Express costs will likely continue to exceed fees collected and recoveries. In a program that currently has high defaults and relatively small recoveries, SBA faces challenges in taking in offsets sufficient to cover the costs of the program. Recoveries are particularly limited in loans of a low-dollar value (below $25,000) because no collateral is attached to these loans. As discussed earlier, 41.2 percent of all Patriot Express loans were for amounts less than $25,000, and 21.3 percent were for amounts less than $10,000.

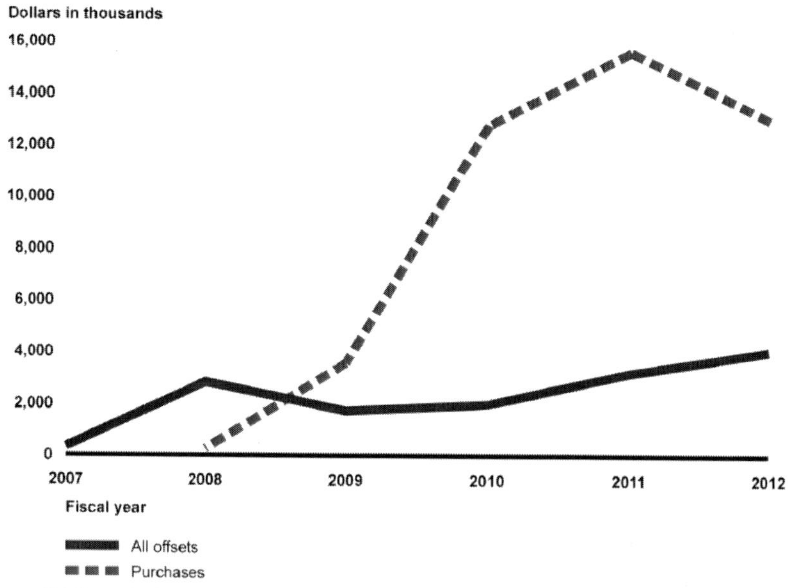

Source: GAO analysis of SBA data.

Figure 13. Patriot Express Purchases and Offsets, Fiscal Years 2007-2012.

Another factor that may affect the net cost of the Patriot Express program is the extent to which SBA has been making improper payments—that is, making guarantee payments that should not have been made—on Patriot

Express loans.[26] According to SBA, the improper payment review for 7(a) includes loans made under the Patriot Express program. In November 2012, the SBA Office of Inspector General (OIG) calculated that the improper payment rate for the 7(a) program could be as high as 20 percent, a significantly higher rate than SBA reports (about 2 percent).[27] According to OIG officials, some of the reasons that SBA did not identify improper payments were that its reviewers were unfamiliar with or misinterpreted agency policies or did not have sufficient time to conduct improper payment reviews. The SBA OIG's higher estimated rate could indicate that SBA is paying more than is necessary on defaulted loans in the 7(a) program, including the Patriot Express program. The SBA OIG found that SBA did not detect all improper payments when conducting improper payment reviews to estimate its fiscal year 2011 improper payment rate for 7(a) guarantee purchases. From a sample of 303 guarantee purchases made between April 1, 2010, and March 31, 2011, originally selected by SBA, the SBA OIG sampled 30 purchases for improper payment review and determined that SBA did not detect 6 loans that were purchased improperly.[28] Although SBA disagreed with the OIG's assessment, SBA acknowledged that the improper payment rate could be as high as close to 10 percent. OIG reviewed and reaffirmed its original methodology as an accurate assessment of SBA's real improper payment rate and concluded that the rate could potentially be as high as 20 percent.[29] The SBA OIG made 12 recommendations to SBA, including that SBA create more comprehensive guidance and policies to better detect improper payments, provide training for SBA staff to conduct reviews, and determine the appropriate amount of time needed for loan reviews to better identify erroneous payments. The SBA OIG indicated that SBA is making progress on these recommendations.

Finally, according to SBA officials, administrative costs directly associated with Patriot Express are minimal because they have no dedicated staff for Patriot Express. The only unique administrative costs they have dedicated to the program were those involved in creating it in 2007. These officials reported that SBA is able to administer the program using existing staff and resources dedicated to 7(a) and SBA Express programs and there are no separate line items for administrative costs for Patriot Express. SBA's administrative expenses for fiscal year 2012 for all business loan programs (which includes Patriot Express) were $148 million.

STAKEHOLDERS REPORTED BENEFITS AND CHALLENGES, BUT SBA HAS NOT EVALUATED THE EFFECTS OF THE PATRIOT EXPRESS PILOT

Selected loan recipients and lenders, as well as veteran service organizations we met with, identified various benefits and challenges to Patriot Express, but SBA has not evaluated the effects of the Patriot Express pilot. Lenders and borrowers we met with most frequently identified supporting veteran businesses and providing veterans with a streamlined application process as benefits of the program. Low awareness among veterans of the program and participating lenders were among the most frequently cited challenges by selected lenders, borrowers, and veteran service organizations. In addition to Patriot Express, veterans also access capital through alternate SBA-guaranteed loan products and other means. SBA provides optional training and counseling through a variety of resources to help veteran entrepreneurs navigate the options available to them. However, as with some of its previous pilot loan programs, SBA has not conducted an evaluation of the Patriot Express program to assess the extent to which it is achieving its objectives, including an assessment of its effect on eligible borrowers. Our previous work has shown that an evaluation gives an agency the opportunity to refine the design of a program and determine whether program operations have resulted in the desired benefits for participants.

Helping Veterans Expand Their Business and Providing a Streamlined Loan Process Were among the Cited Benefits of the Program

Participating loan recipients and lenders, as well as veteran service organizations we met with, identified supporting veteran businesses as a top benefit of the Patriot Express program. Specifically, 21 of the 24 Patriot Express loan recipients we met with said that the loan had enabled them to start their business, expand operations, or keep their business open during challenging times. In addition, four of the six recipients we spoke with who received a line of credit through the program said that having available credit increased their attractiveness as a potential contractor because it signaled to other businesses that they could pay for the costs to complete projects. Ten loan recipients believed that if they had not received the loan, they would currently not be in business because the loan provided capital at a critical point in time. The remaining 14 loan recipients believed that they would still be in business if they had not received the loan but would have faced difficult decisions to cover the costs, including firing staff and foregoing key projects. All loan recipients we met with said that they would apply for the program again based on their experience, and 6 recipients had pursued and received another Patriot Express loan. Likewise, the three veteran service organizations that we met with stated that the program benefited veterans who obtained Patriot Express loans.

The Patriot Express program provides veterans with a streamlined application process, and loan recipients and lenders we met with noted that this was a benefit of the program. Six of the eight lenders and one veteran service organization we met with said that the program provided veterans with a less onerous application process and reduced SBA paperwork requirements, particularly when compared to SBA's 7(a) loan program. For example, SBA requires borrowers to submit additional documents to apply for a 7(a) loan, such as monthly cash-flow projections, income statements, and balance sheets for the last 3 years. Further, since 7(a) borrowers must pledge all available collateral up to the loan amount, SBA requires borrowers to complete a schedule of collateral of all real estate and personal property used to secure the loan and provide supporting documents for such collateral, including real estate appraisals and environmental investigation reports.[30] Almost all loan recipients we met with reported that they had a positive experience with the Patriot Express loan application process, including satisfaction with the amount of documentation required. In addition, nearly all loan recipients said that they received the loan proceeds in a timely manner, ranging from a few days to 3 months from the time they applied for the loan.

Selected loan recipients, lenders, and veteran service organizations also identified other benefits to the program, such as providing veterans with favorable loan terms. For example, nearly all lenders, one veteran service organization, and officials from the National Association of Government Guaranteed Lenders (NAGGL) said that the program provided veterans with more favorable loan terms than an SBA Express loan, such as lower interest rates or higher maximum loan amounts.[31] In addition, seven loan recipients we met with said that the Patriot Express loan terms provided a more cost-effective credit alternative to fund their small business expenses compared to other financing options. For instance, four recipients stated that receiving a Patriot Express loan saved them from using credit cards and other expensive lines of credit to obtain the necessary capital for their business.

Finally, borrowers, lenders, and veteran service organizations we met with said that having a dedicated program solely for those in the military community was a benefit. For example, 10 Patriot Express loan recipients said that they appreciated that the program targeted veterans specifically and noted that it played a large role in their decision to obtain the loan. In addition, one lender said that having a loan program that also targets the business needs of spouses of service members or reservists is valuable, particularly if the business is jointly owned by the couple, because it provides access to capital to expand the business if one spouse is deployed. Further, two veteran service organizations we met with stressed that having a program for veterans also helped to initiate conversations between the veteran entrepreneur and the lender about other small business resources and financing options available.

Low Awareness of the Program and Its Participating Lenders Were Reported as Challenges, among Others

Lack of Awareness of the Program

Selected loan recipients, lenders, and veteran service organizations said that a low awareness of the Patriot Express program among the military community was among the most frequently cited challenges. Specifically, over half of the Patriot Express loan recipients, six of the eight lenders, and two veteran service organizations we met with said that SBA could do more to increase outreach to veteran entrepreneurs and better market the program to the military community. In addition, five loan recipients did not know about the program until they approached a lender for financing and were notified about it. Further, awareness of the program among selected veteran entrepreneurs who have not participated in the program was also low. For example, 11 of the 16 veterans that received 7(a) loans and all 15 SBA Express veteran loan recipients that we were able to contact were unaware that Patriot Express existed.[32]

SBA officials said the agency tries to increase awareness of the program through district offices, resource partners, and lenders. For example, SBA officials noted that there is a veteran loan specialist at each SBA district office who could recommend specific small business resources, including the Patriot Express program, to veteran entrepreneurs. Additionally, SBA officials said that their resource partners, such as Small Business Development Centers (SBDC) and SCORE (formerly the Service Corps of Retired Executives) chapters, could advertise the program through hosted events that discuss potential options for financing small business needs. Five loan recipients we met with said that they learned about the program through an SBA resource partner, including SBDCs and SCORE counselors, and two noted that these resources further helped them to find a participating lender. For example, one loan recipient said that the SBDC staff member who told him about the program also recommended a lender, assisted him with his loan application, and followed up with him after the loan was approved.

SBA officials also said that they have reached out to NAGGL to increase marketing of the program at the lender level. According to NAGGL officials, NAGGL hosted roundtables at its 2013 Lender Leadership Summit and Lending Technical Conference to discuss ways that lenders can better serve veteran entrepreneurs, including the Patriot Express program. Although NAGGL does not participate in marketing SBA programs to borrowers, NAGGL officials said that individual lenders typically advertise certain SBA loans based on their involvement with those programs. For example, some lenders we met with noted that they try to increase awareness by marketing themselves as Patriot Express lenders, particularly if they have branches in locations with large concentrations of veterans. These lenders also partnered with veteran groups at their branch locations and presented their loan products, including Patriot Express loans, to interested members at events hosted by veteran groups. One lender, however, noted that it was difficult to market SBA loan products at their branches because identifying borrowers who can qualify for SBA loans can be challenging. According to this lender, pursuant to SBA's "credit elsewhere" requirement, the lender needs to first evaluate a borrower's ability to obtain credit against their own lending policies for conventional loans in order to determine if an SBA loan product is appropriate for the borrower.[33] This approach is consistent with what we have previously reported regarding how lenders make credit elsewhere decisions.[34]

Low Awareness among Borrowers of Participating Lenders

Patriot Express and 7(a) loan recipients we met with stated that low awareness of which lenders make Patriot Express loans is also a challenge to the program. For example, 7 of the 24 Patriot Express recipients and 3 of the 4 7(a) veteran loan recipients we met with reported that SBA could provide better information about which lenders currently participate in the program. A majority of these 10 recipients found that the search for a participating lender was difficult and required many phone calls and visits to lenders. Three recipients also noted that the SBA resources they used incorrectly identified banks as participating lenders. For example, one veteran said that he spent significant time away from his business to contact six banks—which the district SBA office said were participating lenders—and found that none of them participated in Patriot Express. Additionally, two 7(a) veteran loan recipients said they initially sought financing through the Patriot Express program but they said that they settled for a 7(a) loan when they could not find a participating lender. Further, two Patriot Express loan recipients told us that they paid fees to a third-party entity that could identify lenders that made Patriot Express loans. All 10 of these recipients stated that having a consolidated and up-to-date list of participating lenders would have been helpful to their search for a loan.

SBA officials said that they did not have a list of participating lenders on their website because the agency did not want to appear to be steering borrowers toward financing their businesses through loans, especially loans from particular lenders. Rather, SBA officials stated that prospective veteran borrowers interested in the program should first contact an SBA district office or SBDC to determine if financing through a loan would be suitable for their business. Further, SBA officials said that if financing through a loan was the best solution for the veteran, SBDCs would then give the veteran a list of local lenders that participate in the program. As mentioned previously, two of the loan recipients we met with found a lender through these SBA resources, such as SBDCs and SCORE counselors.

Other Challenges

Other challenges reported by selected borrowers, lenders, and veteran service organizations included high fees associated with the loan, stringent collateral requirements, and limited maximum loan amount.

- *High Fees*: Six Patriot Express loan recipients and five lenders we met with said that the SBA guarantee fees were unaffordable for some veterans and suggested that they should be reduced or waived. These six Patriot Express loan recipients also noted that the lender packaging fees were unaffordable and suggested that they should be reduced or waived as well. According to SBA officials, the guarantee fee plays an important role in the continuation of the loan guarantee program because fees are collected to offset potential losses from defaulted and purchased loans. SBA officials also noted that the guarantee fee is ultimately the responsibility of the lender, though often it is passed on to the borrower.[35] In addition, SBA guidance establishes limits to the amount of packaging and other fees a lender can charge based on a percentage of the loan amount.[36] SBA officials said that issues regarding potentially excessive fees charged at origination could be identified either through complaints from the SBA OIG's hotline or during SBA's 7(a) lender on-site examinations, which are discussed in the next section of this report. According to SBA officials, there has only been one complaint about fees, which was reported to the SBA OIG hotline. SBA officials said they resolved the issue by confirming that the fees were inconsistent with SBA guidance and working with the lender to compensate the borrower.

- *Stringent Collateral Requirements*: Three Patriot Express loan recipients noted that they struggled to meet the collateral requirements for their loans.[37] Additionally, three lenders felt that the SBA collateral requirement for Patriot Express loans above $350,000—for which the borrower must make all collateral available to the lender up to the loan amount— was excessive and a disincentive for prospective veteran borrowers to participate in the program. According to SBA officials, the agency is considering some modifications to the collateral requirements for regular 7(a) that would still maintain a strong underwriting process. To the extent those changes are adopted, they would apply as well to Patriot Express loans in excess of $350,000.
- *Limited Maximum Loan Amount*: Two Patriot Express loan recipients, two veteran service organizations, and one lender we met with said that the current maximum loan amount for the program was challenging because certain projects and contracts require more than $500,000.[38] For example, one veteran service organization we met with noted that veterans who are federal contractors often need a loan for more than $500,000 to win a contract. SBA officials noted that the agency has not considered changing the maximum loan amount for Patriot Express loans.

Veterans Also Access Capital through Alternate SBA Programs and Other Means

Veterans access capital through other SBA-guaranteed loan products, including 7(a), SBA Express, and Small Loan Advantage (SLA) loans.[39] These loan products have some terms that are similar to those of Patriot Express and some that are different, as shown in figure 14.

As shown above, there are several similarities and differences between the programs, and three lenders we met with reported that deciding which SBA loan products to offer veteran borrowers was challenging. For example, Patriot Express loans offer veteran recipients lower maximum interest rates, but higher guarantee percentages and fees compared to SBA Express. Additionally, while regular 7(a) loans can provide veterans with similar loan terms and fees, these loans typically have longer processing times than Patriot Express loans due to the increased SBA paperwork requirements previously discussed.

While Patriot Express and SLA have some similar loan terms, SBA officials identified other differences in the programs.[40] Three of the eight lenders we met with said that deciding what product to offer a veteran entrepreneur was difficult because the loan terms and underwriting process for a Patriot Express loan were similar to those of other SBA loans they offered. Additionally, seven of the eight lenders believed that if the Patriot Express program were not available, veterans could still access capital through these other SBA loan programs.

While 7(a) and SBA Express are alternatives to Patriot Express, loan recipients noted that other ways veterans could access capital were less advantageous and all loan recipients we met with were not aware of any veteran-specific loan guarantee programs aside from Patriot Express. For example, nine recipients said that veterans could finance their small business needs through conventional loans or credit cards, but they stated these options may be more expensive than a Patriot Express loan because they typically have higher interest rates.

Two recipients considered bringing on an investor, which would inject capital into their business, but would require the recipient to give up ownership of a part of the business to the new investor. Finally, five recipients thought about financing their business through their personal savings accounts, but said that this option could have depleted their savings and a few noted that it might not have been enough to cover the amount of capital needed.

	Loan amount	SBA Guaranteed portion of loan amount	Borrower Guarantee fee	Maximum Interest rate	Monthly Payments	Target processing time	Collateral policy
Scenario 1: $10,000, 5-year loan (Prime = 3.25%)							
Patriot Express	$10,000	$ 8,500 (85%)	$170	Prime + 4.25% = 7.5%	$ 200	1 business day	No collateral required
SBA Express	10,000	5,000 (50%)	100	Prime + 6.5% = 9.75%	211	1 business day	No collateral required
7(a)	10,000	8,500 (85%)	170	Prime + 4.25% = 7.5%	200	• Regular 7(a): 6 business days • Delegated 7(a): 1 business day	All available collateral up to $10,000
SLA	10,000	8,500 (85%)	170	Prime + 4.25% = 7.5%	200	1 business day	No collateral required
Scenario 2: $250,000, 5-year loan (Prime = 3.25%)							
Patriot Express	$250,000	$187,500 (75%)	$5,625	Prime + 2.25% = 5.5%	$4,775	1 business day	Follow lender's collateral policy
SBA Express	250,000	125,000 (50%)	3,750	Prime + 4.5% = 7.75%	5,039	1 business day	Follow lender's collateral policy
7(a)	250,000	187,500 (75%)	5,625	Prime + 2.25% = 5.5%	4,775	• Regular 7(a): 6 business days • Delegated 7(a): 1 business day	All available collateral up to $250,000
SLA	250,000	187,500 (75%)	5,625	Prime + 2.25% = 5.5%	4,775	1 business day	Follow lender's collateral policy but at a minimum must obtain lien on business assets of applicant
Scenario 3: $500,000 5-year loan (Prime = 3.25%)							
Patriot Express	$500,000	$375,000 (75%)	$11,250	Prime + 2.25% = 5.5%	$9,551	1 business day	All available collateral up to $500,000
SBA Express	Not available at this loan amount (Maximum loan amount is $350,000)						
7(a)	500,000	375,000 (75%)	11,250	Prime + 2.25% = 5.5%	9,551	• Regular 7(a): 6 business days • Delegated 7(a): 1 business day	All available collateral up to $500,000
SLA	Not available at this loan amount (Maximum loan amount is $350,000)						

Source: SBA.

Note: 7(a) loans refer to (1) regular (nondelegated) 7(a) loans and (2) delegated 7(a) loans made by lenders in the Preferred Lenders Program (PLP).

Figure 14. Examples of Loan Terms for a Patriot Express, Express, 7(a), and Small Loan Advantage Loan to a Veteran Borrower.

SBA Offers Several Veteran-Specific Training and Counseling Efforts

SBA provides training and counseling to veteran entrepreneurs through a variety of resources, although Patriot Express loan recipients are not required to use them. According to SBA officials, the agency delivers training and counseling to veterans through the following ways:

- *Cooperative agreements*: SBA has cooperative agreements with 16 organizations that serve as Veteran Business Outreach Centers (VBOC), which offer services such as business plan preparations and veteran entrepreneur counseling for service-disabled veterans. Additionally, SBA has cooperative agreements with other resource partners through which veteran entrepreneurs can receive training and counseling, including SBDCs, SCORE chapters, and Women's

Business Centers (WBC). According to SBA data on veteran participation in training and counseling offered by the aforementioned resource partners (VBOCs, SBDCs, SCORE chapters, and WBCs) from fiscal year 2008 through fiscal year 2012, overall veteran participation remained steady from 2008 through 2010. However, it increased over 40 percent from approximately 115,000 veterans in 2010 to about 163,000 veterans in 2012. Further, veteran participation in training and counseling offered through VBOCs also increased in 2011, from about 45,000 veterans in 2010 to about 90,000 veterans in 2012. As of June 2013, about 36,000 veterans had received training and counseling through SCORE, SBDCs, and WBCs.[41]

- *SBA-sponsored activities*: According to SBA officials, some SBA-sponsored activities may be provided in coordination with the previously mentioned resource partners, and veterans can also receive training and counseling through these efforts. For example, Operation Boots to Business leverages SBA's resource partner network—VBOCs, SBDCs, SCORE chapters, and WBCs—and SBA's partnership with, among other entities, Syracuse University's Institute for Veterans and Military Families to provide an entrepreneurship training program for transitioning service members.[42] Operation Boots to Business consists of several phases, including a 2-day training session on creating a feasibility analysis for a business plan and an 8-week online course on the fundamentals of small business ownership, including marketing, accounting, and finance. As of March 2013, a total of 1,390 veterans (1,309 for the 2-day session and 81 for the online course) had participated in this effort.
- *SBA participation in third-party activities:* Veteran entrepreneurs can access training and counseling services provided through SBA's participation in third-party activities, including events hosted by other federal agencies and nonprofit entities. For example, SBA awarded a 3-year grant to Syracuse University to create the Entrepreneurship Bootcamp for Veterans with Disabilities (EBV), which provided small business management training to post-9/11 veterans with disabilities.[43] According to SBA, 463 veterans participated in EBV during this 3-year grant period. In 2010, SBA provided Syracuse University with funding for two additional programs that support veteran entrepreneurship: Veteran Women Igniting the Spirit of Entrepreneurship (V-WISE), which focuses on the training and mentorship of women veterans and spouses, and Operation Endure

and Grow (OEG), which features an 8-week online course geared toward National Guard and Reserve members, their families, and their business partners.[44] As of April 2013, 857 women veterans, female spouses and partners of active service members, and transitioning female members of the military community had participated in V-WISE, and 168 reservists had received training through OEG.

Veterans who have participated in certain training and counseling efforts have generally found them to be helpful. For example, SBA's Office of Veterans Business Development (OVBD) conducts an annual VBOC client satisfaction survey, which shows that client satisfaction with VBOC services had increased from 85 percent in 2008 to 93 percent in 2012. 45 According to these SBA officials, the survey results are used to, among other things, identify areas for improvement and new training topics. OVBD officials said they are responsible for collecting feedback surveys for the VBOC program only. Veterans whom we met with who participated in these efforts also found them to be helpful. Specifically, 14 of the 28 loan recipients we met with—Patriot Express loan recipients as well as 7(a) veteran loan recipients—participated in an SBA-sponsored training or counseling session, and the most commonly used resources among these recipients were SBDCs and SCORE counselors. Eight of the recipients said these sessions were helpful in starting and growing their business, such as assisting in the development of business plans and marketing strategies, and they noted that these sessions were free. Two loan recipients suggested that SBA develop more advanced workshops for seasoned entrepreneurs, but acknowledged that these training and counseling resources would be helpful for first-time business owners.

As with Some of Its Previous Pilot Programs, SBA Has Not Evaluated Patriot Express

SBA has not evaluated the Patriot Express program's performance or its effect on eligible borrowers. GAO's guide for designing evaluations states that an evaluation gives an agency the opportunity to refine the design of a program and provides a useful tool to determine whether program operations have resulted in the desired benefits for participants.[46] In addition, evaluations can inform future program decisions. Program evaluations are individual, systematic studies that use research methods to assess how well a program, operation, or project is achieving its objectives and the reasons why it may or may not be performing as expected.[47] Program evaluations are distinct from routine monitoring or performance measurement activities in that performance measurement entails the ongoing monitoring of a program's progress, whereas program evaluation typically assesses the achievement of a program's objectives and other aspects of performance in the context in which the program operates.[48] At a minimum, a well-developed and documented program evaluation plan includes measurable objectives, standards for performance, methods for data collection, and time frames for completion.

Incorporating these elements and executing the plan can help ensure that the implementation of a pilot generates performance information needed to make effective management decisions about the future of the program. In addition, recent legislation has highlighted the importance of program evaluation for federal agencies. Specifically, Congress updated the Government Performance and Results Act of 1993 (GPRA) with the GPRA Modernization Act of 2010 (GPRAMA), which requires agencies to describe program evaluations that were used to establish or revise strategic goals.[49]

When Patriot Express was created in 2007 under SBA's authority to initiate pilots, SBA indicated that it would evaluate the program's performance and make a decision whether to modify or continue the program after December 31, 2010. In December 2010, SBA announced through a Federal Register notice that it would extend the pilot through 2013 in order to have more time to evaluate the effect of the program and determine whether any changes need to be made.[50] According to SBA officials, they have not established any measurable goals for the pilot, but have begun to hold meetings on what information they will need to assess the performance of Patriot Express loans. However, although SBA officials said that they have begun to hold meetings, the program extension ends in only a few months on December 31, 2013. As of August 2013, SBA had not established a plan for the evaluation of the program, and such a plan should include clear and measurable objectives, standards for performance, methods for data collection, and time frames for completion. In addition, SBA has taken several actions in an attempt to increase lending to veterans across its programs, but these initiatives have not been substantiated by findings from an evaluation of the Patriot Express program or the current state of SBA lending to veterans.

As mentioned previously, SBA announced a new initiative to increase loans to veteran entrepreneurs by $475 million over the next 5 years across all SBA loan programs. Because SBA had not conducted an evaluation of the pilot, the agency had little information available to inform such decisions, such as a comparison of benefits that veterans receive from Patriot Express in relation to those received by veterans participating in other SBA loan programs. SBA has conducted performance measurement and monitoring activities—such as internally reporting the number of Patriot Express loans made each quarter and deciding not to renew a top lender's delegated authority to make Patriot Express loans based on ongoing monitoring, as previously mentioned—but these activities are not the same as program evaluation.[51] Because there are many more 7(a) loans, which therefore pose a greater risk to SBA than the smaller volume of Patriot Express loans, SBA officials told us that they have focused more resources on evaluating the performance of 7(a) loans.

In addition to Patriot Express, SBA has authorized other pilot loan programs that it has subsequently not evaluated when making decisions about the future of the program. For example, in 2010, SBA's OIG conducted an assessment of the Community Express program, which was established in 1999, to determine, among other things, whether the program was properly structured to ensure success and minimize the risk of fraud. [52] This assessment was completed in response to a concern presented by SBA to the SBA OIG regarding poor performance of the Community Express program. In this assessment, the SBA OIG found that SBA did not establish measurable performance goals and outcomes for evaluating the Community Express program until 9 years after the pilot's inception. Further, though the OIG determined that these performance measures were adequate, SBA had extended the pilot without using the measures to assess the program's effectiveness.[53] Similarly, in 2006 the OIG found that SBA had not reviewed the SBA Express program—which was initiated in 1995 as a pilot—to determine, among other things, if final rules and regulations would be developed.[54]

Rather than evaluate the program to develop regulations, SBA continued to extend the program as a pilot for 9 years until Congress made it permanent in 2004. Because of this lack of review and establishment of regulations, the OIG recommended in 2006 that the agency issue regulations to, among other things, ensure that that SBA has legally enforceable rules to manage the program. SBA agreed that regulations were needed for the program, but did not establish such regulations, according to OIG officials.

The Administrator of SBA has the authority to suspend, modify, or waive rules for a limited period of time to test new programs or ideas through pilot programs, but this authorization does not include a specific requirement for

SBA to conduct a pilot evaluation.[55] Congress has established an annual limit for the number of loans made through pilots within the 7(a) program. Specifically, no more than 10 percent of all 7(a) loans guaranteed in a fiscal year can be made through a pilot program.[56] According to SBA officials, a pilot program's duration and the number of times the agency can extend it depend on the length of time needed to complete testing of the pilot. However, as shown by SBA's experience with the Patriot Express, Community Express, and SBA Express pilots, SBA does not always test pilots or evaluate their effects when initiating pilot programs under its own authority.

Without designing and conducting evaluations of the pilot programs it conducts under its own authority, SBA has little information to assess the performance of the programs and their effects on eligible borrowers, which could be used in decisions on the future of these pilots, including the Patriot Express program. For example, information on the financial performance of veteran-owned businesses participating in various SBA loan programs could help inform policy decisions. Further, the information drawn from an evaluation of Patriot Express could also be used to inform training and counseling resources for veterans. In turn, input from veteran borrowers participating in SBA loan programs and from counselors at SBA resource partners assisting veteran borrowers could provide a basis for improvements in existing SBA loan programs.

SBA's Internal Controls May Not Provide Assurance of Borrower Eligibility

SBA has two primary internal control activities to ensure lender compliance with borrower eligibility requirements—on-site examinations and purchase reviews. However, these reviews may not provide the agency with reasonable assurance that Patriot Express loans are only made to eligible borrowers. SBA only reviews a small number of Patriot Express loans for eligibility as part of on-site examinations, and although it examines eligibility as part of purchase reviews, these reviews occur only for loans that have defaulted, in some cases long after an ineligible borrower may have received proceeds from a Patriot Express loan. In addition, although SBA officials told us that they expect borrowers to maintain their eligibility throughout the term of the loan, SBA has not developed procedures to provide reasonable assurance that Patriot Express loans continue to serve eligible borrowers after a loan is disbursed. Internal control standards for federal agencies and GAO's fraud-prevention framework state that oversight programs should be designed to ensure that ongoing monitoring occurs in the course of normal operations.[57] Furthermore, the intent of the Patriot Express program is to support eligible members of the military community. Without greater review of Patriot Express transactions during on-site examinations of lenders and requirements for lenders to ensure that borrowers remain eligible after disbursement, there is an increased risk that the proceeds of Patriot Express loans will be provided to or used by borrowers who do not qualify for the program.

SBA Has Reviewed Few Patriot Express Loans during On-Site Examinations of the Largest Participating Lenders

GAO's fraud-prevention framework identifies three elements needed to minimize fraud: (1) up-front preventive controls, (2) detection and monitoring, and (3) investigations and prosecutions.[58] For Patriot Express, SBA addresses the first element of the framework through the steps lenders are required to take under their delegated authority to ensure borrower eligibility at loan origination. It addresses the third element by the steps it must take to refer potential cases of fraud to its OIG for investigation and possible prosecution. However, we found that SBA's detection and monitoring—the second element of the framework— could be strengthened. One of SBA's primary monitoring activities to provide reasonable assurance that Patriot Express loans are made only to eligible borrowers is the reviews it performs as part of its on-site examinations of lenders. However, since the program's inception in 2007, SBA has reviewed only a small number of Patriot Express loans for the 10 largest Patriot Express lenders.[59]

SBA does not conduct specific Patriot Express program examinations. Instead, it reviews a lender's compliance with Patriot Express program eligibility requirements as part of its examination of the lender's 7(a) program or as part of a safety and soundness examination of an SBLC.[60] These examinations are known as risk-based reviews or safety and soundness examinations for SBLCs.[61] During these reviews, SBA draws a sample of loans from a lender's files to assess, among other things, whether the loans met specific program eligibility requirements at the time of approval.[62] For example, if an SBA examiner selects a Patriot Express loan, the examiner is expected to review the lender's documents to determine whether that loan was provided to a veteran or other eligible member of the military community. The lenders must document in their files how they determined the borrower's eligibility for the Patriot Express program, including what Department of Defense and Department of Veteran Affairs documents they used to verify veteran status. Additionally, the examiner is expected to review lender documentation to determine whether the veteran or other eligible borrower owned 51 percent or more of the small business at the time of loan approval. As part of the risk-based review, SBA's examiners are required to compile a list of all eligibility deficiencies by issue type and errors, and identify any trends of deficiencies that warrant lender attention.

We reviewed the most recent 7(a) risk-based examination and an SBLC safety and soundness examination for the 10 largest Patriot Express lenders and found that with the exception of 3 lenders, SBA examined few Patriot Express loans. As table 4 shows, for the first 3 lenders, SBA sampled at least six Patriot Express loans during the examination. However, for the remaining lenders, SBA sampled one or two loans at two of the lenders and did not sample any Patriot Express loans at the other 5 lenders. For the 5 lenders in table 4 for which SBA sampled at least one Patriot Express loan, 4 lenders were found by SBA to be in compliance with eligibility requirements. For the remaining lender, SBA did not report on its assessment of eligibility requirements in the examination.

Table 4. Patriot Express Loans Sampled in Most Recent SBA Examination and Number of Patriot Express Loans Made by Top 10 Lenders from 2007 to the Year Prior to Examination

Lender	Year of most recent examinations	Patriot Express loans sampled
Lender 1	2010	35
Lender 2	2012	8
Lender 3	2010	6
Lender 4	2012	2
Lender 5	2012	1
Lender 6	2012	0
Lender 7	2011	0
Lender 8	2012	0
Lender 9	2011	0
Lender 10	2012	0

Source: GAO analysis of SBA data.

SBA officials said SBA examined few or no Patriot Express loans for 7 of these 10 lenders because Patriot Express comprised a small percentage of these lenders' overall lending. At six of the 7 lenders, the Patriot Express loan volume as of the program's inception to the year prior to the examination ranged from 1 percent to 8 percent of their overall SBA lending activities.[63] However, while these percentages are relatively small, in a program that has a specific target population—veterans and other eligible members of the military community—assessing lenders' compliance with eligibility requirements is particularly important to help ensure that the guaranteed loans are assisting only eligible veteran entrepreneurs as intended. The monitoring of borrower eligibility that occurs through on-site examinations is a key internal control and fraud-prevention element for Patriot Express because the loan program serves a specific population with loan provisions intended only for this population of borrowers.[64]

Another primary internal control that SBA uses to monitor borrower eligibility is the purchase reviews that it conducts for loans that have defaulted and for which the lender is seeking the guarantee payment. [65] As part of the purchase review, an SBA official must review documentation relied upon by the lender to determine whether the borrower was eligible for the program. However, purchase reviews are only conducted for loans that have defaulted and would not identify ineligible borrowers who continue to make their loan payments. Additionally, ineligible borrowers may have the loan for years before ultimately defaulting. Because SBA conducts so few on-site examinations of Patriot Express loans, opportunities to identify these ineligible borrowers prior to a default are limited. For a program with a specific target population, an increased emphasis on reviewing borrower eligibility is important. Without sampling more Patriot Express loans during examinations, SBA may have difficulty identifying deficiencies related to eligibility. This, in turn, could increase the risk to SBA of Patriot Express loans being provided to borrowers who do not qualify for the program.

SBA Has Not Provided Clarity to Lenders Regarding Borrowers' Ongoing Ownership Requirements

Although SBA requires lenders to assess borrowers' eligibility for Patriot Express at the time of loan approval, it does not require them to reassess eligibility, including the 51 percent ownership requirement, after the loan has been disbursed. SBA does not have a stated requirement for borrowers to maintain their eligibility after the loan has been disbursed, but SBA officials told us that they do expect borrowers to maintain 51 percent ownership after a loan has been disbursed to remain eligible for the program. SBA requires that borrowers certify that they will not change the ownership structure or sell the business without the consent of the lender.[66] Additionally, SBA officials told us that in the event of a borrower default, a lender could lose the SBA guarantee if the borrower had sold his or her business to an individual who does not qualify for a Patriot Express loan. However, in the examples below, lenders may not be aware of changes in ownership structure or sale of the business if the borrower has not informed lenders of such actions and the lender is not periodically reassessing Patriot Express eligibility after the loan has been disbursed. Borrowers may initially be approved as meeting Patriot Express eligibility requirements at the time of loan approval, but subsequent events may affect their eligibility and result in the loan being used by an ineligible borrower. For example, according to SBA OIG officials, a business may recruit a veteran to pose as the majority business owner in order to be eligible for a Patriot Express loan and add the veteran to legal ownership documents that would be provided to the lender when applying for the loan. Once the loan is disbursed, however, the business could reduce the ownership interest or remove the veteran as an owner of the business. Such cases could also involve the businesses giving the veteran a kickback after the loan was disbursed. In another example, after the loan has been disbursed, an eligible Patriot Express borrower might sell all or part of his or her ownership interest in the qualifying business. In these examples, an ineligible party benefits from the Patriot Express loan proceeds.

These examples illustrate the importance of effective monitoring and detection activities, which are key internal controls and an element of the fraud-prevention framework. Detection and monitoring controls include activities such as periodically evaluating lender procedures to provide reasonable assurance that only eligible borrowers obtain loans and benefit from the program as intended. Such assurance is particularly important in a program that has specific eligibility requirements and was created to serve a specific population. Four of six lenders we spoke with thought that borrowers needed to remain eligible for the loan after disbursement, but these four lenders stated that they did not think that they needed to check on borrowers to make sure that they remain eligible after loan disbursement. The other two lenders we spoke with told us that they did not think ongoing borrower eligibility was a requirement of the program. In the absence of formal SBA eligibility procedures to ensure that only borrowers who maintain 51 percent ownership receive assistance after a loan has been disbursed, Patriot Express loan proceeds may ultimately be used by those other than the intended program beneficiaries. As a result, SBA may not have reasonable assurance that Patriot Express loans are serving the intended population.

CONCLUSION

Prior to 2007, SBA served the small business needs of veteran entrepreneurs through its 7(a) and SBA Express programs. SBA established the Patriot Express Pilot Loan initiative in 2007 as a targeted effort to provide veterans and other eligible members of the military community access to capital to establish or expand small businesses. However, the effect this initiative has had on the small business financing needs of veterans and other entrepreneurs in the military community is unknown. While SBA recently announced an initiative to increase overall lending to veteran small businesses by $475 million over the next 5 years, the role of the Patriot Express pilot initiative is unclear given that SBA has yet to evaluate the effectiveness of the program. Based on our analysis, with the exception of 2007, Patriot Express loans made to veterans have had a relatively high default rate, and losses for the initiative have exceeded its income. Moreover, SBA has not conducted an evaluation of the pilot initiative that would include standards for pilot performance, comparative measures with other programs that may also serve veterans, methods for data collection, evaluation of data on the performance of the loans, data and analysis from external reports and evaluations, and time frames for completion. Although SBA officials said that they have begun to hold meetings on what information they will need to assess the performance of Patriot Express loans, SBA has not established a plan to evaluate the program, and only a few months remain before the current extension of the program is set to end. Program evaluations can be useful in informing future program decisions, including SBA's planned efforts to expand lending to veterans.

In addition, the lack of an evaluation or an evaluation plan for Patriot Express follows a pattern for SBA pilot loan programs. As with the Patriot Express pilot initiative, SBA has authorized other pilot loan programs in the past that it has subsequently not evaluated when making decisions about the future of those programs. SBA's past experience with pilots raises questions about its commitment and capacity to fully implement pilots that include a rigorous evaluation. Without evaluations of pilot initiatives, SBA lacks the information needed to determine if a pilot program is achieving its intended goals and whether it should be cancelled, modified, or expanded.

Finally, SBA's reliance on lenders to assess borrowers' eligibility for Patriot Express highlights the importance of strong internal controls over lenders to ensure that only eligible borrowers are served by the program. Federal internal control guidance and GAO's fraud-prevention framework indicate that program controls should include monitoring and detection. However, SBA currently samples few Patriot Express loans during on-site examinations. In addition, while SBA expects borrowers to maintain 51 percent ownership after a loan has been disbursed, SBA has not developed procedures to require lenders to verify that the 51 percent ownership requirement is maintained, nor does it monitor the lenders' activities to ensure eligibility after disbursement. As a result, SBA's internal controls may not provide the necessary assurance that Patriot Express loans are made to and used by only eligible members of the military community—the intended mission of the program.

RECOMMENDATIONS FOR EXECUTIVE ACTION

As SBA considers whether or not to extend the Patriot Express Pilot Loan program, we recommend that the Administrator of SBA design and implement an evaluation plan for the pilot program that assesses how well the Patriot Express pilot is achieving program goals and objectives regarding its performance and its effect on eligible borrowers. The evaluation plan should include information such as

- evaluation of SBA data on performance of Patriot Express loans;
- evaluation of borrowers served by Patriot Express in relation to veteran borrowers served by other SBA loan programs; and
- review of relevant SBA OIG reports and other external studies.

To help ensure that SBA makes informed decisions on the future of pilot programs it creates under its own authority, we recommend that the Administrator of SBA require the agency to design an evaluation plan for any such pilot program prior to implementation—including an assessment of the program's performance and its effect on program recipients—and to consider the results of such an evaluation before any pilot is extended.

To help ensure that Patriot Express loans are only provided to members of the military community eligible to participate in the program, we recommend that the Administrator of SBA strengthen existing internal controls, including

- sampling a larger number of Patriot Express loans during examinations;
- developing a requirement in SBA's Standard Operating Procedures for lenders to verify the eligibility of the borrower, including the 51 percent ownership requirement, after the loan has been disbursed; and
- periodically monitoring the lenders' implementation of this eligibility requirement.

Agency Comments

We provided the Administrator of the Small Business Administration with a draft of this report for review and comment. On August 26, 2013, the SBA liaison—Program Manager, Office of Congressional and Legislative Affairs—provided us with the following comment via email on the draft. He stated that the agency will consider the findings from this report as it reviews the extension of the Patriot Express Pilot Loan Program. SBA also provided technical comments, which we incorporated into the report where appropriate.

William B. Shear
Director,
Financial Markets and Community Investment

Appendix I: Objectives, Scope, and Methodology

Our objectives were to examine (1) trends in the Patriot Express program and related Small Business Administration (SBA) guarantee programs, including performance of these loans, and what is known about the costs of the Patriot Express program, (2) the benefits and challenges of the Patriot Express program for members of the military community eligible to participate as well as training and counseling opportunities available to them, and (3) what internal controls SBA has in place to ensure that the Patriot Express program is available only to eligible members of the military community. To describe trends in the Patriot Express program, including how Patriot Express loans approved from 2007 through 2012 have performed, we obtained SBA loan-level data on loans approved from the second quarter of 2007 through the fourth quarter of 2012 for Patriot Express and from the first quarter of 2007 through the fourth quarter of 2012 for the 7(a), and SBA Express programs. We took a number of steps to develop a dataset we could use for our analyses.[1] We excluded loans with missing disbursement dates unless they had positive balances at some point in their history, which to us indicated loan activity. Additionally, we excluded loans that in December 2012 were indicated to have been cancelled. Once we arrived at our final dataset, we analyzed it for various performance measures, including default rates.[2] A loan was defined as defaulted (purchased) if it had a purchase date on or after the approval date. Specifically, we analyzed the default rates by the following categories:

- *Cohort analysis*—Using the loan approval date data field, we identified loans for all three programs and grouped them in calendar year cohorts reflecting loans approved from 2007 through 2012. Once these loans were identified, we calculated the default rates, total number of loans, and total loan values approved from 2007 through 2012 for all three programs.
- *Loan amount*—Using the gross amount approved data field, we identified the number of loans by loan amounts that were approved for all three programs from 2007 through 2012. We grouped these loans into major categories based on requirements of the programs. For example, we focused on loans below \$25,000 because the Patriot Express and SBA Express programs require no collateral for these loans. We selected the next category, loans valued between \$25,001 and \$150,000, based on the guarantee percentage change from 85 percent to 75 percent for Patriot Express and 7(a) that occurs at \$150,000. We selected the next two categories of loans valued between \$150,001 and \$350,000 and between \$350,001 and \$500,000 to capture the maximum allowable loans for SBA Express and Patriot Express, respectively. Additionally, we focused on loans valued between \$500,001 and \$1,000,000 and between \$1,000,001 to \$5,000,000 to account for the larger loan amounts for 7(a). Once these loans were identified by loan amounts, we calculated the default rates for all three programs based on loans approved from 2007 through 2012.

- *Lender concentration*—Using the main bank data field, we identified the top 11 lenders based on the number of approved Patriot Express loans from 2007 through 2012. Once these lenders were identified, we calculated the default rates, average loan amounts, and total loan amounts approved from 2007 through 2012. Additionally, we calculated the relative percentage of loans made by each of the top 11 lenders compared to the overall number of Patriot Express loans approved from 2007 through 2012. After we identified that one lender accounted for 26 percent of all Patriot Express loans approved, we calculated the relative percentage and default rates of this one lender compared to all other lenders from 2007 through 2012.
- *Veteran status*—Using a data field that identifies borrowers based on their veteran status, we identified borrowers that self-identified as either a veteran, service-disabled veteran, or Vietnam-era veteran from each of the three programs. Once these loans were identified, we calculated the default rates, total number of loans, and total loan values approved from 2001 through 2012 for SBA Express and 7(a), and 2007 through 2012 for Patriot Express.
- *New Business*—Using the new or existing business data field and information provided by SBA, we identified new businesses that had been in operation 2 years or less prior to loan approval, and existing businesses that had been in operation for more than 2 years at time of loan approval. Once these loans were identified, we calculated the relative percentage of new businesses for loans approved from 2007 through 2012.
- *Use of Proceeds*—Using the loan proceeds data field and information provided by SBA, we identified the most common use of loan proceeds for Patriot Express loans approved from 2007 through 2012.
- *Small Business Portfolio Scores (SBPS)*—Using a data field that identifies borrowers by their SBPS scores, based on available data, we grouped businesses based on having a low (139 or lower), medium (140-179) or high (180 or greater) SBPS score. We then calculated the default rates, total number of loans, total value of loans, and relative percentage of loans for Patriot Express, SBA Express and 7(a).

For all of our analyses on the performance of Patriot Express, 7(a), and SBA Express loans, we did not weight default rates by loan amount. In addition, for each analysis we did not include loans with missing values. To assess data reliability, we interviewed SBA representatives from the Office of

Performance and Systems Management and the Office of Credit Risk Management about how they collected data and helped ensure data integrity. We also reviewed internal agency procedures for ensuring data reliability. In addition, we conducted reasonableness checks on the data to identify any missing, erroneous, or outlying figures, and when necessary, submitted follow-up questions to SBA officials at the Office of Performance and Systems Management and the Office of Credit Risk Management to clarify our understanding of the data. Through our electronic data testing, we identified irregularities in the data in a small percentage of cases, such as loans with approval amounts in excess of what we understood to be the limits of the program or loans with disbursal dates, but zero dollars disbursed. However, SBA was able to explain these cases as being due to periods in which the limits of the program were temporarily expanded, or provided other explanations. We did not find more than a minimal amount of missing values in fields relating to approved amount, approval year of purchase, and key variables for our analysis of performance. As such, we determined that the data were sufficiently reliable for our purposes.

To describe what is known about the costs of the Patriot Express program from 2007 through 2012, we obtained and analyzed SBA cash-flow data on SBA purchases of defaulted loans, as well as data on offsets, which include the following three categories: (1) upfront fees generated by the program at time of approval, (2) annual fees based on loans in a lender's portfolio in good standing, and (3) recoveries either from the proceeds of attached collateral to the defaulted loans or subsequent payments on loans following purchase by SBA. Additionally, we reviewed SBA guidance, the agency's standard operating procedures, and inspector general reports to obtain more information on cash-flow data. To assess data reliability, we interviewed SBA representatives from the Office of Financial Analysis and Modeling, the Office of Performance and Systems Management, and the Office of Credit Risk Management to understand how they collect data and help ensure the integrity of the cash-flow data, as well as how they use these data for budgetary purposes. We also submitted follow-up questions to SBA officials at both the Office of Financial Analysis and Modeling and the Office of Credit Risk Management to clarify our understanding of the data. We determined that the data were sufficiently reliable for our purposes. To assess the effect of the Patriot Express program on members of the military community eligible to participate in the program, we conducted semi-structured interviews with a sample of 24 Patriot Express loan recipients about how the Patriot Express loan affected their businesses and their views on how the program could be improved.[3] We selected this nongeneralizable, stratified random sample of loan recipients to reflect two factors: the recipient's loan amount and the number of Patriot Express loans their lender has made since the program's inception to 2012. While the results of these interviews could not be generalized to all Patriot Express loan recipients, they provided insight into the benefits and challenges of the program.[4] Table 5 below highlights selected characteristics of the Patriot Express loan recipients we interviewed.[5]

Table 5. Selected Characteristics of Loan Recipients Included in Our Sample

Characteristic	Number of loan recipients insample[a]
Patriot Express loan amount	
Less than $20,000	9
$20,000-$149,999	10
Greater than $150,000	5
Lender	
Top 11 Patriot Express lenders[b]	13
Remainder of lenders	11
Loan approval year	
2008	3
2009	8
2010	4
2011	5
2012	4
Type of eligible borrower	
Veteran	19
Spouse	5
Type of loan product	
Term loan	18
Line of credit	6

Source: GAO analysis of SBA data.

[a] The number of loan recipients within each characteristic category total to 24 and individual loan recipients are categorized into multiple categories.

[b] These are the top 11 lenders that made the most number of Patriot Express loans from 2007 through 2012.

To obtain the perspectives of veteran entrepreneurs who were aware of the Patriot Express program and appeared to meet the eligibility requirements for a Patriot Express loan but instead obtained an SBA Express or 7(a) loan, we attempted to contact a nongeneralizable sample of veterans who participated in these two other programs.[6] Of the 15 SBA Express veteran loan recipients and 16 7(a) veteran loan recipients whom we were able to contact, we interviewed 4 veteran entrepreneurs who obtained a 7(a) loan.[7] We conducted interviews with these recipients to inquire about their experiences with the 7(a) loan and to obtain their views on the Patriot Express program.

We also interviewed a sample of lenders to obtain their perspectives on the benefits and challenges of the Patriot Express program. We selected the top 10 lenders that made the greatest number of Patriot Express loans from 2007 through 2012. [8] The selected lenders made approximately 48 percent of the Patriot Express loans over this period and consisted of various types of lending institutions, including large banks, a credit union, and a small business lending company (SBLC).[9] While the results of these interviews could not be generalized to all lenders participating in the Patriot Express program, they provided insight into the key differences in administering the program as compared to other SBA loan programs. To obtain a broader set of lender perspectives on the program, we interviewed representatives from the National Association of Government Guaranteed Lenders (NAGGL), a trade organization representing SBA 7(a) lenders. We also interviewed representatives from three veteran service organizations with an interest in veteran entrepreneurship, namely the Veteran Entrepreneurship Task (VET) Force, Veteran Chamber of Commerce, and American Legion, to gather information on the benefits and challenges of the program that their members have experienced. Finally, we interviewed SBA officials from the Offices of Capital Access and Veterans Business Development who are responsible for managing and promoting the program. We interviewed these officials to obtain their perspectives on identified benefits and challenges to the program, promotion of the program and its lenders, and efforts to evaluate the program's effect on members of the military community eligible to participate.

To describe other ways in which veteran entrepreneurs accessed capital, as part of our interviews with Patriot Express and 7(a) loan recipients, as well as selected lenders and veteran service organizations, we also inquired about other ways in which veterans can gain access to capital. To describe the training and counseling efforts SBA has in place for veteran entrepreneurs, we obtained and reviewed reports by the Interagency Task Force on Veterans Small Business Development from 2011 and 2012.[10] We also reviewed SBA documents related to training and counseling resources and SBA information on the number of veterans that have used these resources from 2008 through 2012. We also interviewed SBA officials responsible for these efforts. To describe the perspectives of veteran entrepreneurs on the effectiveness of

SBA's training and counseling efforts, we reviewed results from SBA's annual Veteran Business Outreach Center client satisfaction survey from 2008 through 2012. We also interviewed the selected veteran service organizations and Patriot Express and 7(a) loan recipients on their perspective on the quality of training and counseling efforts sponsored by SBA.

To determine SBA's prior experience with pilots initiated under its own authority, we obtained and reviewed pertinent regulations on SBA's authority to initiate pilots and applicable limitations. We also reviewed two SBA Office of Inspector General (OIG) reports pertaining to SBA's experience with the Community Express and SBA Express pilot programs.[11] To assess how well SBA has conducted pilot programs, including Patriot Express, we reviewed components identified in our previous work as key features of a program evaluation and an evaluation plan.[12]

To evaluate SBA's internal controls related to ensuring that the Patriot Express program is available only to members of the military community eligible to participate in the program, we reviewed SBA's standard operating procedures related to borrower eligibility requirements. Also, as part of our interviews with the selected lenders and borrowers previously discussed, we inquired about the documentation used to establish eligibility for the program. To determine how SBA oversees lenders to ensure they are complying with the Patriot Express eligibility requirements, we reviewed SBA's standard operating procedures related to lender oversight. We also obtained copies of examination reports for the top 10 Patriot Express lenders (based on the number of loans made) from 2007 through 2012. We reviewed these reports to determine the number of Patriot Express loans sampled during the examination and SBA's disposition on whether the lender was complying with SBA rules and regulations related to borrower eligibility. Additionally, we interviewed officials from the Office of Credit Risk Management to inquire about SBA's oversight of its lenders as it relates to the Patriot Express program. To determine how SBA reviews defaulted loans as part of its purchase review, we reviewed SBA's standard operating procedures related to these reviews, as well as an SBA OIG report on improper payments, which also described the purchase reviews. [13] We also met with officials from SBA's Office of Financial Program Operations to understand how SBA staff review submissions from lenders requesting that SBA purchase defaulted loans. Finally, to help assess the extent to which the Patriot Express program could be susceptible to fraud and abuse, we reviewed SBA's internal control standards related to ensuring that Patriot Express loans were made to eligible members of the military community. We compared these internal controls to federal internal control standards, as well as to GAO's Fraud Prevention Framework.[14] We also interviewed officials from SBA's Office of Inspector General to learn about scenarios under which the Patriot Express program could be susceptible to fraud and abuse. We conducted this performance audit from November 2012 to September 2013 in accordance with generally accepted government auditing standards. Those standards require that we plan and perform the audit to obtain sufficient, appropriate evidence to provide a reasonable basis for our findings and conclusions based on our audit objectives. We believe that the evidence obtained provides a reasonable basis for our findings and conclusions based on our audit objectives.

APPENDIX II: COMPARISON OF SBA'S 7(A), SBA EXPRESS, AND PATRIOT EXPRESS LOAN PROGRAMS

In addition to the Patriot Express pilot program, there are several delivery methods within the SBA 7(a) program, including regular (nondelegated) 7(a), delegated 7(a) loans made by lenders in the Preferred Lenders Program (PLP), and SBA Express loans.[1] While all delivery methods provide a borrower with an SBA-guaranteed loan, there are several similarities and differences between these three programs, such as eligibility restrictions, maximum loan amounts, and percent of guarantee. Table 6 below compares the key features of these three loan programs discussed throughout this report.

Table 6. Comparison of 7(a), SBA Express, and Patriot Express Loan Programs

	7(a)	SBA Express	Patriot Express
Type of loan	Short-term (12 months) or long-term loan. No revolving features.	Same as 7(a) or may be used for revolving lines of credit (up to 7 years).	Same as SBA Express.
Use of loan proceeds	SBA-guaranteed loan proceeds may be used for the following purposes:[a]	Same as 7(a) plus Renewable Energy and Energy Efficiency Loans.	Same as 7(a).

	7(a)	SBA Express	Patriot Express
	1. Acquisition of land or purchase, construction or renovation of buildings 2. Improvement of a site 3. Acquisition and installation of fixed assets 4. Inventory 5. Supplies 6. Raw Materials 7. Working Capital 8. Refinancing		
Loan decision process	Regular (nondelegated) 7(a) loans: SBA approves the loan for both credit and eligibility. Delegated 7(a) loans made by PLP lenders: Lender is delegated the credit decision and completes a checklist for eligibility which SBA reviews.	Authorized lenders make loan approval decisions, including credit determinations, without prior SBA review.	Same as SBA Express.
Target processing time	Regular (nondelegated) 7(a) loans:6 business days Delegated 7(a) loans made by PLP lenders: 1 business day	1 business day.	Same as SBA Express.
Eligibility restrictions	1. The small business applicant must:[b] a. Be an operating business b. Be organized for profit c. Be located in the U.S. d. Be small (as defined by 13 C.F.R. 121) e. Demonstrate a need for the desired credit 2.Lender must certify that credit is not available elsewhere on reasonable terms.[c]	Same as 7(a).	Same as 7(a). In addition to meeting the eligibility requirements of the 7(a) program, the business must be 51% or more owned and controlled by one or more of the following:

Table 6. (Continued)

	7(a)	**SBA Express**	**Patriot Express**
	3.Applicant must show that funds are not available from alternative sources, including personal resources of the principals.[d] 4. The business must be an eligible type of business.[e]		•Veteran, certain active-duty military, reservist or National Guard member
			•A spouse of any of the above groups, or •A widowed spouse of a service member or veteran who died during service, or ofa service-connected disability.
Maximum loan amount[f]	$5,000,000	$350,000	$500,000
Percent of guarantee	•85% for loans $150,000 or less. •75% for loans over $150,000.	50%	Same as 7(a).
Collateral policy	Available collateral (liquidation value) up to loan amount.	No collateral is required for loans $25,000 or less. Lenders may use their own collateral policies used for their non-SBA-guaranteed loans for loans more than $25,000.	•Same as SBA Express for loans $350,000 or less. •Same as 7(a) for loans more than $350,000.

	7(a)	SBA Express	Patriot Express
SBA guarantee fees	**Lender's Annual Ongoing Fee:**[g] Not to exceed 0.55% of the outstanding balance of the guaranteed portion of loan **Lender Guarantee Fee:**[h] Loans with maturities of 12 months or less:0.25% of the guaranteed portion Loans with maturities of over 12 months: •$150,000 or less: 2% of the guaranteed portion •$150,001 - $700,000: 3% of the guaranteed portion •$700,001 - $5,000,000: 3.5% of the guaranteed portion up to $1,000,000 plus 3.75% of the guaranteed portion over $1 million	Same as 7(a).	Same as 7(a).
Borrower Packaging and Other Services Fees[i]	•Packaging and other service fees that a lender charges a borrower based on a percentage of the loan amount cannot exceed: •3% for loans $50,000 or less •2% for loans between $50,001 to $1 million and an additional 0.25% on the remaining amount over $1 million (maximum fee of $30,000).	Same as 7(a).	Same as 7(a).
Maximum Interest rates[j]	**Loans less than 7 years:** •$0 - $25,000: Base Rate[k]+ 4.25% •$25,000 - $50,000: Base Rate + 3.25% •Over $50,000: Base Rate + 2.25%	**Loans $50,000 or less:** Cannot Exceed Prime[l]+ 6.5% **Loans over $50,000:** Cannot Exceed Prime + 4.5%	Same as 7(a)[m]

Table 6. (Continued)

	7(a)	SBA Express	Patriot Express
	Loans 7 years or longer: •0 - $25,000: Base Rate + 4.75% •$25,001 - $50,000: Base Rate + 3.75% •Over $50,000: Base Rate + 2.75%		

Source: SBA.

[a] 13 C.F.R. 120.120.

[b] 13 C.F.R. 120.100.

[c] 13 C.F.R. 120.101.

[d] 13 C.F.R. 120.102.

[e] 13 C.F.R. 120.110.

[f] Amounts listed are gross loan amounts.

[g] This fee cannot be passed to the borrower and SBA may charge the lender a late fee if the ongoing guarantee fee is not paid in a timely manner.

[h] This fee can be passed on to the borrower and is a one-time fee paid when the loan is approved or after initial disbursement.

[i] Packaging services" include the lender assisting the applicant with completing the application and preparing cash-flow projections and other documents related to the application. "Other services" include consulting as to what financing is needed and what type. The fees must be reasonable and customary for the services performed and must be consistent with those charged on the lender's similarly sized, non-SBA-guaranteed commercial loans. In addition, fees for packaging and other services may be based on a percentage of the loan amount.

[j] Lenders are permitted to add an additional 2 percentage points to the maximum interest rate listed for loans of $25,000 or less and an additional 1 percentage point to the maximum interest rate listed for loans between $25,000 and $50,000.

[k] For standard 7(a), there are three acceptable base rates: (1) the Prime Rate; (2) One Month London Interbank Offered Rate (LIBOR) plus 3 percentage points (LIBOR Base Rate); or (3) the SBA Optional Peg Rate.

[l] For SBA Express, a lender may use the same base rate of interest it uses on its similar non-SBA loans as long as the resulting interest rate does not exceed Prime + 6.5% or Prime + 4.5%, depending on the loan amount. However, if the loan is sold in the secondary market only the Prime Rate, LIBOR, and SBA Optional Peg Rate are permitted.

[m] Similar to SBA Express, a lender may use the same base rate of interest it uses on its similar non-SBA loans as long as the resulting interest rate does not exceed the amounts stated in the 7(a)'s maximum interest rates. However, if the loan is sold in the secondary market, only the Prime Rate, LIBOR, and SBA Optional Peg Rate are permitted.

End Notes

[1] Section 7(a) of the Small Business Act, as amended, codified at 15 U.S.C. § 636(a).

[2] Other eligible members of the military include service-disabled veterans, active duty military participating in the military's Transition Assistance Program, reservists or National Guard members or a current spouse of any of these groups, a widowed spouse of a service member who died while in service, or a widowed spouse of a veteran who died of a service-connected disability.

[3] The proceeds of 7(a) loans may be used for working capital and other general business purposes. The program is intended to serve small business borrowers who could not otherwise obtain credit under reasonable terms and conditions from the private sector without an SBA guarantee. The 7(a) program provides an 85 percent guarantee on loan amounts of $150,000 or less and a 75 percent guarantee on loan amounts over $150,000.

[4] In this report, we define the default rate as the number of loans that SBA has purchased from the lender divided by the outstanding number of loans approved.

[5] The SBA Express program is a subprogram of the 7(a) loan program and was established as a pilot program by SBA on February 27, 1995. The program was made permanent through legislation in 2004. The program was designed to increase the availability of credit to small businesses by permitting lenders to use their existing documents and procedures in return for receiving a reduced SBA guarantee on loans. It provides a 50 percent loan guarantee on loan amounts up to $350,000.

[6] Section 7(a) of the Small Business Act, as amended, and now codified at 15 U.S.C. Section 636(a), provides the authority for the 7(a) program.

[7] SBA has limited legislative authority to make direct loans to borrowers unable to obtain loans from conventional lenders.

[8] In addition to depository institutions, SBA has authorized other types of lenders to make SBA-guaranteed loans. These lenders include SBLCs, which are generally not subject to oversight and examination by a federal financial institution regulator. SBLCs are nondepository lenders that enter into agreements with SBA to provide 7(a) loans and microloans to qualified small businesses. By statute, SBA is the primary federal regulator for SBLCs and conducts safety and soundness examinations of these institutions.

[9] In establishing size standards, SBA considers economic characteristics of the industry, including degree of competition, average firm size, start-up costs and entry barriers, and distribution of firms by size. It also considers growth trends, competition from other industries, and unique factors within an industry that may distinguish small firms from other firms. SBA's size standards seek to ensure that a firm that meets a specific size standard is not dominant in its field of operation. In addition, the Small Business Act specifies that SBA shall not make or guarantee loans for borrowers who are able to obtain credit elsewhere, which is defined as "the availability of credit from non-Federal sources on reasonable terms and conditions taking into consideration the prevailing rates and terms in the community in or near where the concern transacts business, or the homeowner resides, for similar purposes and periods of time." See, 15 U.S.C. § 636(a)(1); 15 U.S.C. § 632(h). Further, SBA requires lenders to ensure that the borrower or any principal of the business do not have the personal resources to cover the needed funding.

[10] The 7(a) program formally includes all subprograms, including Patriot Express and SBA Express. However, in this report, when we make comparisons of loan volume, performance, and benefits and challenges of Patriot Express to SBA Express and 7(a), we use "7(a) loans"

to refer to both (1) regular (nondelegated) 7(a) loans and (2) delegated 7(a) loans made by PLP lenders but excluding Patriot Express and SBA Express, unless otherwise noted.

[11] SBA's collateral policies for Patriot Express loans vary depending on the loan amount. For example, no collateral is required for Patriot Express loans of less than $25,000. However, lenders that make Patriot Express loans above $350,000 are required to collateralize the loan to the maximum extent possible up to the loan amount. If business assets do not fully secure the loan, the lender must take available personal assets of the principals as collateral. SBA considers liquidation of business personal property collateral to be completed when a lender has exhausted all prudent and commercially reasonable efforts to collect upon these assets.

[12] Credit subsidy costs represent the net present value of expected lifetime cash flows, excluding administrative costs. The subsidy rate reflects the net present value cost for each dollar of credit assistance. According to SBA, the Patriot Express program does not have a separate subsidy rate. The 7(a) subsidy rate is also applied to the Patriot Express program.

[13] Prior to reorganization in May 2007, the office was called the Office of Lender Oversight.

[14] The American Recovery and Reinvestment Act of 2009 (ARRA). Pub. L. No. 111-5 Division A. Title V. §§ 501, 502, 123 Stat. 115, 151-153 (2009), enacted on February 17, 2009, permitted the temporary reduction of fees in the 7(a), Patriot Express, and 504/CDC loan guarantee programs until September 30, 2010, or until $375 million of appropriated funds was expended and increased the 7(a) program's maximum loan guarantee percentage to 90 percent for all standard 7(a) loans except for SBA Express loans.

[15] For example, the Small Business Jobs Act of 2010, Pub. L. No. 111-240. §§ 1111,1114, 124 Stat. 2504, 2507, 2508 (2010) provided funding to extend the fee subsidies and 90 percent loan guarantee percentage through December 31, 2010 or until available funds were exhausted. Also, the Continuing Appropriations and Surface Transportation Extensions Act, 2011, Pub. L. No. 111-322. § 1(a)(2), 124 Stat. 3518, 3520 (2011), authorized SBA to continue the fee subsidies and the 7(a) program's 90 percent maximum loan guarantee through March 4, 2011.

[16] We calculated defaults by examining the number of loans that were purchased by SBA (as of December 31, 2012) based on the year that the loan was approved. As mentioned earlier, lenders can request that SBA purchase a loan if a borrower is in default on an SBA loan for more than 60 calendar days and if a borrower is unable to cure the loan after working with the lender. A loan is in default when a borrower fails to make a regular installment of principal and/or interest when due to the lender.

[17] The average time to default, as measured by the time period from approval to purchase of the defaulted loan by SBA, was 34 months for 7(a) and SBA Express, and 28 months for Patriot Express.

[18] SBPS is a credit score specific to small business that each SBA loan receives on a quarterly basis. It is an off-the-shelf product produced by the Fair Isaac Corporation (FICO) and Dun & Bradstreet. It uses Dun & Bradstreet's commercial and TransUnion's consumer credit bureau data for all disbursed and outstanding 7(a) loans. It includes business data reported by third parties, such as venders, utilities, and insurance companies. SBPS is categorized by risk (high, medium, and low) and contains a range of credit scores consistent with each level of risk.

[19] The SBA loan-level data for these three programs include a field that indicates whether a loan has been made to a veteran, service-disabled veteran, or Vietnam War veteran. However, unlike borrowers in the Patriot Express program—which requires lenders to confirm a veteran's status for eligibility purposes—veterans who receive 7(a) or SBA Express loans

self-report their veteran status to SBA, and the lender is not required to verify this information. Because this information is self-reported, SBA officials indicated that the veteran status field for 7(a) and SBA Express borrowers may not be accurately or consistently capturing all veterans who have received a loan through these programs.

[20] As mentioned earlier, the higher number of 7(a) and Patriot Express loans approved in 2009 and 2010 may be attributable, in part, to ARRA and subsequent legislation, which provided funding to temporarily subsidize the 7(a) guarantee programs' fees and to increase the programs' maximum loan guarantee percentage from 75 or 85 percent to 90 percent.

[21] As indicated earlier, the guarantee was increased to 90 percent as part of ARRA and subsequent legislation for 7(a) loans made from February 17, 2009, through March 4, 2011.

[22] According to SBA guidance, the guarantee portion of the loan is 85 percent for loans of $150,000 or less, and 75 percent for loans above $150,000.

[23] As stated earlier in figure 2, according to SBA, for loans approved on or after May 14, 2007, a lender may demand in writing that SBA honor its guarantee if the borrower is in default on any installment for more than 60 calendar days and the default has not been cured, provided all business personal property securing the defaulted SBA loan has been liquidated.

[24] As mentioned earlier, SBA considers liquidation of business personal property collateral to be complete when a lender has exhausted all prudent and commercially reasonable efforts to collect upon those assets.

[25] The estimated recovery rate was calculated from 2008 because no recoveries or purchases occurred in 2007. The recovery rate is calculated by dividing the total of all recoveries from 2008 to 2012 by the total purchases for the same time period. Recoveries include proceeds from the sale of any collateral attached to the loan at the time of purchase, including other payments from the borrower following purchase.

[26] When a loan goes into default and the lender requests guarantee payment from SBA, SBA reviews loan documentation to evaluate the lender's compliance with program rules and regulations to justify the guarantee purchase. According to Office of Management and Budget (OMB) guidance, an improper payment is any payment that should not have been made or that was made in an incorrect amount under statutory, contractual, administrative, or other legally applicable requirement.

[27] SBA, Office of Inspector General, *The Small Business Administration's Improper Payment Rate for 7(a) Guaranty Purchases Remains Significantly Underestimated*, Report No. 13-07 (Washington, D.C.: Nov. 15, 2012).

[28] According to the OIG audit, the OIG's statistician tested the sampling methodology used by SBA and the OIG to ensure it would produce a statistically valid estimate of the rate of improper payments.

[29] In response to SBA's written response stating that OIG's estimated improper payment rate was based on a flawed statistical approach, OIG noted that it would be extremely unlikely—1 chance in 1.72 million—that the deficiencies would only exist in the subsample of 30 and nowhere else.

[30] Patriot Express loans of less than $25,000 do not require collateral and lenders may use their own collateral policies for their nonguaranteed loans for Patriot Express loans over $25,000 but below $350,000. For loans greater than $350,000, the lender must take all available collateral up to the loan amount. As mentioned previously, 41.2 percent of Patriot Express loans made since the program's inception were less than $25,000 and are, therefore, uncollateralized.

[31] NAGGL is a trade organization that represents SBA 7(a) lenders.

[32] In addition to the 24 Patriot Express loan recipients, we attempted to contact veterans who were aware of the program and have received SBA 7(a) and SBA Express loans. As part of our attempt to contact these veterans, we found that some were not aware of the Patriot Express program, and we did not interview them as part of our review.

[33] For purposes of this report, a conventional loan is a loan without a federal guarantee.

[34] GAO, *Small Business Administration: Additional Guidance on Documenting Credit Elsewhere Decisions Could Improve 7(a) Program Oversight*, GAO-09-228 (Washington D.C.: Feb. 12, 2009).

[35] The President's 2014 budget waives guarantee fees on loans of less than $150,000 in SBA's 7(a) loan program, including the Patriot Express program. However, existing fees on loans $150,000 and greater will remain, and SBA's budget would need to be adjusted accordingly in order to offset the fees that would have been collected from loans less than $150,000.

[36] SBA SOP-51-10 5(E) states that packaging and other fees must be consistent with those charged on the lender's similarly sized, non-SBA-guaranteed loans. For more information on maximum allowable fees, see appendix II.

[37] SBA's collateral policies for Patriot Express loans vary depending on the loan amount. For example, no collateral is required for Patriot Express loans of less than $25,000. On the other hand, lenders that make Patriot Express loans above $350,000 are required to collateralize the loan to the maximum extent possible up to the loan amount. If business assets do not fully secure the loan, the lender must take available personal assets of the principals as collateral. See appendix II for more information on the program's collateral policies.

[38] As previously discussed, the maximum loan amount for the Patriot Express program is $500,000.

[39] Announced in 2010, the SLA initiative was aimed at increasing lower-dollar SBA loans in underserved communities by offering lenders a prescreen credit score from SBA that the applicant's business has sufficient creditworthiness to warrant giving the applicant full consideration for financing.

[40] SBA officials identified differences in the programs such as differences in the credit analysis used by the programs and the type of loan products allowed. For example, SBA officials said that lenders could use their own credit analyses for Patriot Express loans, but had to follow specific credit analysis requirements for SLA loans. Additionally, SBA officials noted that the Patriot Express program allowed revolving lines of credit, but the SLA program did not.

[41] Veteran participation figures in VBOCs have not yet been collected through fiscal year 2013. As of the third quarter of 2013, 28,119 veterans had been counseled and 13,619 veterans had been trained at VBOCs.

[42] The full title of the program is "Operation Boots to Business: From Service to Startup" and it was launched in 2012. Operation Boots to Business is currently in its pilot phase and is currently being tested in four Marine Corps bases before a complete national rollout to all branches of the military later in 2013.

[43] The 3-year grant period began on November 11, 2009, and was terminated on November 10, 2012.

[44] The funding period for the V-WISE and OEG grant ends on September 30, 2013.

[45] The Office of Veterans Business Development's mission is to maximize the availability, applicability, and usability of all SBA small business programs for veterans, service-disabled veterans, reserve component members, and their dependents or survivors.

[46] GAO, *Designing Evaluations: 2012 Revision*, GAO-12-208G (Washington D.C.: Jan. 31, 2012).

[47] GAO, *Managing for Results: 2013 Federal Managers Survey on Organizational Performance and Management Issues*, GAO-13-519SP (an E-supplement to GAO-13-518) (Washington D.C.: June 26, 2013).

[48] GAO, *Program Evaluation: Strategies to Facilitate Agencies' Use of Evaluation in Program Management and Policy Making*, GAO-13-570 (Washington D.C.: June 26, 2013).

[49] Pub. L. No. 111-352, 124 Stat. 3866 (2011).

[50] 75 Fed. Reg. 77935 (Dec. 14, 2010).

[51] On July 23, 2013, SBA provided us documentation on some calculations of performance (as of Jan. 31, 2009) of Patriot Express loans originated from July 2007 through January 2009.

[52] SBA, Office of Inspector General, *Assessment of the Community Express Pilot Loan Program*, Report No. 10-12 (Washington, D.C.: Aug. 25, 2010). The Community Express program authorized approved lenders to adopt streamlined and expedited loan procedures to provide financial and technical assistance to borrowers in the nation's underserved communities.

[53] SBA terminated the Community Express program on April 30, 2011.

[54] SBA, Office of Inspector General, *Management Advisory Report: Policies and Procedures for the SBA Express and Community Express Loan Programs*, Report No. 6- 34 (Washington, D.C.: Sept. 29, 2006).

[55] 13 C.F.R. § 120.3.

[56] 15 U.S.C. § 636(a)(25).

[57] See GAO, *Standards for Internal Control in the Federal Government*, GAO/AIMD-00-21.3.1 (Washington, D.C.: November 1999) and *Service-Disabled Veteran-Owned Small Business Program: Fraud Prevention Controls Needed to Improve Program Integrity,* GAO-10-740T (Washington, D.C.: May 24, 2010).

[58] GAO-10-740T.

[59] These are the top 10 lenders based on the number of Patriot Express loans made since the program's inception.

[60] In this context, 7(a) refers to (1) regular (nondelegated) 7(a) loans, (2) delegated 7(a) loans made by PLP lenders, and (3) all subprograms including Patriot Express and SBA Express.

[61] The risk-based review and examination process allocates on-site review resources to SBA lenders with higher-risk characteristics in terms of credit risk, portfolio performance, SBA exposure, and compliance.

[62] Based on our review of examinations of the 10 largest Patriot Express lenders, SBA selected the sample of loans based on (1) a random sample of the lender's SBA loans and (2) a judgmental sample to ensure that loans from different SBA programs (e.g., 7(a), SBA Express, Patriot Express) were selected.

[63] For the other lender, Patriot Express loan volume as of the date of the examination was 45 percent of their overall SBA lending activities.

[64] Regular (nondelegated) 7(a) loans, delegated 7(a) loans made by PLP lenders, and SBA Express loans do not have any comparable specific targeted borrowers, other than the common goal of serving small businesses.

[65] More broadly, the purchase review is SBA's primary control for ensuring lender compliance and preventing improper payments.

[66] Borrowers who own at least 51 percent of the business must personally guarantee all loans, including Patriot Express loans. In order for borrowers to be released from this guarantee, such as through the sale of their ownership interest in the business, lenders must obtain SBA's approval.

End Notes for Appendix I

[1] Because SBA provided us with loans from Patriot Express, 7(a), and SBA Express in one file, we used the subprogram code field to identify loans from the different programs. In the process of inquiring with SBA about SBA Express loans, SBA identified 55 loans that according to the subprogram code were SBA Express loans but that SBA, through the use of another field we did not have access to, identified as Export Express loans.

[2] In this report, we define default rate as the number of loans that SBA has purchased from the lender divided by the outstanding number of loans approved.

[3] In order to arrive at our final sample of 24 Patriot Express loan recipients, we contacted or attempted to contact 132 Patriot Express loan recipients. We found that a high percentage of SBA's contact information on these borrowers was inaccurate or missing. SBA officials told us that they do not contact borrowers but that if they needed to and found that the borrower's contact information was inaccurate or missing in SBA's data, they could get the correct contact information from the lender.

[4] For loan recipients that we contacted who received multiple Patriot Express loans, we only analyzed the experiences drawn from the Patriot Express loan included in our sample.

[5] All 24 loan recipients we met with were still in business at the time we interviewed them. In contacting Patriot Express loan recipients, we encountered some borrowers who had gone out of business or declared bankruptcy, and they declined to speak with us.

[6] To sample veteran entrepreneurs who appeared to meet the eligibility requirements for a Patriot Express loan, we limited our sample to veterans who received SBA Express and 7(a) loans that were $500,000 or less (the same loan amount range as Patriot Express) and made after June 2007, when the Patriot Express program was initiated. Information on veteran status for SBA Express and 7(a) loan recipients is self-reported by the borrower and is not verified by the lender. Therefore, this information may not accurately or consistently capture all veterans who have received a loan through these programs.

[7] As part of our attempt to contact these veterans, we found that some were not aware of the Patriot Express program. Because we wanted to obtain perspectives of veteran entrepreneurs that received other SBA loans and could share their views on Patriot Express, we did not interview those that were unaware of the program.

[8] Two of the top 10 lenders we contacted declined to speak to us.

[9] The term "large bank" refers to banks with over $10 billion in assets.

[10] The Interagency Task Force on Veterans Small Business Development was created in 2010 by the President and is chaired by the Administrator of SBA. It is tasked to, among other things, develop proposals related to improving access to capital for veteran-owned businesses and increasing training and counseling services provided to veteran entrepreneurs. For the task force's annual reports, see Interagency Task Force on Veterans Small Business Development, *Report to the President: Empowering Veterans Through Entrepreneurship*, (Washington D.C.: Nov. 1, 2011) and Interagency Task Force on Veterans Small Business Development, *Heroes on the Home Front: Supporting Veteran Success as Small Business Owners* (Washington D.C.: Nov. 29, 2012).

[11] SBA, Office of Inspector General, *Assessment of the Community Express Pilot Loan Program*, Report No. 10-12 (Washington, D.C.: Aug. 25, 2010) and SBA, Office of Inspector General, *Management Advisory Report: Policies and Procedures for the SBA Express and Community Express Loan Programs*, Report No. 6-34 (Washington, D.C.: Sept. 29, 2006).

[12] GAO-13-519SP, GAO-13-570, and GAO, *Designing Evaluations: 2012 Revision*, GAO-12-208G (Washington D.C.: January 2012).

[13] SBA, Office of Inspector General, *The Small Business Administration's Improper Payment Rate for 7(a) Guaranty Purchases Remains Significantly Underestimated*, Report No. 13-07 (Washington, D.C.: Nov. 15, 2012).

[14] See GAO, *Standards for Internal Control in the Federal Government*, GAO/AIMD-00-21.3.1 (Washington, D.C.: November 1999) and GAO, *Service-Disabled Veteran-Owned Small Business Program: Fraud Prevention Controls Needed to Improve Program Integrity*, GAO-10-740T (Washington, D.C.: May 24, 2010).

End Note for Appendix II

[1] As mentioned previously, when we refer to 7(a) loans, we are referring to (1) regular (nondelegated) 7(a) loans and (2) delegated 7(a) loans made by PLP lenders, unless otherwise noted.

INDEX

D

E

F

G

H

I

O

P

Q

R

S

T

U

V

W